READING AUSTRALIAN POETRY

Born in 1940 in Victoria, Andrew Taylor has taught in the English department of Adelaide University since 1971. He is a graduate of Melbourne University, where he was Lockie Fellow in Australian Literature and Creative Writing. In 1975 he was one of the founders of Adelaide's Friendly Street poetry readings. More recently he has been a member of the Literature Board of the Australia Council, and twice chairperson of Writers' Week at the Adelaide Festival of Arts.

He is the author of eight books of poetry, the latest being *Travelling* (UQP 1986) which won the British Airways Poetry Prize, Australian-Pacific section, in 1986. He has also written a children's book, edited a collection of contemporary short fiction, and collaborated with Beate Josephi on a volume of translations of contemporary German poetry, *Miracles of Disbelief* (1985). He has published numerous articles on Australian and American literature, and has recently written two opera libretti.

He has lived in Italy, Germany and the USA, and lectured extensively in Europe. In Adelaide he teaches American and Australian literature, and literary criticism and contemporary theory.

READING AUSTRALIAN POETRY

Andrew Taylor

University of Queensland Press

First published 1987 by University of Queensland Press
Box 42, St Lucia, Queensland, Australia
Reprinted 1989

Typeset by University of Queensland Press
Printed in Australia by The Book Printer, Melbourne

Distributed in the USA and Canada by
International Specialized Book Services, Inc.,
5602 N.E. Hassalo Street, Portland, Oregon 97213-3640

Cataloguing in Publication Data

National Library of Australia

Taylor, Andrew, 1940– .
Reading Australian poetry.

Bibliography.
Includes index.

1. Australian poetry — History and criticism.
2. Australian poetry — 20th century — History and criticism. I. Title.

A821'.009

PR9610.T38 1987 821 86-27246

ISBN 0 7022 2062 0

Contents

Acknowledgments

Some of the chapters of this book have appeared elsewhere in earlier versions. Chapter 2 was printed as "A Book on Australian Poetry" in *Poetry of the Pacific Region* edited by Paul Sharrod (Adelaide: Centre for Research into New Literatures in English, Flinders University, 1984). Chapter 3 drew heavily on my essay "Bosom of Nature or Heart of Stone: A Difference of Heritage" which first appeared in *The Literary Criterion* Mysore, India, nos. 3 & 4, 1980, and later in *An Introduction to Australian Literature* edited by C. D. Narasimhaiah (Brisbane: John Wiley and Son, 1982).

"A. D. Hope: The Double Tongue of Harmony" was printed in *Southern Review* March, 1984. "Gwen Harwood: The Golden Child Aloft on Discourse" appears in *Gwen Harwood* edited by Robert Sellick (Adelaide: Centre for Research into New Literatures in English, Flinders University, 1987). "Dorothy Hewett as Poet" was printed in *Southerly* no. 4, 1984. "Past Imperfect?: The Sense of the Past in Les A. Murray" was published in *Southern Review* March 1986. "War Poetry: Myth as De-Formation and Re-Formation" was written at the request of Dr Laurie Hergenhan, editor of *Australian Literary Studies*, and published in vol. 12, no. 2, October 1985. "John Tranter: Absence in Flight" was printed in *Australian Literary Studies*, vol. 12, no. 4, October 1986.

Considerable changes have been made to the text of these essays between their first appearance and their form in the present volume. I acknowledge my gratitude to these journals and their editors for publishing my earlier, stumbling versions, and for their permission to reprint here.

In a study of this length, I must acknowledge my particular debt to Vincent Buckley who, both as critic and as poet, was my first guide into the world of Australian poetry. Chris Wallace-Crabbe has, for many years, also provided essential assistance and stimulation, as has Ken Ruthven more recently. This book was conceived and started during a period of study leave at Cornell University, where Jonathan Culler was an invaluable guide to recent critical theory and practice. John Tranter's comments on my discussion of his poetry were both generous and fascinating, and I am grateful for his permission to quote from them. Robin Eaden gave essential assistance with the preparation of the bibliography. And Beate Josephi, who insisted that I write this book, has proved to be a patient source of perceptive criticism and encouragement. My thanks go to all of them.

1

Introduction

The American poet Wallace Stevens once remarked of a poem of his that it had a lot of theory behind it, or words to that effect. The same could perhaps be said of this book. But since I have tried to lay the theory on as lightly as possible in the actual essays which deal with the poetry, it is essential that I say a few words about my guiding ideas by way of introduction.

Just as societies are said to get the government they deserve — at least in democracies — it could also be claimed that literature receives the criticism it deserves. Ever since Vincent Buckley's *Essays in Poetry, Mainly Australian* appeared in 1957 Australian poetry has received the thoughtful attention of critics too numerous to mention. A number of these have been poets themselves: Judith Wright and Chris Wallace-Crabbe have made particularly significant contributions, while the less systematic comments by A.D. Hope, James McAuley, Thomas W. Shapcott, and Les A. Murray have frequently been provocative and stimulating. Although — but it might be more accurate here to say because — many of these poet-critics have also been academics, I think it is fair to claim that the majority of their comments have been guided by two principles: a humanistic belief in the moral significance and value of poetry, and an adherence, by and large, to the reading practices roughly associated with the New Criticism. This has resulted in a series of readings of poems, and oeuvres, which seek to reveal their moral and human significance, and to reconcile it with artistic or aesthetic excellence considered in terms of coherence of statement, unity (sometimes "organic unity") of form, and logic (again, sometimes "imaginative logic") of development. This endeavour has thus been in line with the critical practices which prevailed until recently in universities both in Australia and abroad. Other critics, particularly within the universities, have been more concerned with the social, political and biographical provenance of Australian poetry. As a result of their researches, a great deal of material dealing with this aspect of literature has been amassed, some of it useful, some of it of more relevance to the historian than to the reader of poetry.

This is not the place to engage in a detailed analysis of the critical work of these writers, especially since some of the relevant issues are touched on in chapter 2. But recent years have seen a number of major challenges to their undergirding principles, not the least of which has been the realization that any consistent practice implies a theory and a guiding ideology. By and large, earlier criticism of Australian poetry regarded itself as non-theoretical and largely free of ideologies. Perhaps the most basic principle underlying the present study is that this claim to a non-ideological practice was, and always will be, an illusion. As Fredric Jameson has pointed out, following on the work of Louis Althusser, ideology is to be found beyond the limits of conscious political or value systems, in their suppressed "other side", in what he has called, tellingly, "the political unconscious".[1]

The subtleties of recent Marxist criticism have been little reflected in academic studies of Australian poetry, which have tended to consider the relationship of literary text to social formation as relatively unproblematic, and have rarely investigated the consequences of the reader's and/or critic's ideological position. Similarly, the work of those recent French and American thinkers and writers generally called post-structuralist has been treated with a suspicion occasionally bordering on hostility. After all, while Roland Barthes's declaration of "the death of the author" patently defies common sense, Jacques Derrida's programme of deconstruction seems to render meaningless all claims to meaning, and to permit any reading whatever of particular texts. And as for the neo-Freudian psychoanalyst Jacques Lacan, who can understand him anyway?

In the past decade a number of Australian critics have shown an increasing willingness to engage with the work of these thinkers, including — belatedly — several critics of Australian literature. This book is one such attempt at reading Australian poetry in the light of what a number of post-structuralist thinkers have to say about some things deeply relevant to it: in particular, the nature of language and of poetry, and the nature of the subject, the "experiencing I" of poet and reader, in relation to them both. But I have tried to avoid interlarding my consideration of the poetry with long passages of detailed theoretical argument, and I am reluctant to preface the whole study with what some readers may find a deterrent to further interest. Instead I have clung to the old belief that the value of any theory is only as good as its practice. Thus I have attempted to exemplify my theoretical principles within the discussion of the poetry itself, referring the reader by means of end notes to relevant sources and supporting reading. I have been encouraged to do this by the fact that little of the theory I employ here is actually now very new or out-of-the-way. It may be still unfamiliar to some readers, but it has now been debated so thoroughly that there seems little point in my debating it all over again.

It is only proper, however, to note here in as brief a form as possible certain notions which have guided me in the following discussion. A fully reasoned account of them would be a book in itself, one which I have neither the time nor, probably, the expertise to write. For the source of these ideas, where they are not original, I refer the reader to my bibliography and to the end notes mentioned above. The value of these ideas, as far as I am concerned, is in their ability to produce readings of poetry which are interesting in themselves, and in their capacity — while remaining attentive to the linguistic and psychological complexities of individual poems — to permit a wider consideration of Australian poetry to take place. I have tried to avoid technical language (what is called "jargon" by unsympathetic readers) as much as possible. However if there should still be readers who find the next few paragraphs excessively technical, smacking of jargon, then I suggest they turn to my discussion of the poetry, where these notions are put into practice. I list these points in no order of priority:

* Jacques Derrida's development of Ferdinand de Saussure's theory of language. Language is not the vehicle or locus of truth, but a system of signs which signify only because they differ from other signs. Language does not, therefore, enable truth to be present in some eidetic fashion, but is a mediating system which takes the place of the truth it signifies, standing in for it and deferring it indefinitely.
* A notion of intertextuality. No text, however one defines a text, exists in and of itself, but only and always in relation to other texts, one of which is always the reader's complex subjectivity. This notion is obviously closely related to the first, since it implies that meaning is not simply internal to a text, but is generated by a text's impingement on other texts.
* A consequent notion of poetry not as truth but as text, not as the aesthetically pleasing embodiment of determinate meaning but as a series of linguistic operations subject to further linguistic operations (e.g., reading).
* A notion of literary development, as set out in chapter 2, which accords literature an active role as a series of "possible solutions" to problems existing outside literature, but which considers it also as operating always within a dynamic socio-historical *and* literary intertextuality.
* A notion of the other: that which, by being different, other than, permits anything to be distinct, to be perceived as being what it is and not indistinguishable. The other is both antagonist or rival,

and also the only thing that enables a sense of identity to be experienced. It is important to remember that "identity" is *only* difference from the other — difference is therefore integral to, and internal to, identity.

* The notion, drawn from Jacques Lacan, that the subject is constituted by its reliance on language as that mediating system which enables all transactions between itself and itself, and between itself and its other. This is because the subject is not a simple entity, but the play of forces resulting from the essential "internal difference" (to use a phrase of Emily Dickinson's) that the previous notion entails.
* A notion of poetry particularly (due to its complexity) as consisting of language which signifies an excess of meaning that furnishes multiple and conflicting readings.
* The notion that while theoretically *any* reading of poetry may be achieved within the complex of texts which is the reading subject in its socio-historic situation, powerful conventions of reading serve to limit the conception of what is a "meaningful" reading of any text within any context.
* The notion that no reading of a text is "final" or "definitive", any more than any theoretical framework is. To long for such finality is to succumb to the impossible lure of the transcendental signified — that truth which needs no mediating system to make itself manifest. This would mean an escape from language — and from the human condition — entirely.
* The notion that in the intertextual operation which is reading, some readings of texts bear more relevantly on the reader than on what is being read, and vice versa. While text and other are inseparable and inextricably implicated in each other, they can only be so, and fulfil their constitutive functions, *because* they are not identical. In the case of text and reader, they occupy different socio-political and historical positions.
* The notion that a thorough reading of poetry involves, in Barbara Johnson's words, "the careful teasing out of warring forces of signification within the text itself". Only then can something of its fully dynamic quality be apprehended, particularly its relation to the apparently contradictory but enabling other.[2]
* A belief that if one loves words and poetry enough — which means, simply, accepting the central role of language in our lives that these notions indicate it has — such a reading is neither perverse nor capricious. It is an indication that we are, in the words of the late Paul de Man, "only trying to come closer to being as rigorous a reader as the author had to be in order to write the [poem] in the first place".[3] As someone who writes poems myself, I can see little wrong with such an aspiration on the part of a reader or critic.

I have called the above points "notions" because, for reasons I have already explained, I have not tried here to argue them rigorously. It may turn out that they are not all true. One example will suffice. The exact place that Lacan accords language in the constitution of the subject may be faulted by later psychoanalytic investigation. It none the less seems to me that when it comes to poetry we are discussing language or nothing at all — and, what is more, we are discussing it *in* language. It is hard to imagine the subject engaging in intelligibility without language; it is impossible to imagine poetry doing so without it. Whether or not Lacan is factually true about the subject, his observations seem to be of particular value to a discussion of poetry — especially when taken in conjunction with Derrida's discussion of language.

There is a further reason why I have not tried to argue the above points through into a rigorous system, although I have tried to avoid anything which looks like an obvious inconsistency or debilitating self-contradiction. Such an enterprise — laudable though it may be — would be yet another expression of that longing for the Absolute, the System which contains all systems which is impossible because it cannot contain itself. Throughout the history of thought such a system has eluded far better minds than mine, and will always do so, just as the history of "definitive" readings of texts has inevitably revealed their provisionality. As T.S. Eliot put it so provocatively in "Tradition and the Individual Talent":

> . . . what happens when a new work of art is created is something that happens simultaneously to all the works of art which preceded it. The existing monuments form an ideal order among themselves, which is modified by the introduction of the new (the really new) work of art among them.[4]

All meaning, just as all poetry and all systems of thought, exists within an intertextual space which is not finite, never complete.

Which brings me, finally, to the question of a canon of Australian poetry. I have considered the question of defining such a canon in chapter 1, but would like to add this briefly. The establishment of a literary canon involves the creation of a hierarchy of texts by means of value judgments. One of the strictures directed at recent post-structuralist criticism has been its apparent inability to determine any new canon, no matter how radically it may question old ones. Such criticism is based on a failure to grasp the radical nature of that questioning, which challenges the very notion of a canon. By posing such questions in relation to the forming of value judgments as "Valuable for whom?" and "Valuable within what social formation?" post-structuralist critical theory demands of the reader a consciousness of ideological location which had previously been assumed as neutral. A canon is only a canon *for* a readership.

Matthew Arnold's notion of a canon as the best that has been thought and said or Coleridge's the best words in the best order leaves unquestioned the position of who does the judging, who decides what is best.

I have therefore left the establishment of a new canon of Australian poetry to those who feel more confident than I that they speak authoritatively with the voice of the whole of Australian society. For myself, I have chosen to write on a number of poets whose work I have read with pleasure and involvement over many years. Their reputation has been, for the most part, established by commentators on Australian poetry with no knowledge of post-structuralist criticism or theory, and my own interest in them has dated from before my acquaintance with it. These poets are by no means the only Australian poets worthy of careful attention and I hope to be able to write something on others in the future. My present task, however, is a deliberate attempt to cast a new light on those who have had critical scrutiny play on them before, and to see what this new light reveals.

2

A Book on Australian Poetry

It is not so long ago that mention of a book on Australian poetry would have been greeted by a certain kind of academic with the comment "I didn't know there was any Australian poetry, much less a book on it". The implication was not, of course, that no poetry had been written in Australia, but that no poetry written here was good enough or interesting enough to warrant a book on it. Manifestly foolish as such a comment would be today, it serves nonetheless to raise the whole problematic of Australian poetry — just what is it and, equally important, how do we know what it is?

Things are very different today from thirty, or even twenty, years ago. The notion that there is some unitary tradition of English literature with its capital still in London has been replaced by the acceptance of a multiplicity of traditions. Even the image of literature in English as some kind of tree — the great trunk, consisting of Chaucer, Shakespeare, Milton, and so on, branching at various historical moments into American, Australian, Canadian, etc., literature — seems a little antiquatedly colonialist. Rather, the English language — and perhaps one should say languages — is or are seen as seed, scattered in different places and at different times, and over differing races, cultures, and social classes or groups; thus it germinates into a variety of literatures which include not only the "high" but also the popular which almost always coexist with it. Thus we no longer feel guilty when we study — or teach — Brennan instead of Wordsworth, Slessor instead of Eliot. Brennan and Slessor have their places within a field designated Australian literature (sub-section Australian poetry), a field which to a considerable extent provides the frame within which they can be read as Australian poets. Yet at the same time the field itself is also to a large part constituted by their presence within it.

How this field is accounted for (if for the present we can set aside the ideology of the value judgments that determine which texts constitute it, are permitted entry) varies somewhat from critic to critic. But by and large the format of the Pelican volume, *The Literature of*

Australia, edited by Geoffrey Dutton,[1] exemplifies a procedure which explicitly or otherwise still underlies the practice of many Australian critics. A social, political and historical matrix (the "history of Australia") is invoked, in relation to which a number of writers judged to be important are considered in such a way that the "development" of Australian writing from convict days to the present is shown to have taken place. Although none of the contributors to *The Literature of Australia* can ultimately account for a writer's output totally in terms of them (and in fact none of them actually tries to do so), the motivating assumption of this model is that literature grows out of, or is produced by, society and history. Most studies of Australian writing have stressed this "commonsense" priority of society and history to literature; John Docker's[2] concern with the two-way formative processes of cultural history is only a more recent sophistication of an approach which has long distinguished commentators on Australian literature from the erstwhile New Critical or Leavisite practice of some of their academic colleagues, who tended to isolate literature from any political-historical matrix. But this re-insertion of Australian literature into history has rarely taken into account the sophistications of contemporary Marxist criticism, in particular the fact that history as we know it is not an empirical "given", but our reading of our past. Without dwelling on this point in any detail at the moment, I would argue that history is available to us only as a text, as yet another text among a multiplicity of texts. As Fredric Jameson writes in a recent and sophisticated account of this notion:

> What Althusser's own insistence on history as an absent cause makes clear, but what is missing from the formula as it is canonically worded, is that he does not at all draw the fashionable conclusion that because history is not a text, the "referent" does not exist. We would therefore propose the following revised formulation: that history is not a text, not a narrative, master or otherwise, but that, as an absent cause, it is inaccessible to us except in textual form, and that our approach to it and to the Real itself necessarily passes through its prior textualization, its narrativization in the political unconscious.[3]

Thus how we read history — which means, simply, what history is for us at any given moment — depends in some measure on how we have learned to read it by means of our practice with it and other texts.

For example, Patrick White's *Voss*, although loosely based on the historical story of Leichhardt, is not itself history in any verifiable sense; yet it has become a powerful influence on the way many Australians of the present see their country's past and, therefore, on the way they inhabit its present. Similarly, the various "cultural" readings of the Anzac story (from Alan Seymour's *The One Day of The Year*, for example, to Peter Weir's film *Gallipoli*) provide influential interpretations of that event to today's Australians, almost none of whom actually participated in it. No Australian historian with any claim to a knowledge of his field can plausibly be untouched by these cultural readings of the past, any more than he can be by similar readings of the present. Therefore I want to suggest that to treat history as prior to, and thus in some way productive of, literature involves a hierarchical ordering of the duality "history/literature" in which history is the privileged term, an ordering which could be readily subverted so as to indicate that literature contributes to and thus helps to generate our (reading of) history.

A less debatable matter is the general consensus that Australian culture has developed under the progressively weakened dominance of its parent culture — the English — in a process endemic to all colonial cultures. This process of maturation is conveniently outlined by Elaine Showalter in her book on women's literature, *A Literature of Their Own*:

> In looking at literary subcultures, such as black, Jewish, Canadian, Anglo-Indian, or even American, we can see that they all go through three major phases. First, there is a prolonged phase of *imitation* of the prevailing modes of the dominant tradition, and *internalization* of its standards of art and its views on social roles. Second, there is a phase of *protest* against these standards and values, and *advocacy* of minority rights and values, including a demand for autonomy. Finally, there is a phase of *self-discovery*, a turning inward freed from some of the dependency of opposition, a search for identity.[4]

Given the peculiar beginnings of white settlement in Australia as a convict colony, one can perceive elements of the second phase of this development right from the start. Nonetheless this model is as apt for Australia, in its general outlines, as it is for any of the cultures Showalter mentions. Beginning as a process of submission yet imitation, then giving way to a rebellion leading finally through self-discovery to independence, it is clearly akin to the development of a child through adolescence to adulthood. In many respects it resembles Harold Bloom's Oedipal or Promethean model of the development of a "strong" poet, particularly when we bear in mind that any culture which successfully wins its independence from the powers of influence has become, in Bloom's sense, a "strong" culture.

The gist of Bloom's rather complex argument is that any poet (and for the purposes of this discussion we could substitute the word culture for poet) who becomes "strong" does so not by neglecting his or her precursors but as a result of an obsession with a parental figure whose work he or she must wrestle with and ultimately rewrite, wrench askew, in order that it might be made right, got right. As Bloom writes:

> The meaning of a strong poem is another strong poem, a precursor's poem which is being misinterpreted, revised, corrected, evaded, twisted askew, made to suffer an inclination or bias which is the property of the later and not the earlier poet. Poetic influence, in this sense, is actually poetic misprision, a poet's taking or doing amiss of a parent poem . . .[5]

In order to gain a place for himself, the younger must displace the older; the success of the younger is won "at the expense of his forebears as much as his contemporaries".[6] One could translate this into Oedipal terms by saying that the young culture or "strong" poet must in some sense deform or destroy his father in order to take possession of his father's wife, who in this case is the muse, his own true mother. Obviously the terms of this model could be changed from he to she without damaging its structure.

Although in the long run it is nothing more than a trope, such a model seems to be of considerable use, particularly when deployed simultaneously on an individual and on a national level. It provides an account, for example, of the failure of Christopher Brennan ever to displace Milton, the dominating father figure, from the centre of his poetic world and to create a space at Milton's expense within which he could mature as a strong poet. In this respect Brennan was manifestly less a "strong" poet than Milton himself, who was prepared to grapple with no less a father figure than the Protestant god himself in order "to justify the ways of God to men". Brennan's tactic, on the contrary, was to evade, rather than seek out, confrontation. Writing in the last decade of the nineteenth century when Australia, as a federated nation, was not yet in existence, Brennan was further disadvantaged by writing within a poetic culture which had barely embarked on adolescent rebellion against parental authority. Whether any poet could have achieved Brennan's ambition at that moment of Australia's cultural development is problematic, though one must not ignore the achievement of his contemporaries in other fields, notably in fiction and painting. One could hazard the hypothesis that in prose that necessary rebellion was already further advanced, as could be easily enough demonstrated by the nationalism apparent within it. Consequently Lawson's and Furphy's aim would have been less to emulate British precursors than to subvert them and render them unfit for their role as dominating father. Certainly some such operation seems to be going on in Furphy's satire and parody. Their ultimate aim was thus to write Australian literature; whereas Brennan's was still to win himself a place within English or, more grandly still, within European literature.

This trope or model of cultural development also offers a way of discussing the tensions within a culture at any particular time as new writers develop by testing their strength against their precursors. And it enables us to read Australian poetry in relation to

English precursors and contemporaries, and Australian poetry of one period of development in relation to Australian poetry of another. But it also entails certain problems. When it is applied to a young culture (as distinct from an individual writer) in the process of its development toward maturity, it could be seen as serving to support or underwrite the notion of poetry as a "corpus", even a kind of "body politic", united at any historical moment in some adversary relationship with parental tyranny. It would be a naive critic indeed who would claim that all Australian poetry of, for example, the last decade of the nineteenth century was unified and coherent in its position vis-à-vis English poetry. Nonetheless the common habit of characterising poetry in terms of decades ("the poetry of the nineties", for example) indicates a deep-rooted tendency to classify in terms of likeness and to minimize disparities and differences. It seems more congenial to characterize a body of poetry in terms of similarity rather than in terms of its internal differences: the corpus of Australian poetry thus consists less of a diversity of parts, each adapted for specific ends, than of what fits together, what shares common characteristics. This stress on what is common underlies many attempts to define the corpus. Definition is — by definition — the establishing of limits, the erection and policing of boundaries around a common ground. Within these limits we have Australian poetry. Beyond them we have something else.

To define the corpus is, psychologically, an attempt to eliminate diversity, to establish inner coherence by excluding what is discordant, disruptive, other. (To continue the Oedipal comparison, it is an attempt to rid Thebes of all that would corrupt and subvert its purity: ostensibly the Sphinx but, as we should know, really Oedipus himself.) The corpus of Australian poetry thus consists of those poets and those poems sharing a family likeness, those which are akin. This does not mean, of course, that they are all absolutely alike, and critics and anthologists — those organizers of family reunions — pride themselves on the diversity of the family members they manage to assemble in one place. Still, they all must have some kinship; and it is when one asks of what, precisely, this kinship consists, that difficulties arise. Few critics or anthologists today would insist on some more or less explicit quality of "Australianness" in the way that Douglas Sladen did in his *A Century of Australian Song*, published in 1888. Still, writers as diverse as Les A. Murray and John Tranter have firmly held ideas about what direction they wish to see Australian poetry going and thus what, properly speaking, is or is not part of that family.

Murray wishes to eradicate or discourage certain qualities he considers alien to some kind of genuine Australianness which he sees exemplified in rural or small town life and threatened by urban sophistication, excessive intellection and the seductions of mere faddishness. Deeply distrustful of the academy, he champions a "fundamentally democratic style" which is "the central and best tendency of Australian poetry, an enlightened, inclusive, civil mode of writing which belongs ultimately to the middle style".[7] Criticizing John Tranter's poetry for being "mannered, controlled, discussing feeling rather than evoking it and disciplined out of any simplicity or largesse", he claims that "the memory and aspiration of community . . . have kept the best Australian poetry humane in a time when it has often seemed more natural to accept the apparent drift of things and become wholly elitist". His wide-ranging choice of poems in *The New Oxford Book of Australian Verse*, with its generous selection of Aboriginal material, exemplifies this position.[8]

Tranter, on the other hand, wishes to lop off developments which he sees as antiquated, enfeebled and incapable of vigorous new growth, and to graft onto the old stock a cosmopolitan awareness of new possibilities: to arrange a good marriage for Australian poetry, in other words. Combating Murray's endorsement of a national tradition, he promotes a poetry involved in the developments of international modernism:

> The poets of the Generation of '68 have left the duties of priest, psychotherapist and moral administrator to those who feel they are best trained to enact them. They have instead devoted their energies to that field of human action where their skills and talents arm them with a unique authority, where meaning embodies itself as speech, and words emerge as that most ancient yet most contemporary voyage of discovery, literature.[9]

Despite his explicitly cosmopolitan and anti-conservative stance, Tranter, just as much as Murray, is attempting an ideologically based purification of the family of Australian poetry, in that the spouse he chooses for it is seen as eminently capable of producing offspring whose vigour will unequivocally proclaim them as the true heirs to, and rightful possessors of, this country's poetic inheritance. It should not surprise us that the definitions of Australian poetry underlying both Murray's and Tranter's procedures result not from simple exclusion of the unfamilial, but from expulsion of members of the family deemed unworthy of their place within it. Only by rejecting, excluding Australian poetry, it seems, can Australian poetry be defined.

Another way of attempting to define the corpus or family of Australian poetry — and it is, of course, inextricably intertangled with what Murray and Tranter are doing too — involves some more or less defined criteria of literary quality, that is, goodness or badness. And here we enter onto hazardous ground indeed. The fact that judgments of literary quality have a very large — and largely unconscious — ideological dimension is something that critics, reviewers, anthologists, and even writers in Australia are still reluctant to come to terms with. The concealment of ideology as common sense, or as sensibility, is still so widely practised that it is rarely recognized for what it is. Critics praise what is moving, profound, powerful, invigorating, vital, and so forth — without adding the essential qualifications, "for whom" and "why for whom". Therefore it was heartening to read, at the end of her introduction to *The Oxford History of Australian Literature*, Leonie Kramer's declaration that "We have tried to take a clear view of the very large body of literature before us, and to expose the critical assumptions upon which our judgments rest".[10]

It is consequently disappointing when we turn to Vivian Smith's section on poetry in *The Oxford History* to find that nowhere within its one hundred and fifty-five pages is this exposure actually made. When he claims, early in his essay, that "somewhere between the pressures of inherited forms which need to be individually mastered and not simply imitated, and the burdens of a culture in perpetual difficulties, individual work of considerable value and impressiveness has been created" he does not go on to give an explicit account of how value is constituted.[11] One suspects that value here has something to do with being impressive, but there is no real attempt at a careful theoretical analysis of who is being impressed, particularly in relation to subjectively held social or other values that are not explicitly acknowledged. Similarly the whole problematic of "inherited forms" — suggesting the interlocking questions of a writer's relation with previous writing and a young culture's relation to an older one which I have touched on earlier — receives little rigorous attention. One would also welcome some analysis of what is meant by "a culture in perpetual difficulties". If one were to find food for thought in Fredric Jameson's provocative thesis that "a given style [is] a projected solution, on the aesthetic or imaginary level, to a genuinely contradictory situation in the concrete world of everyday social life"[12], then those "perpetual difficulties" — whatever they might be — might be read as culturally productive rather than as "burdens" to be sloughed off.

When one turns to actual critical analysis in Smith's essay, one finds that evaluation is performed by means of an impressionistic and frequently metaphorical language which leaves untouched the deeper questions of value formation. Several examples, taken almost at random, can illustrate this. Discussing James McAuley, he writes:

> If many of the later lyrics are slight the best are by no means superficial, and in the finest like "At Rushy Lagoon" and "In Northern Tasmania" the valedictory mood — the sense of a fading life — comes together with the sense of a vanishing way of life to achieve a poignant music.[13]

One cannot take issue with his thematic analysis, although one should remind oneself that the words "slight" and "superficial" when applied to poetry — as they so often are — are actually metaphors. But it is the reference to "poignant music" which is of interest here. Music is devoid of semantic significance: it is less answerable to its listeners' demands for signification than poetry is, since the apparent offer of "meaning" is one of the things we habitually ask of poetry. (In fact in the poem that Smith is discussing McAuley makes his meaning quite clear: "A way of life is in decline, / And only those who lived it know / What it is time overwhelms . . .") The implication of the image Smith uses to praise McAuley is that his finest late poetry gains in quality as it leaves semantic signification behind, in so far as it becomes something other than poetry. What we have here, concealed behind an impressionistic evaluative characterization of the poem's quality, is an apparently unconscious endorsement of Pater's dictum that poetry aspires to the condition of music.

Elsewhere, in his discussion of David Campbell, Smith praises him in these terms:

> It is the strength of Campbell's art (as of the lyric in general) to affirm the paradoxical resistance of the small and frail in front of the great and overwhelming, in a poem that avoids both sentimentality and preciosity; to demonstrate how a sustaining truth may be perceived through the apparently insignificant.[14]

The resident values of a conservative liberal humanism are closer to the surface here, more explicit. Campbell's poetry is good because of the values it thematizes: a championing of the underdog, a mistrust of the big, a dislike of both sentimentality and the precious, a belief in sustaining truth. But Smith then goes on to discuss Campbell's later poems in this way:

> His poems have become smoother and rounder but more deliberately random. He no longer writes with the plucked staccato tension of *Speak with The Sun*, but his poems have retained one quality throughout: the capacity for looking at the commonplaces of nature and life with a fresh eye. His imagery is always clear and alertly observed in the manner of folk songs.[15]

Implicit in the description of the poems becoming "smoother and rounder" is the image of water-worn stones, water-worn stones which look, incidentally, "with a fresh eye". Again, as with the McAuley passage, the poems are praised in terms of what they are not, in terms this time of passivity, inertness, non-signification. The reference to folk songs is also interesting. Contrary to what is claimed, "the manner of folk songs" is not one of clear and alert observation — "a fresh eye" — but of clear and alert reference to social and cultural codes immediately retrievable. Folk song's stock of tropes is small when compared with that of "high" literature, and they function by familiarity and convention, unlike the tendency of "high" literature towards originality and unfamiliarity. If such tropes appear vivid to middleclass university educated people such as Vivian Smith and myself — readers rather than singers — it is because they are not so familiar to us as they are to habitual singers and listeners of folk songs. Transposed into a different social context, they acquire the unfamiliarity and hence the vividness that we praise in "high" literature. Implicit in Smith's remarks, therefore, is a failure to take account of the complex social and conventional operations at work in any reading of literature, and the role they play in any kind of evaluation.

I have written at some length on these three passages, not because Smith is a particularly flagrant example but because he is so representative of commentators on Australian poetry who, eschewing a rigidly historical approach, attempt a definition of the field of Australian poetry in terms of literary values.[16] Literary values, literary standards, are themselves conventional and ideological, and are not absolute. Yet rarely are the ideological bases for their value judgments made explicit. Ideology, in general, masquerades as common sense, good taste, a firm knowledge of literature and an appreciation of what it means to be an Australian, or some such apparently self-explanatory quality. Needless to say, the picture of Australian poetry which emerges is nonetheless intimately related to the ideologies so disguised, and not to any chimerical absolute sense of literary worth.

James McAuley employed another metaphor in attempting a definition of Australian poetry when he titled his book *A Map of Australian Verse.*[17] But for all its implicit claim to a technical impartiality, a scientific disinterestedness, mapmaking is not an innocent activity. A map is a deployment of conventional signs which are simultaneously passive (their signification assigned to them by society and history) and active (they signify certain things by excluding the signification of others). Any map, whether it be of Australian verse or of Australia itself, is thus interpretation, a reading of the field, in which certain features are omitted in order that other features become visible. The signs themselves are not passively obedient to the cartographer's will. They help to determine not only what form his expression will take but also what he will find to map in the first place. In addition, this cartographic reading is itself subject to further factors not originating within it, and not the product of what is read either, as "pure" or "innocent" response. As Jonathan Culler states in *The Pursuit of Signs*, "Meaning is not an individual creation but the result of applying to the text operations and conventions which constitute the institution of literature".[18] These "operations and conventions" which make reading "an interpersonal activity" originate neither in McAuley nor anyone else, nor in the text itself, but in society and history (history which is accessible to us only as a text). They constitute themselves within us as ideology, or as the pathways along which ideology advances itself. To an extent that "commonsense" or sensibility critics would consider preposterous, they actually determine what will be seen as poetry, what will be read as poetry at any moment, and how that poetry will be read. In this way it is they that draw the map, determining what can appear on it and what cannot. McAuley's "map", therefore, is really a reading of a map already drawn, in that the conventions and signs determining his interpretation of Australian poetry are always — and always already — in place.

By way of concluding this part of my discussion, I would just observe that it is one of the paradoxes of literary studies that while we claim that one of literature's greatest qualities is its ability to unsettle and disturb, the urge to relate, integrate and even unify — the urge to privilege the familiar and the familial, that which works on us in ways which we can understand because it does not subvert what our understanding is grounded in — still activates most studies of literature. This integrative activity, I want to stress, consists simultaneously and necessarily of its opposite: of a divisive, exclusive drawing of limits. The irreducible, and largely unexamined, ideological subjectivity, (what Jameson calls "the political unconscious"), determining the drawing of these limits in no way prevents them from being drawn. In fact, it may be organic with the wish to locate the other as outside the self, rather than as radically within it, constitutive of it.

Thus when the locus of poetic discourse is actually claimed to be the other itelf, this is an ideological act which not only challenges orthodox versions of the corpus of Australian poetry, but also reveals their ideological formation. This is the effect of anthologies such as *Off the Record* and *The Penguin Book of Australian Women Poets*.[19] Both books can be seen as specific interventions aimed at changing common perceptions of Australian poetry. Although questions of poetic quality are addressed by the editors, neither anthology is concerned primarily with them. Instead, they aim to make heard voices which common preconceptions of Australian poetry have rendered inaudible. *Off the Record* paradoxically is a collection of poems which are in most cases not primarily intended for printed presentation, but meant to be presented orally — performance poetry. The irony of this is not lost, of course, on its editor who, in a lengthy introduction, claims that print-oriented poetry in Australia is the product and the property of the middle class establishment and the academic support system which controls its production and distribution. Performance poetry, on the other hand, is not so much the voice of another class as the voice of those who challenge this perceived hegemony: "Poetry was losing its high-art nose, its meaningful pause and its class-diseased larynx . . . It was now in the hands of chemists, carpenters, teachers, housewives, journalists, architects and factory hands."[20] *The Penguin Book of Australian Women Poets* is, like similar anthologies elsewhere, an attempt to rescue the voices of women from the obscurity to which a patriarchal critical apparatus would condemn them. It challenges the assumptions of value-formation which have served to privilege male poets over female, or to favour that poetry by women which best consorts with male-defined conceptions of female gender. These two anthologies claim to speak from "outside" a perceived social establishment or received discourse, and in doing so they draw attention to the ideological bases — and hence limits — of what until recently was regarded as a largely aesthetic practice. Their essentially partisan nature is thus a challenge to any unitary conception of Australian poetry which earlier practices may have fostered.

In a way that is in no sense exhaustive, I have attempted to suggest several of the problems that emerge when critical discourse attempts to engage with the notion of Australian poetry in some sense conceived as a whole: as a body of work emerging from a colonial situation and akin to a child developing towards maturity and independence from parental authority; as a family held together by kinship and defining itself in terms of its difference from what is "outside" while being still, as families are apt to be, fraught with internal differences and incompatibilities; as a terrain and as a reading of a terrain. For the last part of this discussion I want to turn to those two words "Australian poetry" which are responsible for, and constantly vex, the critics' and the anthologists' nightmare: whom to include, whom to exclude. The mention of anthologists here is deliberate because the anthology, like the critical study, is a signifier, both in its production and in its consumption. And it works, like all other signifiers, by exclusion. An anthologist's reading of Australian poetry is, inevitably and simultaneously, a writing of it: a writing out of it by means of a writing off of (parts of) it. I have already touched on the way this reading is effected by putting into play certain operations and conventions which are to a greater or lesser extent as unconscious as those we both activate and conform to while driving a car; and I have pointed to the fact that these are ideological, often unconsciously so. So the further question remains: just what is it that the critic and the anthologist are reading/writing?

The obvious answer to this question is, of course, Australian poetry. But at this point we must tackle the question of what this phrase means. Take the second term, poetry, first. M. H. Abrams's invaluable handbook, *A Glossary of Literary Terms*, does not list it, and wisely so.[21] For despite the fact that enormous attention has been paid to the structures and language of literature in recent years, no fully satisfying definition of poetry has emerged. Nor can it. What will be acknowledged as poetry is what the conventions of reading operative within a reader in a given place and time permit him or her to read as poetry. Although this may sound tautological, it is not meaningless. To start with, it indicates that whatever it is that constitutes poetry is not to be sought in formal structures which can typologically exclude unwanted intruders, in the way that A.D. Hope, as one amongst many, once attempted.[22] Nor can it be located in "the words on the page", where English departments in Australia were — and largely still are — wont to look for it. Rather, it is to be found in what happens to those words when they go off the page, when they are read. This formulation also indicates that how the words will be read is not a matter of simple, innocent response, but depends on the activity of numerous codes available to and operating through the reader and which ultimately must be ascribed to society and history.[23] The meaning of a poem therefore is not something "contained" within it, manifestly inherent in its words, to be apprehended by a "judicious" or "sensitive" reading (the "content" of a literary "form"); rather, meaning is what happens in the encounter of a text with a reader, when the text of, for example, a poem is inscribed within the ambit of that complex web of texts, textual activities, which is the reader, by means of the act of reading. For as Roland Barthes says, "this 'I' which approaches the text is already itself a plurality of other texts, of codes which are infinite or, more precisely, lost (whose origin is lost)".[24]

A simple illustration will serve to show how not only poetic meaning is generated by reading, but also how what is poetry is determined extrinsically rather than intrinsically. When the Ern Malley poems were first devised by James McAuley and Harold Stewart in 1944, they were intentionally conceived by their authors as not poetry. The "poems" deliberately failed to satisfy their expectations of intelligibility, formal clarity and a certain coherence or "logic" of imagery. Devised specifically to frustrate these expectations, their purpose presumably was to demonstrate that the editors of *Angry Penguins* and its readers either failed to hold these laudable expectations or held them at such a low level of importance that even pastiche satisfied them. However it seems that one convention operative (largely unconsciously) in any act of reading poetry is an expectation of unity or coherence. Without that expectation and the resultant willingness to search for coherence and even to construct it when it is not immediately manifest, our reading of poetry would fall apart at the first metaphor. In the case of the Ern Malley poems, the editors of *Angry Penguins* clearly placed less importance on manifest coherence in the text, and more importance on the readers' activity of searching for it, struggling to find it within the poems' (deliberate) attempts to frustrate them. What has happened, since 1944, is that readers now expect to have to work harder in making coherence of the poems they read than McAuley and Stewart then felt they should. The result is that we can now read the Ern Malley poems as poetry. They have become poems, even if not major or particularly good ones, because their incoherences no long exclude them from the space our reading habits allocate to poetry.

If a definition of poetry can be approached only circuitously, by assigning it a place within the reading process and simultaneously assigning to the reading process certain cultural (in the widest as well as the narrower sense) and historical determinants, which themselves result from an individual's reading of culture and history, how do we fare when we approach that other term of our problematic phrase, "Australian poetry"?

At perhaps the simplest level, do we mean poetry written by Australians?[25] If so, then we would have to exclude all poetry written in Australia by holders of British, New Zealand, Canadian or American passports, not to mention those residents from countries whose language is other than English and who have not taken out Australian citizenship. If and when such writers acquired Australian citizenship, would only their subsequent poetry be Australian or could their earlier poetry (involved, possibly, with the problems of a new resident in Australia) be admitted along with the poet? Clearly there is something wrong with this method of determining the Australianness of poetry according to the passport of its author. Could we then say that any poetry written within Australia is Australian? But Australia as a nation has existed only since 1901, so we would have to exclude all poetry written before then. We could counter this one by claiming all poetry written within the land-mass of what is now Australia, and in doing so manage to recover the Aboriginal poetry as well. But we would have to exclude all poems written by Australians abroad, for example A.D. Hope's "A Letter from Rome" which was not only written, as it tells us, in Italy, but is about Italy too. And we would have to include all poems written here by visitors, irrespective of whether these were in English or any other language spoken here, and of whether they were ever published, let alone read, here. Even if we were to relax the guidelines a little, and say that Australian poetry is all poetry written by people normally resident in Australia, we still have problems. What, for example, does "normally" mean? Ninety-five per cent, seventy per cent of one's time? Where would this place Peter

Porter, or Randolph Stow? Or J.R. Rowland who, as a diplomat, normally spends much of his time overseas and yet who, also as a diplomat, represents, even signifies, Australia in that obscure grammar which is diplomacy?

Since all these attempts at determining by way of provenance what the word "Australian" in this context means, it may be necessary to look within the poetry itself. In terms of content, A.D. Hope's "Australia" is clearly Australian. Just as clearly, the same poet's "Imperial Adam", "The Double Looking Glass" and "In Memoriam: Gertrude Colmar", all poems which "Australian poetry" would be poorer without, are not. Could it then be a matter of linguistic or stylistic characteristics that we need to be looking for? But Bruce Dawe's colloquialism and air of chat is in these respects far closer to the American Frank O'Hara than he is to Christopher Brennan who, in turn, is closer to the periodic non-colloquiality of Milton than to any recognizable version of Australian linguistic practice. Could it be, in fact, that neither Dawe nor Brennan writes Australian poetry? What we can be sure of, to cut this vexing matter short, is that any attempt at defining Australian poetry in terms of qualities inherent in the poetry will, as with our attempts at defining it in terms of provenance, external qualities, inevitably fail. If the phrase "Australian poetry" has any meaning at all, it is, like what it signifies, conventional, approximate, and subject always to revision.

Because, in one sense, we all know what Australian poetry is. It is that body of poetry, expressing certain themes in certain formal ways, and in certain linguistic modalities (although to be accurate, for "certain" we must also read "uncertain") which, as a result of our reading, our education and even our conversation, we have come habitually to associate with the country and the nation we call Australia. If we wish to be a little more precise, we would have to say that Australian poetry is that poetry selected from this field at its widest extent by critics, reviewers, teachers, readers, and the poets themselves, to signify, to stand for (by means of substitution) the field itself. And, as we have seen, this signification is done by a process of exclusion, frequently based on unconscious ideologies. Only by excluding Australian poetry can Australian poetry be signified. Only in terms of what it is not can Australian poetry actually *be*.

So it seems that the apparently innocuous and self-explanatory term "Australian poetry" is not only hard but actually impossible ultimately to pin down. Australian poetry reveals itself both as a kind of individual developing to maturity, to freedom from a parental culture, and also as a family within which this Oedipal revolt and others are already and always occurring; it is both a terrain and the map of the terrain; it is both something which defies definition and its definition which substitutes itself for it as both signifier and signified. It is, by excluding itself as much as by excluding what is extrinsic to it (what is written in another country and in another language, for example). Australian poetry is, always and inextricably, in terms of what it is not; it is always being overtaken and supplanted by its own definitions, and always being excluded in order that it be manifest. Furthermore, while it is in one sense deeply and inescapably historical, its historicity is constituted by our immediate and contemporary acts of reading.

It should not be surprising, therefore, that a book on Australian poetry, any discourse which attempts to engage meaningfully with whatever that phrase means, is necessarily problematic. Any book on Australian poetry is both a reading of it and a signification of it; it is both an inscription and an exclusion; finally, and perhaps foremost, it is both personal and inescapably cultural and historical.

3

A Case of Romantic Disinheritance

Australian poetry in English is now almost two hundred years old. White settlement was first established here the year before the French Revolution began in 1789, a date frequently seen as marking also the start of the great period of romanticism in Germany and England and, later, in other European countries and the United States. Romanticism left such an indelible trace on the literary and cultural consciousness of these countries that all their subsequent literature must be seen as inescapably post-romantic. This is so even of those further crucial literary movements, modernism and post-modernism, which at first glance might seem so revolutionary in their aspects towards romanticism as to have achieved independence from it.

A full account of romanticism, modernism and post-modernism is clearly far beyond the scope of the present study. Instead, I would refer the reader to the account given by Charles Altieri in *Enlarging the Temple*, especially in his introduction and first chapter.[1] While the critical literature on romanticism and modernism is virtually endless, the virtue for my purposes in Altieri's account is in his distinguishing post-modernism from modernism in terms of their respective re-readings of romanticism. Briefly, Altieri argues the origin of the romantics' notion of the Imagination in the inability of late eighteenth century language to "reconcile value and fact by integrating abstract and empirical orders". This inability, Altieri suggests, following Whitehead, is a result of the philosophical traditions (rationalism and empiricism) inherited by the romantics, traditions which separated mind from world, value from fact:

> This leads to the need for inventing special categories of the mind like imagination, which justify claiming special status for the modes of discourse they produce. Hence the imagination can be said to produce symbolic structures that reconcile fact and value because they are not primarily descriptions of the world but occupy a distinctive epistemological and ontological space. (P. 31)

However it would be a mistake to see the Imagination, in romantic thought and practice, as meaning the same thing for everybody. In chapter 13 of his *Biographia Literaria* Coleridge claims that the Imagination "dissolves, diffuses, dissipates, in order to re-create; or where this process is rendered impossible, yet still at all events it struggles to idealize and to unify".[2] But for Wordsworth, the Imagination is that faculty which enables him to "see into the life of things" and to hear "the still, sad music of humanity" in subtle harmony with Nature, a conception of the imagination which Altieri characterizes as "immanentist".[3]

> Both poets seek to reconcile subjective and objective, to find value within fact, but while Wordsworth emphasizes reorienting the subjective consciousness by teaching it ways of attending to its participation in objective laws, Coleridge tries to redeem the objective by pointing to the ways it is formed and structured in creative acts of consciousness. (P. 37)

According to Altieri this latter, Coleridgean, notion of the Imagination proved more durable than Wordsworth's during the Victorian period. While empirical "certainties" were crumbling, the Coleridgean attitude drew attention to the mind's own powers. In the modernist period this essentially symbolist[4] (as distinct from the Wordsworthian immanentist or, one might say, metonymic) notion of the Imagination prevailed, with its concomitant valuation of culture or tradition as that which has, and can, put a meaningful human expression onto the flux, even the chaos, of human experience. As T.S. Eliot put it in his essay on James Joyce, "Ulysses, Order, and Myth":

> In using the myth, in manipulating a continuous parallel between contemporaneity and antiquity, Mr. Joyce is pursuing a method which others must pursue after him . . . It is simply a way of controlling, of ordering, of giving a shape and a significance to the immense panorama of futility and anarchy which is contemporary history.[5]

Myth, tradition, the symbolist Imagination — all these can "control", "order", "give shape and significance" where shape and significance are lacking. It is only with the passing of the classic modernist period, Altieri argues, that we find again an immanentist, Wordsworthian poetic, one which "stresses the ways an imaginative attention to common and casual experience can transform the mind and provide satisfying resting places", where "poetic creation is conceived more as the discovery and the disclosure of numinous relationships within nature than as the creation of containing and structuring forms".[6] This, according to Altieri, is the characteristic post-modernist mode, one which, with Wordsworth, recognizes "nature and the language of the sense" (that is, sensory experience) as the foundation of moral, spiritual and psychological well-being.

Altieri's account is a persuasive one, despite his tendency to simplify the dynamics of literary inheritance. There can be no denying the overwhelming influence of Emerson as a transmitter of romanticism into the main stream of mid-nineteenth century American writing. But Emerson's thought was, at times, closer to Wordworth's than, as Altieri implies, to Coleridge's. As Ezra Pound's grudging praise of Whitman might indicate, American modernism was as much a swing against an earlier generation's ahistorical immanentism as it was as affirmation of a neo-Coleridgean impulse to make sense where no sense, empirically, existed, and to affirm the value of culture and tradition as more than a mere momentary stay against confusion. None of this, however, denies the fact that romanticism underwent a second birth in the United States which prevented it from falling into the sear, the yellow leaf, of an Arnoldian melancholy, and this paved the way for the later achievements of Pound, Eliot, Stevens and others. But the fate of romanticism in Australia was very different indeed, with far-reaching consequences for the subsequent development of Australian literature generally, and for poetry in particular.

Near the end of March 1845, Henry David Thoreau borrowed an axe and went down to the woods by Walden Pond to build himself a cabin. After living there for two years, he gave us his reasons for doing this:

> I went to the woods because I wished to live deliberately, to front only the essential facts of life, and see if I could not learn what it had to teach . . . and if it proved to be mean, why then to get the whole and genuine meanness of it, and publish its meanness to the world; or if it were sublime, to know it by experience, and be able to give a true account of it in my next excursion.[7]

Anyone who has read *Walden* knows that Thoreau found life in the woods to be more sublime than mean; to such an extent, in fact, that his lifestyle became the model for a whole generation of young people more than a century after his death:

> I learned this, at least, by my experiment; that if one advances confidently in the direction of his dreams, and endeavors to live the life which he has imagined, he will meet with a success unexpected in common hours. He will put some things behind, will pass an invisible boundary; new, universal, and more liberal laws will begin to establish themselves around and within him; or the old laws be expanded, and interpreted in his favor in a more liberal sense, and he will live with the licence of a higher order of beings. (P. 214)

Not many years after Thoreau's excursion, Henry Lawson was dispatched from Sydney to acquire some first-hand knowledge of life in the outback. It is hard to imagine a picture of human solitude within nature differing more from Thoreau's than Lawson later gave in "The Drover's Wife":

> Bush all round — bush with no horizon, for the country is flat. No ranges in the distance. The bush consists of stunted, rotten native appletrees. No undergrowth. Nothing to relieve the eye save the darker green of a few she-oaks which are sighing above the narrow, almost waterless creek. Nineteen miles to the nearest sign of civilization — a shanty on the main road.
>
> The drover, an ex-squatter, is away with the sheep. His wife and children are left here alone.
>
> Four ragged, dried-up-looking children are playing about the house. Suddenly one of them yells: "Snake! Mother, here's a snake!"[8]

Grouped together at the start of Lawson's most famous story are the elements which have become almost definitive of Australia's reading of Nature and — consequently — of the relationship between Nature and the human. First, there is the bush itself. Australia produces native trees as grand in their own way, and as beautiful, as any elsewhere. Australian painting has amply demonstrated this, particularly the painters of the Heidelberg School who were contemporary with Lawson — a point to which I wish to return shortly. But Lawson's "native appletrees" are not fruitful and nourishing; they are stunted and rotten, quite unlike the useful "tall, arrowy white pines"[9] Thoreau found at hand when he decided to build his cabin. They are also monotonous. Lacking North America's seasonal differentiation, the Australian bush's featureless anonymity mocks our human desire for detail and distinction. Then there is the isolation. Whereas Thoreau is wrapped in a seclusion which is protective rather than threatening, the drover's wife and her fragile band of children are nineteen miles from the nearest civilization which is, ironically, a shanty, a place where liquor is sold. (Drunkenness, madness and suicide are the recurring fates of so many characters in early Australian fiction, and most notable in the work of Lawson.) In contrast to the "bottomless" Walden pond teeming with fish, there is the near-dry creek: water, the source of life, is capricious, almost malicious in its scarcity. Also, whereas the woods around Walden Pond abound with bird and animal life, in the Australian story there is the snake, that ancient symbol of evil. Somehow inseparable from the "native apletrees", the snake is here the focus for all of Nature's apparently pointless mercilessness.

And, of course, there is "the gaunt, sunbrowned bushwoman [who] . . . snatches her baby from the ground . . . and reaches for a stick". At the end of the story she hugs her son "to her worn-out breast . . . while the sickly daylight breaks over the bush". If A.D.

Hope's later depiction of Australia as "A woman beyond her change of life, a breast / Still tender but within the womb is dry" recalls the drover's wife to us, it is not by accident. In the latter part of the nineteenth century three writers — Lawson, Furphy and Barbara Baynton — established an intimate connection between the Australian country and a figure of haggard female endurance suffering at the hands of the male. For example in "Squeaker's Mate" by Barbara Baynton[10] the barren but grimly enduring woman is the victim of her husband's laziness and later of his obnoxious callousness. Deserted by all human consideration — not to mention kindness — the only emotional bond remaining to her is between herself and her dog. She and nature belong together, in a pathetic pact of mutual self-defence against her husband. A similar bond between the female and Nature is found in "The Chosen Vessel", where the murdered mother's natural counterpart is the ewe and her lamb. In this story the male is doubly antagonistic in that the woman is derided and left alone and defenceless on the farm by her husband, and raped and murdered by an intruder. In Joseph Furphy's *Such Is Life* the solitary Nosey Alf, living in seclusion in the remoter parts of the land, is in fact the hideously disfigured Molly whose chance of marriage to Alf Morris was wrecked by the loss of her conventional female good looks.[11] Finally, to return to "The Drover's Wife", the woman is the victim of her husband's absence: she has to endure her ordeal because he — like the men in the three other stories — has abandoned any role as protector and partner. One must not ignore, either, the traditional maleness of the snake/serpent. In Lawson's story therefore, as in those of Baynton and Furphy, the woman's antagonist is not Nature, the Australian bush, but the male. The woman can then be seen as sharing in the qualities of Nature, unattractive though they may seem: she is gaunt and sunbrowned, harsh and lacking in traditional female beauty, exhausted yet enduring, of a piece with Nature's isolation.

Only rarely in American literature do we get a comparable picture of the privations suffered by women isolated in nature: for example, in Robert Frost's studies of farm women, "The Fear" and "The Hill Wife", or the women in John Steinbeck's novel, *The Grapes of Wrath*. By contrast to her Australian sisters, Hester Prynn, banished to the outskirts of Boston for her adultery, and thus set free to wander a "moral wilderness", receives from Nature a degree of support and guidance towards a strengthened integrity unthinkable in Australian writing. Her famous liberation in the paradoxical privacy of the New England woods in chapter 18 of Nathaniel Hawthorne's *The Scarlet Letter* is, however, only part of the picture. The momentary freedom she experiences in the woods when she tears off the badge of her guilt cannot be sustained, for she must inevitably return to her role within the world of human sociality and resume her confining headdress, claiming again the scarlet letter of her shame. There are two good reasons for this. Firstly, although an outcast of society, she is not free of it: her social role, in fact, is to be cast out, to be the scapegoat whose expulsion from within Boston is intended to purge the settlement of guilty sexuality. Her manifest guilt proclaims the settlement's purity. Secondly, no matter what correspondence there may be between the human and the natural, guilt is human and cannot be washed away by pathetic fallacy. It is the strangely sprite-like, seemingly cruel yet apparently innocent figure of her daughter Pearl who has, in fact, the most complete identification with Nature, possibly because she has not yet entered the social world. And it is Pearl who provides us with the clue to why Hester and Dimmesdale cannot simply escape their guilt:

> A wolf, it is said — but here the tale has surely lapsed into the improbable — came up, and smelt of Pearl's robe, and offered his savage head to be patted by her hand. The truth seems to be, however, that the mother-forest, and these wild things which it nourished, all recognized a kindred wildness in the human child.[12]

Pearl has the wildness of Nature herself. Her own nature's demand for a father to complement her mother — her demand for a balance of female and male cooperating publically within the social as well as the private world — is a compelling motivating force in the novel's moral and psychological economy. For the bulk of the novel she is incompletely social — so incompletely social, in fact, that the point is made several times that she is more like a spirit-child than a human one. Strange though it may seem, female Nature impels her away from herself (that is, away from Nature) and towards the balance of male and female which could (ideally) be found in the social world, in the world of relationships between people:

> "Doth he love us?" said Pearl, looking up with acute intelligence into her mother's face. "Will he go back with us, hand in hand, we three together, into the town?"[13]

Childlike, even cruel, as her question may seem, it points the way to a line of action which, if persevered with, would lead Dimmesdale publically to confess his guilt in proclaiming his parenthood, purging the leech-like Chillingworth from his soul. This "wildness" of Nature in impelling the human away from herself and towards the balance of an ideal sociality is what transforms Hester's "moral wilderness" into a meaningful pattern of confession and redemption. Nature, explicitly female, is not meaningless, but the script of a moral and spiritual order which must be acted upon in the social, male-dominated world, and in *The Scarlet Letter* it is legible in the female figure so thoroughly identified with it. The "mother-forest" recognized "kindred" in the human child.

Hawthorne's identification of Nature with both the female and with moral and spiritual pattern is, of course, common in much romanticism in English. What now seems characteristically American in Hawthorne, however, is the powerfulness of this female force, which seems to be a necessary counterpart to the stern authority of the Puritan God the Father. Behind Hawthorne, of course, stands Emerson's essay *Nature*:

> 1. Words are signs of natural facts.
> 2. Particular natural facts are symbols of particular spiritual facts.
> 3. Nature is the symbol of the spirit.[14]

And

> Spirit is the Creator. Spirit hath life in itself. And man in all ages and countries embodies it in his language as the FATHER.[15]

In Hawthorne, Nature's message is her own: its tidings of innocence, freedom and harmony differ from the stern burden of authority and law signified by the Puritan God and the patriarchy which is His social expression. But in Emerson, Nature, "her text", is the spokeswoman for the Father.[16] She is the language He speaks and she signifies His divine plan. It follows for Emerson that being "the symbol of the spirit" means that she is constituted by the fact that she signifies not herself, but the Father, who remains ineffable without her mediation. "Spirit hath life in itself", and that is about as far as it goes until Nature takes upon herself the role and function of language, mediating that divine self-sufficiency as purpose, order, plan. In Emerson, the hierarchical dominance of the male (God) over the female (Nature) is clear.

Behind Emerson stands the considerably more subtle Wordsworth who affirmed that "Nature never did betray / The heart that loved her" and who declared he was

> . . . well pleased to recognise
> In nature and the language of the sense
> The anchor of my purest thoughts, the nurse,
> The guide, the guardian of my heart, and soul
> Of all my moral being.[17]

For Wordsworth, that peculiar

> . . . motion and a spirit, that impels
> All thinking things, all objects of all thought,
> And rolls through all things

is not so explicitly male as it was to be for Emerson. Instead, we have a powerful coordination of the female, of spiritual power, and of immanent moral and psychological order, within a figure of nature as nurse, guide and guardian. This coordination, quite obviously, does not originate with Wordsworth but draws on a very ancient tradition indeed, to be found as much in the female divinities of, for example, Greek antiquity as in the contemporary clichéd appellation, "Mother Nature". There is little to be gained, for my present purpose, in tracing its provenance further back. It is enough simply to point out that it was an important element in English romanticism, and that in those crucial years in which the modern tradition in American literature was being forged, it was an important element in the United States also. So powerfully was America's conception of Nature inscribed within this tradition that its impress can be discerned today in a wide spectrum of American post-modern poets.[18] And a profound disappointment with this tradition, a sense of having been duped and betrayed by it, is a crucial element in American modernism.

It goes without saying that even if Emerson, Thoreau and Hawthorne were not widely read in Australia in the nineteenth century, the English romantics were. Thus the existence of a very different configuration of the female and Nature in Australia bears thinking about, particularly since it seems that this difference was not inevitable. For example Lawson's predecessor, Charles Harpur, depicted Nature in a way that shows close affinities with Wordsworth's. In his introduction to *The Colonial Poets*[19], G. A. Wilkes follows Judith Wright in her essay on Harpur in *Preoccupations in Australian Poetry* and points out that Harpur is the only Australian poet of any note to show much influence of Wordsworth. It is perhaps not surprising that he should, writing as he was at a time when Wordsworth was still, comparatively, alive. Even in Harpur's more sombre pictures, such as "The Creek of the Four Graves" and "A Storm in the Mountains", nature is revealed as an active, even a sentient force. In a less dramatic mood, as in "A Mid-Summer Noon in the Australian Forest", he creates an antipodean reflection of the Lake District, idyllic in its sense of warmth and luxurious repose:

Every other thing is still,
Save the ever-wakeful rill,
Whose cool murmur only throws
A cooler comfort round Repose;
Or some ripple in the sea
Of leafy boughs, where, lazily,
Tired Summer, in her forest bower
Turning with the noontide hour,
Heaves a slumbrous breath ere she
Once more slumbers peacefully.

O 'tis easeful here to lie
Hidden from Noon's scorching eye,
In this grassy cool recess
Musing thus on Quietness.[20]

Nature, personified here as Summer, is female, nurturing and protecting, hiding the subject in her "grassy cool recess" from the intrusive, would-be penetrating, "scorching eye" of the sun. But even in this brief Waldenesque tranquility Nature is neither the script of a Patriarchal Divine nor the dwelling place of a "great Universal spirit". Wordsworthian though this passage undoubtedly is in some respects, it remains stubbornly secular, with traces of a genteel eighteenth century pastoralism showing through. And even this trace of romantic influence proved to be short-lived. Harpur died in 1868, and by the time Lawson started to publish, Wordsworth and the other English romantics were not only foreign but also a little old-fashioned. Even in England their influence was in the eclipse. As Judith Wright wrote:

> One reason for the neglect of Harpur's work, among many, was probably that when he wrote his mentor, Wordsworth, was falling out of fashion and the impulse of the early Romantics was already almost spent. The poetic influence of the 'forties and 'fifties was Alfred Tennyson.[21]

The consequences of this are significant. Harpur was writing after the great period of English romanticism had given way to the increasing pessimism of a Victorian loss of faith, and in a society which he himself castigated for its secular devotion to money. As he wrote in his old age "During my whole manhood I have had to mingle daily amongst men . . . who have faith for nothing in God's glorious universe that is not, in their own vile phrase, 'money's worth' ".[22] As a result he was unable to inscribe into the beginnings of Australia's poetic tradition his own antipodean version of romanticism in which Nature is a sentient female power nurturing and cherishing humanity. The subsequent neglect of Harpur's poetry compounded this, so that an unbridgeable gap was opened between this romantic aspect of Nature and Australian poetry. By the time Harpur was "rediscovered" — and Judith Wright is as much responsible for this as anyone else — Australian poetry was firmly headed elsewhere. Yet it would be a mistake to attribute the secularism and, particularly, the pessimism of subsequent Australian writers' reading of nature simply to this failure of a Wordsworthian influence to "take", important though it is. Just as importantly, it would also be a mistake to see them simply as responses to the physical realities of the Australian landscape which, as we all know, is neither the Lake District nor Walden Pond.

There can be no doubt that the picture of rural hardship presented by Lawson, Furphy, Baynton and, later, Henry Handel Richardson was not unfaithful to the experience of many settlers. Life was harsh and often primitive; distances were vast and isolation was often extreme and punishing; the seasons were capricious, and good farming country was not always easy to find. The absence of any equivalent to the American frontier tradition is certainly related to the absence of wide stretches of habitable land waiting to be opened up. But the colonies did grow and even flourish; by no means did all those on the land battle against insuperable odds; and it was not only the rich who grew richer at the expense of the poor. Colonial literature has plenty of stories of the successful rise to riches, capricious though fortune often was. Furthermore, there is little reason to suspect that the good weather and generally enjoyable climate which Australians today are so proud of is a twentieth century innovation. Our forebears lacked air conditioning; but they also lacked the bitter winters taken as commonplace in many other parts of the world.

More significantly, a group of artists virtually contemporary with Lawson created an image of Australian nature which is strikingly in contrast to the writers'. The landscapes of the Heidelberg School, Australia's approximate equivalent of impressionism, show splendid vistas, sculpturally massive and powerfully individualistic trees, and most significantly an invigorating, even exhilarating, display of light. The sun, from which Harpur was granted refuge by a beneficent Nature in "A Midsummer Noon in the Australian Forest", and which was to beat down mercilessly in subsequent Australian writing until suntans were redeemed by being de rigueur for all, became the guiding spirit lighting the path of the painters out of the gloom of colonial derivativeness. McCubbin might paint sentimental narratives of bush privation and suffering, but these were conscious transpositions of European sentimental narrative painting into a local setting. His other canvases, and particularly his small sketches of light on tangles of vegetation, are every bit as exhilarated as the depictions of nature by his contemporaries. There is nothing sickly, barren or malevolent about the landscapes of Tom Roberts or Arthur Streeton in the 1880s and 1890s. As the name of the group suggests, these painters worked near Melbourne in a region which was certainly different from the outback that Lawson visited so briefly. The landscape they painted was temperate, and being hilly it provided the capacity for vista and visual drama which a flat landscape lacked, and which it continued to lack until seen by Fred Williams. But it was not totally different from landscape elsewhere in the settled parts of Australia. In fact, many of the Heidelberg School painted other parts of the country in such a way as to bring out the same qualities. But as Robert Hughes points out,[23] the crucial, liberating influence on these painters was most probably Tom Roberts's acquaintance with the works of Whistler, acquired during Roberts's period in Europe in the 1880s. This, together with the Impressionists' practice of painting not in the studio but in the open air, opened the way for the Australian painters to celebrate to the full a colour and a light which had no European counterpart. These were something powerfully and possibly uniquely Australian.

The Heidelberg School's brush with European impressionism might have been slight, but it was enough to give the painters the technical means, and with them the stimulus, to celebrate something which no other group of painters at that time, at least within their knowledge, could. They used the new means they had acquired from Europe to signify something that was not European but, in fact, distinctly other than European. Given new eyes with which to see light, colour and atmosphere, they saw Australia in a way which liberated them from nineteenth century European models. Streeton's landscapes might still suggest Giorgione in their overall composition, and McCubbin's and Roberts's poorer narratives might look like sentimental versions of English paintings of the period. But they also painted Australia as we can see it today, almost any day, when we go outside.

What is curious here is that while the Heidelberg School landscapes are still recognizably Australian, so too is the very different landscape of Lawson, Baynton and the other writers. The point is not simply that Australia is large enough to encompass contradictions, although it certainly is that. The fact is that within literature, nature has remained largely as it was written in the 1890s. It is worth looking at it again briefly in order to see just what that is.

First, in contrast to English or American conceptions of Nature, it has remained secular. The consequences of this for all Australian writing, including Australian poetry, are far-reaching and crucial. I want to comment on this shortly. Second, it is female. The drover's wife is only one of a long list of women whose association with Nature is so close as to be virtually a personification, and which achieves a powerful confirmation in the work of Patrick White. One thinks of Miss Hare snuffling through her overgrown garden in *Riders in the Chariot*, or the Aboriginal women in *A Fringe of Leaves*, or even Marcia Lushington in *The Twyborn Affair* with her apparent ability to evade the alienation felt so strongly by the male characters in the bush. Two figures of Aboriginal women from earlier novelists provide a link between Lawson and White. The diseased, perishing figure of Coonardoo in Katharine Susannah Prichard's novel of that name, and the skeletons of Tocky and her baby on the final page of Xavier Herbert's *Capricornia* clearly signify more than the fate of the Aboriginal people at the hands of the whites. Both novels stress the Aboriginals' close understanding of the Australian continent and their previously undisturbed ability to live in spiritual and physical harmony with it. Thus the fate of these women signifies the irreversible degradation and subjugation of a natural (that is, non-European) Australia — a nature which was female, harmonious and nurturing — before the onslaught of a patriarchal European "civilization".

The complexion which Nature in Australian writing displays, therefore, does not stem simply from the failure of a Wordsworthian version to take root. Nor is it simply the product of the "harsh" and "un-European" nature of the country, undeniable though this has at times been. Despite both these factors, Nature in Australia is still female — but secular, stubborn, and usually not very friendly. What is making itself apparent here is Nature's role as the other of the male colonizer. The land, and Nature herself, are what men exercise power over: it is what they penetrate tame, subdue, control, rape, open up, explore and, of course, possess. Exiled, either voluntarily or involuntarily, from the "mother country", it is not surprising that the colonists should both covet and despise this new and unfamiliar terrain. Just as understandably, they immediately turned their energies towards subjecting her to their wills. Moreover, although Britannia may have been female, as indeed Queen Victoria was, Westminster, paradoxically dubbed "the Mother of Parliaments", consisted of men voted for by men. In turning away from Westminster's patriarchal domination in the latter part of the nineteenth century, the Australian colonies were rebelling against their Father but only in order to take over his role, to appropriate his image as their own. Australia adopted British law and its political institutions, (though to our credit women gained the suffrage in Australia long before they did in England). Australia's cities were built along English lines and were given English names, and even the most casual acquaintance with Australian public buildings of the nineteenth century — buildings which housed and signified political and ecclesiastical power — reveals the directness with which the colonies' rebellious sons arrayed themselves in their Father's imperial robes. Paradoxically this may account for the popularity of the bush as both subject matter and setting in early Australian writing. Unlike the cities, the bush was distinctively Australian. And as the other of the colonizing Male, it was alternately inviting and mysterious, friendly and threatening, open for exploitation and capriciously — even vengefully — malicious. The bush — which meant, quite simply, all of Australia beyond the immediate proximity and influence of the cities and thus Nature herself — both entices and threatens male consciousness. She is to be subjected to his will and dominated by him: that way she will be rendered fertile. But she is also faithless and violent, and can capriciously repay his advances with nothing but barrenness.

More recent portrayals of Nature may be less negative than Lawson's, but her role in poetry can remain virtually unchanged. For example, in David Campbell's poem "Delivering Lambs" divinity is explicitly attributed not to nature, but to the farmer-subject:

> Delivering lambs, *you're* god: tug at the forelegs
> And drag it, yellow, by the tight lips of the ewe

> Until she starts to lick and the lamb starts butting.
> Walk home as tall as your shadow in the dew.[24]

One can respond positively to this excitement in helping life to happen by becoming a kind of divine, male midwife. But the ambiguity of the last line (in the evening one's shadow stretches a long way due to the low angle of the sun; one's shadow is only as tall as the dew on the grass, which is not tall at all) measures the height of such apotheosis against a natural scale (the dew) which renders two antithetical results. Nature, even here, is no unequivocal supporter of a male sense of grandeur.

Les A. Murray's poem "Laconics: The Forty Acres" is even more explicitly practical and male:

> That interior machinegun,
> my chainsaw, drops dead timber.
>
> Where we burn the heaps
> we'll plant kikuyu grass.
>
> Ecology? Sure.
> But also husbandry.[25]

The militarily aggressive action of the farmer husbanding, or of the husband (of the land) farming, makes clear the antagonistic roles of male subject and female Nature. That Campbell and Murray are widely regarded as belonging to the more "traditionalist" side of Australian poetry is no accident. They have both been concerned with specifically rural life in much (though not all) of their poetry, and have been seen as providing a continuity with the rural past, despite their obvious sophistication. Les Murray has himself been quite explicit about this. But the tradition they continue inscribes its ramifications in their poetry in ways which are not always obvious.

Thus we can see that in fulfilling the antagonistic role within which she was cast, Nature in Australia was unable to perpetuate the role she had in England and the United States as the willing language, script or spokeswoman of a male god. Threatening to stifle his divine patriloquy she must, as in A.D. Hope's poem "On an Engraving by Casserius",[26] be cut open so that her female nature can be forcibly displayed by a male's "elegant dissection". But neither is she mere inert matter; she is a vital force which, in the works of Patrick White or Francis Webb, can enter into a life-and-death struggle with the male subject. But she is secular, for all that. She is not pattern or plan, embodiment of an immanent divine order, but the other: the antagonist/protagonist (it depends on which side you see her from), who is both lover (beloved) and enemy. Thus, for example, in Kenneth Slessor's poetry Nature in her guise as the sea, "the old floundering sea, / The old, fumbling, witless lover-enemy," takes the breath and, with it, the language and the meaning of the lives of Cook and Joe Lynch and, in the case of the "unknown seamen" of "Beach Burial", even their names. Nature provides no support for the imagination in its search for order: search as the imagination may, she reveals not divine coherence, but continuing conflict. As a maternal and nourishing entity she underscores her absence: "Mother Nature" dwells in Europe or Asia or America, and probably in the past. That Nature is what we read about, not what we experience. (Though to be fair, poetry in the last ten or fifteen years has started to approach a non-patriarchal relation to her.) Only in our own peculiar version of the myth of Eden does she signify coherence and order: as the site of the Aboriginal peoples' life within a pre-European harmony marked by a deep spiritual coincidence of people and place. But that harmony is now not only irretrievably lost: it was never ours in the first place since it was our, European, arrival which marked its end by inscribing division in the name of patriarchal power.

Thus our forebears wrote out of our literary tradition the concept of an immanent order whose romantic avatar was the great precursor of modernism in England and America. In Australian writing Nature endures, rather than protects or nourishes. We may have led the western world in this perception, which has now become an ecological commonplace due to the worldwide and aggressive onslaught on her capacity to sustain human life and culture as we know it or would wish it to be. If some of our more recent writers position themselves less antagonistically in relation to her, it is only in the light of a sensitivity to her possible death — and therefore ours. It is therefore unlikely that Nature will emerge within Australian writing as the vital and nourishing force she once was in England and which, by and large, she still is in the United States. But one may now be on the way to realizing why, to realizing that she has undergone that process of rape and subjugation and domination which has marked her up until now as she who doggedly, often rebelliously, and violently endures. But almost two hundred years on from the beginnings of romanticism in England, coming to Nature's rescue should not be confused with Wordsworth's understanding of how Nature could come to ours.

4

Christopher Brennan's Double Exile

I have tried to point out how the image of Nature in relation to humanity that is found in Australian literature differs significantly from that in English and American literature, and have suggested that this difference is at least partly accounted for by the absence of any firm romantic heritage in Australia, and the vigorous presence of one in America. One consequence of this has been that, at least until recently, the dominant mode of most Australian writing has been a kind of realism, and this has been apparent as much in the poetry as in the prose. When a poet of the late nineteenth century in Australia set his aims — rightly or wrongly — on a more ambitious task than a depiction in verse of the land in all its ambiguous newness and ancientness, then the consequences of this absence of romanticism become apparent.

Axel Clark's excellent biography of Christopher Brennan[1] makes abundantly clear that, for all his knowledge of classical and European languages, for all the width and depth of his reading in nineteenth century literature, particularly French and German, Brennan was essentially an exile or, to choose a more modern term which locates him in the context of more recent writers such as Peter Porter and Randolph Stow, an expatriate. There are several obvious senses in which this term applies to him. For example, as a young postgraduate student supposedly working toward a PhD in Berlin (though not, in fact, doing so) Brennan was isolated from his family, his country and, of course, from the English language. One surprising aspect of this two year stay in Europe is that, for all his love of nineteenth century French literature, he did not visit Paris at all, or anywhere else in France. Considering the expense and difficulties of travel from Australia to Europe in the last decade of the nineteenth century, such an omission seems strange, to say the least. It may well be that Brennan was short of cash, and in love with his landlady's daughter, as Clark points out, facts which might induce him to combine economy with pleasure by staying in Berlin. It is also true that Brennan was not a typical tourist: in so far as he explored it at all, he explored the world through books, rather than by train. But the fact remains that during his stay in Europe not only was he far from the country of his birth and of his subsequent career; he also chose to keep the country whose poetry meant so much to him at a remove, unvisited, unseen.

On his return to Australia in 1894, Brennan was an expatriate in another sense. His deep love of, and knowledge of, European literature could not have failed to reflect adversely on the current literary situation in Australia. Important as the nineties are in the history of Australian literature, their aggressive and frequently raw nationalism can have seemed little congenial to a mind whose hero, for many years, was Stéphane Mallarmé. This is borne out not only by Brennan's poetic practice, which was so different from that of his Australian contemporaries, but also by the significantly scant attention that Australian writing receives in his collected prose works. These are dominated by his critical writings on philosophy and aesthetics, on French, German and Italian literature (though mostly French) and on the classics. Terry Sturm claims to have included "all of Brennan's published writings on Australian authors and artists, more than half of them previously uncollected in book form" in his admirably edited Portable Australian Authors edition of Brennan's work.[2] These comprise thirteen pieces, one of which discusses the scansion of his own poetry, another the painter Julian Ashton. "Some Makers of Australia" (1927) is the most substantial in its comments on the poets Kendall, Daley, "Bartie" Paterson, Lawson, Quinn, Mackellar, and Gilmore; however by today's standards it is nothing more than a medium length review article and was "jotted down in such order as might be, at short notice and without any books".[3] The more ambitiously titled "The University and Australian Literature" (1902) mentions no Australian writers by name and discusses the work of none. All told, Brennan's "Writings on Australian Arts and Letters" occupy fifty-four pages of Sturm's edition of Brennan's work, and most of the pieces are occasional and lack the breadth and coherence of thought which characterize his writings on European romanticism. These fifty-four pages on Australian matters are not much compared with the four hundred and forty-four devoted to other subjectmatter in Chisholm and Quinn's earlier edition of Brennan's prose.[4]

It should be clear from this, even if it were not already abundantly clear from any account of his life, that Brennan's life in Australia was also a time in exile, a time spent as an expatriate from the countries and cultures whose literatures he had chosen to adopt as his own, his birthright. It is possible to suppose that he made this choice at least partly from dissatisfaction with contemporary Australian writing. In choosing a culture not that of the country of his birth, Brennan has been by no means alone: it has been the mark of the expatriate from Martial to the present, most of whom have chosen to live actually within the ambit of their adopted culture. What is of interest in Brennan's case is that, by making his adopted *patria* a country which he could readily have visited yet failed to do so, he made himself doubly an exile. Neither at home literally in Europe nor, patently, in Australia with his German wife, Brennan was at home only in a country he had never visited, never seen, and whose culture outside of literature he seems to have had little knowledge of or interest in.

In this respect Brennan is not dissimilar to the American poet Wallace Stevens. As a man of immensely more material well-being than Brennan, Stevens too could have visited the country whose literature he admired, whose language he inserted so playfully into his own poetry, and whose paintings he purchased through an agent. Stevens too wrote extensively on philosophy and aesthetics, and comparatively little about contemporary American writers. Even further, during the bulk of his career with the Hartford Accident and Indemnity Insurance Corporation, Stevens, unlike Brennan, spent little time in the company of other writers, preferring the imaginative world of his own creation. Like Brennan, Stevens has been criticized (misguidedly, in his case) for an absence of "real things" or "real events" in his poetry (the lingering preference for realism, particularly in Australia, emerging again in such a criticism). But unlike Brennan, Stevens was heir to a romantic tradition whose apparent inability to account adequately for the realities of twentieth century life vexed him into writing one of the most productive accounts of the role of the imaginative life that this century has seen, a revisionary romanticism which can now be acknowledged as central both to modernism and also to much post-modernism.

Any adequate account of Stevens is clearly outside the scope of the present work. But the most casual familiarity with his poetry reveals an abiding exploration of the relationship between the real ("things as they are") and the imagination, between the sensible and the intelligible, between the chaotic world beyond the mind and the imaginative world with its tropism to order within which we try to live. For much of his career, Stevens's writing expressed the modernist conviction that the world was chaotic and, in and of itself, meaningless and largely unbearable. Conceding that "The poetic process is psychologically an escapist process" it goes on to say that the "nobility" one expects and finds in major imaginative art:

> . . . is not an artifice that the mind has added to human nature. The mind has added nothing to human nature. It is a violence from within that protects us from a violence without. It is the imagination pressing back against the pressure of reality. It seems, in the last analysis, to have something to do with our self-preservation; and that, no doubt, is why the expression of it, the sound of its words, helps us to live our lives.
>
> (P. 36)[5]

In this respect, Stevens can be seen as a major exponent of the "symbolist" imagination typified in the romantic period by Coleridge (as discussed in chapter 3). On the other hand, his major poem "Notes toward a Supreme Fiction" declares that "To impose is not to discover"; and much of his late poetry testifies to the imagination as that faculty which attentively lies in wait to apprehend those "moments of inherent excellence — when / We more than waken": a position much closer to Wordsworth's sense of an immanent coherence within the phenomenal world, and one central to much post-modern writing and theory. But whichever position Stevens takes (and when, at times, he consciously vacillates, playing the various attitudes against each other) his concern with chaos, our human need for order, and the power and role of the imagination all mark him as the most explicit heir to European romanticism in English of the century. And this inheritance, as I have pointed out, was passed on to him as a result of the central place of romanticism (transcendentalism) in American writing in the middle of the nineteenth century.[6]

Turning back to Brennan, we find nothing comparable to Stevens's near-obsession. This does not mean, of course, that Brennan was ignorant of European romanticism. Far from it: of all people writing in Australia in the last decade of the nineteenth century, he was probably the best informed about the philosophical and aesthetic theories of the romantics, and he wrote extensively on Blake, Novalis, Swedenborg, Heine, German romantic philosophy (and particularly Schlegel), and E.T.A. Hoffman. But he views romanticism, understandably enough, very much from the point of view of the Symbolist poet of the latter part of the nineteenth century. In his essay "Vision, Imagination and Reality" he states:[7]

> . . . imagination itself is to us a symbol of the spiritual principle, a closer approach to it than any other form of conscious life; being an intensive union and fusion of all the modes of mental activity . . . Imagination, then, by its own nature, is a symbol of the unity which is our true spiritual being: by that scheme of correspondences which is the law of its activity, it symbolizes for us our living relation to that true being, and makes plain to us, but through delight and not through demonstration, the ideal kinship and unity of all things.
>
> (*Prose* pp. 38 and 39)

The Symbolist bias of this account of the imagination is obvious, particularly when the above is linked with an earlier passage from the same essay:

> The images of which the artist makes use are not invented by him; they exist already in the world of sense: his imaginative labour consists in perceiving them in relation to their significance; in perceiving that arrangement of them which is demanded by their significance . . . the

> artistic imagination simply perceives, in the disorder of sensuous facts, the arrangement, or rhythm, required for the embodiment of a certain significance . . .
>
> (*Prose* pp. 31 and 32)

For images thus to have meaning, he continues, "these matters of sense must have the capability of symbolizing" which, he points out, entails "the theory of correspondences, that the things above are as the things below" (*Prose* p. 32). In a somewhat later essay, "German Romanticism: A Progressive Definition" (dated at around 1909 or 1910, but not published until 1920) he states:

> We might here, then, *define Romanticism* as *a theory and practice of poetry which seeks to make explicit the transcendental object and activity of the imagination* . . . The world then becomes a web of "analogies", relations other than those of ordinary knowledge or practice, purely spiritual or expressive. This is the adoption into literature of an old mythical idea, formulated in the so-called Smaragdine Table of Hermes, "*Omnia quae superius sicut quae inferius*": "The things above are as the things below."
>
> (*Prose* p. 387)

I have argued earlier that romanticism has not been a live force, not even a vital though dormant or recessive power, in Australian writing ever since Charles Harpur's Wordsworthian example failed to take root here. Yet in Brennan we seem to have a poet with a clear intellectual grasp of one branch of romantic thought, someone who not only could articulate many of its complexities but who also, it seems, was writing some of his most important poetry at roughly the same time as he was formulating these ideas in his prose. Why did not this second influx of romantic thought bear fruit here, and leave a lasting heritage within Australian poetry? To answer this, we must look at the kind of romanticism that so exercised Brennan, both in his prose and in his poetry.

When one looks at Brennan's collected prose works, one is struck by how little attention he gives to the English romantics. Where W.E. Henley is the object of three essays, only Blake among the romantic poets is given any real consideration. Tennyson, Browning, Rossetti, and "The English Decadents" all figure, and we know that Brennan was an admirer of the Yeats of the "Celtic Twilight". But when Yeats turned from the charming romanticizing of his earlier work to embark on the revisionary critique of romanticism which was his contribution to modernism, Brennan lost all interest in him. On this evidence it would be plausible to claim that Brennan's espousal of a German romanticism was not a means of rebelling against or rejecting a dominanting English one, but the act of someone trying to fill the gap in Australia's literary consciousness that I pointed to earlier. A Wordsworthian absorption in the objects and actions of this world with all its immanent spiritual vitality —

something as different from the "realism" of Brennan's contemporaries as it was from the symbolism he so much admired — simply was absent from (or within) Australia's — and Brennan's — literary awareness.[8] Brennan's claim that "Art is the expression of the imagination, and the imagination . . . is the indivisible energy of the spirit expressing itself in the only way possible, the creation of organic form. Within the world there is another one forming itself whose intention is absolute perfection" (*Prose* p. 181) speaks out of that absence, in fact speaks it out.

Another point is suggested by Brennan himself in his essay "A Progressive Definition of German Romanticism" when he quotes Schlegel writing to his brother: "I can't send you my definition of Romanticism, as it runs to 125 quarto pages" (*Prose* p. 394). There are, in fact, many romanticisms. Lacking a sturdy native tradition on which to build (and, of course, Brennan was not alone in this in the late nineteenth century) he self-consciously adopted a strand of romantic thought of far more prominence within German and French literature and philosophy than within English. That his "progressive definition" of German romanticism accords very closely with his own conscious poetic theory is attested to by the similarity of thought in his various essays, both early and late. Significantly, Brennan's constant stress is on the more transcendental, even mystical aspect of German romanticism, with its close alignment of poetry and the imagination with religious and mystical vision. As he says in "Vision, Imagination and Reality", "Vision is imagination intensified" (*Prose* p. 29). In more recent years, we tend to associate the theory of Correspondences primarily with Baudelaire; but Brennan takes it back (rightly, of course) to Hermes. The emphasis he places on "Novalis's mystical theory" in his essay on German romanticism (*Prose* p. 390) underlies the idealizing nature of Brennan's ideas. The trend of his argument is that, as with Novalis, "man is the mediator between the divine and the natural; man has attained the moral plane and must seek to transcend it . . . nature must yet be brought up to the moral plane" (P. 392). Transcendence here already seems to mean something very different from the down to earth involvement in the natural world of Walden Pond and its surroundings which typifies Thoreau's transcendentalism, or the loving enumeration of American detail that fills Whitman's poetry. Brennan's desire for perfection, while an expression of one romanticism, implies not only that man must transcend the moral world, but that Nature must transcend the natural. Only in its capacity as symbol — as signifier — has Nature true value.

This last point will need to be looked at more closely when I turn soon to Brennan's poetry. But another point needs to be raised first, and that is the contradiction, or at least the gap, between Brennan's poetic theory and his poetic practice. Axel Clark has already drawn attention, in his biography of Brennan, to the discrepancy between the facts of the poet's life and the poetry he was writing, particularly in relation to "The Wanderer" sequence.[9] Brennan warmly endorses a view of art which claims "that [imaginative] genius is the power of coming, at moments, into direct and living contact with the ultimate perfection" (*Prose* p. 386) and that "Art here is the *analogy* of perfection there: its ways and means are the same as those with which we must strive to perfect outselves, '*Mensch werden ist* eine Kunst' " (*Prose* p. 392). But his actual poetry is far from being a celebration of an achieved perfection; it is not even notable for the intensity with which it anticipates perfection. The dominant note is one of loss and nostalgia, tempered at times with a willful attempt at heroic self-projection, or self-projection in the heroic mould. In fact I would argue that the motivating occasions of Brennan's poetry grew out of his inevitable failure to achieve the perfection his theories point toward. Far from realizing perfection or at least an anticipation of it, at its heart Brennan's poetry embodies a doubled absence. Thus it could be fair to claim that Brennan's obsession with perfection and its inaccessibility — Eden, as he called it — was as much the cause of his attraction to an idealist romantic theory, as a product of it. In other words, the poetry and the theory are divergent expressions of this central absence, not coherent, mutually supporting discourses. This does not mean, however, that the theory was totally without effect on the poetry.

The foregoing discussion has been an attempt at locating aspects of Brennan's work within the wider context of romanticism. I have chosen to discuss him, so far, in this way because of all Australian poets he is the one who would seem, on first examination, to represent some continuation of a romantic tradition within Australian poetry, a tradition which would include as its English forebears not only Blake, and even Coleridge, but also Wordsworth. I hope it is now clearer that Brennan's continuation of this tradition is largely an illusion — an illusion, which was moreover, held to an extent by Brennan himself. It may partly help to account for why Brennan was never able to outgrow his Victorian poetic vocabulary and follow Yeats into modernism. A prominent aspect of modernism, as with romanticism, in the English language has been a concern with the things of this world, even if, as in Stevens, they tend to be nominated as "things as they are" without further specification. For Brennan to have become a modernist he would have had to transform his sense of a lost (unattainable) perfection into a concern for chaos and order, his nostalgia for the Absolute into concern for the contingent, his idealist and archaic vocabulary into a precise nomination of "things as they are". William Carlos Williams's dictum "No ideas but in things" could not have been further from Brennan's practice.

But it is now time to turn, briefly, to Brennan's poetry itself. If this entails a change in the terms of discourse, moving from the refinements of romantic philosophy to the particulars of late nineteenth century poetry, it is because I feel that the kind of discussion I have conducted in the earlier part of this chapter has got us about as far as it can. Having brought us, finally, to the poetry, we can strike out in a slightly different way, though to perhaps the same ends.

A symptomatic poem, one which provides a convenient point of entry, is No. 25, of which these are the first three stanzas:

I am shut out of mine own heart
because my love is far from me,
nor in the wonders have I part
that fill its hidden empery:

the wildwood of adventurous thought
and lawns of dawn my dreams had won,
the riches out of Faery brought
are buried with our bridal sun.

And I am in a narrow place,
and all its little streets are cold,
because the absence of her face
has robb'd the sullen air of gold.[10]

The conventional interpretation of this poem is that Brennan is separated from the woman he loves and, as a consequence, his world seems dull and lacklustre. The fact that the poem is dated 1897 and in all probability precedes the arrival of his future wife in December of that year corroborates this interpretation. Taken thus, the poem is a charming tribute to the woman whose arrival will bring meaning and colour back into the poet's life. His immediate surroundings are "narrow", "little", "cold", and "sullen" because her "absence" has robbed them of their richness, "gold".

This poverty also takes another form, which is exile from the heart, from which he is "shut out". As the poem goes on to make clear, the heart is not only a site of "broader day" and "undying spring": it is also "home", resplendent with "the riches out of Faery":

My home is in a broader day:
at times I catch it glistening

> thro' the dull gate, a flower'd play
> and odour of undying spring:
>
> the long days that I lived alone,
> sweet madness of the springs I miss'd,
> are shed beyond, and thro' them blown
> clear laughter, and my lips are kiss'd:
>
> — and here, from mine own joy apart,
> I wait the turning of the key:-
> I am shut out of mine own heart
> because my love is far from me.

As the second, fourth and fifth stanzas of the poem should make quite clear, this heart/home does not, in reality, designate a state of coherent and harmonious integration with the world of adult life, a transfiguring of mundane reality by a lucid resolution of the conflicts inherent in it. It presents, rather, a dream world ("lands of dawn my dream had won") of ceaseless origin ("undying spring"). This is that pre-linguistic, pre-symbolic state prior to desire which Jacques Lacan located before the end of the "mirror-stage", at about eighteen months of age, from which we are all, as a condition of our being, exiled for the remainder of our lives. As Lacan writes, "This moment in which the mirror-stage comes to an end inaugurates . . . the dialectic that will henceforth link the I to socially elaborated situations. It is this moment that decisively tips the whole of human knowledge into mediatization through the desire of the other . . . and turns the I into that apparatus for which every instinctual thrust constitutes a danger, even though it should correspond to a natural maturation . . ."[11] According to Lacan, desire enters irreversibly into the child's psychological economy at this moment because this is the moment when the child first recognizes that there is no seamless unity of itself (subject) and the world around it (object). The child now gains its first inklings that its inescapable relation to the world will henceforth be one of disjunction between subject and that subject's other. This same moment therefore also inaugurates the mediatization of knowledge through language, that system of differences which in the growing child as well as in the adult must symbolically "stand for" — and hence stand in for — reality in so far as it participates in intelligibility. As Lacan writes, "the moment in which desire becomes human is also that in which the child is born into language" (*Ecrits* p. 103). The desire to reverse this process is therefore one to return to a pre-social and pre-linguistic state in which desire itself does not exist. This is — psychologically — an infantile regression, and — metaphysically — a response to the lure of the transcendental signified, a longing for a realm of meaning which exists of and for itself in a self-sufficiency which requires no signifier to make it manifest.[12]

Turning back to Christopher Brennan, one can now say that his poem thus states that his desire, his love for another person who is far from him, exiles him from an infantile world of unmediated knowledge in which the I is free of all socially elaborated situations: Eden, as it is so often called. It also, interestingly enough, states the opposite. If we take the word "love" in the poem to signify not "beloved" but love itself, the act or condition of loving, then the poem is saying that its subject does not experience it, since it is "far" from him. The absence of love thus has the same effect as its presence: it submits the subject to a social world ("little streets") experienced as exile. Following this line of interpretation, the presence of love, the ability to love, would release the subject from the inadequacies of the adult, social, condition in just the way that he would be released if he were not, as the other line of interpretation would have it, at present in love. And so, indeed, would the presence of the beloved. What kind of love, and what kind of beloved, could thus annihilate the social, the non-unitary nature of existence? Surely only a beloved, and a condition of loving, which attend as non-presence, as absence. In this way the subject, loving with a love which is not itself, which is not loving, would not be shut out from his heart; and the beloved, attending by not being, (not being herself), would not threaten the subject's long-for solipsism.

The consequent figure of the beloved not as absent, but as absence itself, thus makes her entry into Brennan's poetry and soon comes to dominate it. We come across her trace as the absent Virgin Mary, represented by "this pale absence of the rose" in No. 56 and as the "leaning maid" who is no longer included within "the tawny desert's level ring" of No. 57. And she signifies an oceanic, maternal rejection in No. 41 as "The mother-deep, wise, yearning" from which the poet now feels himself "lock'd" by "mighty hands" so that for him "there lies no way into the deep". But it is, of course, in the Lilith poems that she manifests herself most fully in the dubious splendour of her absence.

As the "Argument" of the Lilith poems makes clear, following tradition, Lilith is prior to Eve, who inhabits her absence. Supposedly of Babylonian origin, Lilith is the contrary of Eve, associated with menstruation and a danger to infants and to women in childbirth. Her own children by Adam, Brennan tells us, are not physical, but mental monstrosities:

> . . . the worm-brood of terrors unconfest
> that chose henceforth, as their avoided nest,
> the mire-fed writhen thicket of the mind.

But the poem hastens to inform us that her evil reputation is a misreading, "in the folk's scant fireside lore misread". She is, in essence, the figure of the female who evades family, is prior to sociality and even to our fallen (that is, mediated, human) condition. Both universal and invisible (her "smile eludes our sight / in her flung hair that is the starry night") she is indeed the female as absence. Her proto-Edenic nature identifies her with the mother as lover, and she can proffer the delights of incest without guilt, when "read" aright, since she is not there.

In fact, the poetry goes to considerable effort to stress her absence. In the long section X of No. 68 (No. 68 is, in fact, the whole Lilith sequence) she is the anti-Eve or anti-wife, the eternal Other Woman, who proclaims

> But I have set my hand upon his soul
> and moulded it to my unseen control;
> and he hath slept within my shadowy hair
> and guards a memory how in my far lair
> the forces of tremendous passion stir:
> my spectral face shall come between his eyes
> and the soft face of her, my name shall rise,
> unutter'd, in each thought that goes to her.

Her control is "unseen", her face "spectral", her name "unutter'd". Intervening between Adam and his new bride Eve, the earthly and mortal woman, Lilith introduces absence there as well by ensuring that "he shall not know her nor her gentle ways / nor rest, content, by her sufficing source". Lilith is "the eternal lack", "the anterior silence" and "the round of nothingness". But also she is "the silence of our thought" as Mallarmé, "he that sleeps in hush'd Valvins hath taught", and is the "pale and thrilling silence" which marks the limit of "song".

It is therefore less than precise to say that Brennan's poetry, in the figure of Lilith, celebrates a perfection, a perfect womanhood, to which real women measure up only rather fitfully and never fully. It would be more to the point to say that (within this poetry) woman achieves perfection to the degree to which she is absent. The index of her absence is her disappearance into the role of signifier of an "Edenic" or infantile state of unmediated narcissism, the condition in which she perfects her role by annihilating herself in her signification of what she, and nobody else, is — that is, not herself, not even someone, but the absence of all someones. Her ultimate manifestation of that role is as "the silence of our thought", the perfection and immediacy just beyond the noise of intellection, just beyond the point at which language begins its mediating, and hence "fallen", task. The poetry then sings her apotheosis as the universal narcissism in which "gods and stars and songs and souls of men / are the sparse jewels in her scatter'd hair".

I remarked earlier on the curious fact that during the two years of his stay in Europe Brennan did not visit France, the country whose poetry meant so much to him. This meant that on his return to Australia — in fact, for the rest of his life — he was an exile not only from a Europe he had seen (that was Germany, in fact, which he came to loathe during the Great War with the hysterical hatred not uncommon to the exile or expatriate); he was also an exile from a country which he had chosen not to see. To put that another way, just as the only true beloved for Brennan was the woman as absence, so too with his only true homeland: it was a country which existed for him as absence. The consequence of this is that for him to be truly at home he had to inhabit that absence: to be nowhere.

And this, I would claim, is the burden of "The Wanderer" sequence: Nos. 86 to 99. The title itself clearly suggests exile, and the explicit import of the poems is unmistakeable. Shut out now, not only from his own heart but also from his own hearth, the subject is "driven everywhere from a clinging home" (No. 88) and "would spread the sail to any wandering wind of the air" (No. 87) because he has embraced the role of

> the wanderer of the ways of all the worlds,
> to whom the sunshine and the rain are one
> and one to stay or hasten, because he knows
> no ending of the way, no home, no goal. (No. 99)

The topography and general tone of much of this sequence is reminiscent of early Anglo-Saxon poetry, and in particular of "The Seafarer", that saddest of all poems. Yet Brennan's poetry also attempts a heroic note which is an odd amalgam of early Germanic heroism and Nietzsche's *Zarathustra*. Addressing those suburban souls at whose table he has sat and whose windows he passes in the dusk, the subject attempts to rouse them from their domestic timidity:

> Go: tho' ye find it bitter, yet must ye be bare
> to the wind and the sea and the night and the wail of birds
> in the sky;
> go: tho' the going be hard and the goal blinded with rain
> yet the staying is a death that is never soften'd with sleep. (No. 95)

The message is clear enough: for those who see the world rightly, Eden ("Yes, Eden was my own, my bride") is understood to be unattainable, "promis'd only" (No. 105). A state of exile is the true human condition, and a heroic "courage to front the way" (No. 98) is the only acceptable moral attitude towards it.

If one were to ask, however, just what the subject of "The Wanderer" is exiled from, and just what he is exiled to, one might be able to take this reading of the sequence a step further, and possibly link it with some of the points made earlier in this essay. Clearly the Wanderer is exiled from domesticity: from "the hearth with its glow and the roof that forbids the rain" (No. 89); from the tables of others at which he has eaten (No. 93); from family, "her eyes in the rosy face that bent over our first babe!" (No. 92). He has left the town behind him (No. 86), and wanders — and this point is stressed by the whole sequence — alone. At a later point in the sequence (Nos. 98 and 99) the subject seems to have left behind him some vaguely Arthurian (or heroic early Germanic) world of battle:

> . . . on the ground and out of livid pools
> wreck of old swords and crowns glimmer'd at whiles;
> I seem'd at home in some old dream of kingship. (No. 99)

This, the poem makes clear, was in the past. In the preceding poem, it is even suggested that this might be the *Götterdämmerung*, a

> battle against the eternal foe,
> the wronger of this world, and all his powers
> in some last fight, foredoom'd disastrous,
> upon the final ridges of the world. (No. 98)

But this too is in the past. The world of heroic allegiance and duty has been abandoned as surely as that of domestic or any other kind of sociality. Thus we can say that the subject is not so much thrown back onto its own discreteness by some overwhelming recognition of metaphysical aloneness, as evading the world of "socially elaborated situations" which, as Lacan has pointed out, inescapably constitute mature experience.

This can be further clarified by looking at where the subject, the Wanderer, has been exiled to. Search as we may through the sequence, we find little definition of where he is beyond the fact that it is outside (echoes of Lear on the heath?), cold, windy, usually evening and near the coast. That this vagueness is not simply the result of a late Victorian generality is made clear by the ending of the sequence:

> I know I am
> the wanderer of the ways of all the worlds,
> to whom the sunshine and the rain are one
> and one to stay or hasten, because he knows
> no ending of the way, no home, no goal,
> and phantom night and the grey day alike
> withhold the heart where all my dreams and days
> might faint in soft fire and delicious death. (No. 99)

The point of this passage is that all places except death are the same for the Wanderer; they are distinguished, one from the other, by no particularity, nor can they be. In fact, the only particularity obtaining to the "land" where the Wanderer wanders is precisely its lack of particularity; it is defined by its absence of definition, by the logical impossibility of its definition. If the Wanderer were "somewhere", he would not be wandering.

If we ask, therefore, where the Wanderer is, we would have to concede first of all, on his own testimony, that he is not dead. Equally, since he has eschewed both the world of human sociality and that of natural, and human, particularity, he is not here. The most precise way to formulate this condition is to say that he is, in fact, absent, and that the world he wanders is absence itself. Just as the woman could only be loved as absence, so this exile finds his home only in what is not home; his true *patria* is a homeland which is neither home nor, rightly called, land as, at the end of the sequence he declares: "I feel a peace fall in the heart of the winds / and a clear dusk settle, somewhere far in me". The Wanderer is at home nowhere. But he is also nowhere; and at home in it.

Anyone who has made even the most fleeting acquaintance with Brennan must have noticed that for all his admiration of French and German poetry the echoes that recur so frequently throughout his verse are from Milton. These range from the phrasing of his description of the "eternal foe" I have already quoted from No. 98 to such a passage as this, despite its rhyme:

> Lo now, beneath the watch of knitted boughs
> he lies, close-folded to his newer spouse,
> creature of morn, that hath ordain'd its fresh
> dew and cool glimmer in her crystal fresh
> sweetly be mix'd . . . (No. 68, X)

And, of course, there is the concern with Adam, Eve, and Eve's precursor which makes it inevitable that Brennan's poetry must be read in some relation to Milton's treatment of our first parents. That Milton should be an influence is not surprising: even Keats claimed to have given up his attempt at writing an epic because it had "too many Miltonic inversions in it". But a brief comparison of Milton and Brennan shows some striking differences.

If, as Milton claimed, his intention was "to justify the ways of God to men", *Paradise Lost* was just as much an anatomy of rebellion against an unreasonable and parental tyranny, a tyranny which defined right in accord with its own will to power and evil as the will to power of others. Duplicitous as Milton's poem is, it is deeply concerned with power, the clash of claims, and naturally, politics. Central to his enterprise is an examination of authority; and if today

Milton's god seems capricious and tyrannical, that is because at least since Nietzsche authority can be read in terms of power rather than in terms of moral absolutes. Brennan's poetry, on the other hand, while in an obvious way concerned with — even obsessed by — the notion of an Absolute, reveals it to be not power but an absence of power, not action but the absence of action, not even thought but the silence beyond thought. For Milton, the Absolute is eternally related to authority as that which commands unquestioning obedience or provokes equally unquestioning opposition. For Brennan, the Absolute is absolute in so far as it is related, intimately and indissolubly, only to nothing. Is it any wonder that Brennan's poetry then, at its most confident, articulates the subject's relation with nothing?

Brennan's attraction to the more mystical, certainly the most idealist, side of German romanticism may have encouraged his pursuit of such an Absolute. But, as I have argued earlier, this pursuit may have been undertaken because of the absence of a more Wordsworthian element in the tradition available to him. Certainly there is little interest in Nature displayed in Brennan's poetry, and in this respect he is widely divergent also from the Australian painters who were his contemporaries. In "Poems 1913" he shows, in fact, little concern with the material world at all: the world of objects, people and events. Wordsworth's poetry articulated a sense of spiritual force immanent in the material, drawing towards coherence and significance, as the famous Simplon Pass passage showed. As "Tintern Abbey" makes clear without any doubt, no matter how spiritual that spirit was, it dwelt in

> the light of setting suns,
> And the round ocean and the living air,
> And the blue sky, and in the mind of man.

But Brennan's sense of the spiritual was ultimately transcendent, to be located — if at all — not within this world nor, even, beyond it, but only in absence. Not surprisingly, the physical world rarely appears in his poetry. Where it does, as in No. 10, it is fraught with a Baudelairean repugnance culminating in a wish for it to be destroyed. In No. 105, it enters the discourse only to be overtrodden by abstraction. Even the most recognizably "Australian" of his poems in setting, No. 54 ("Fire in the heavens . . ."), reveals the physical to be a source of pain in its culminating "cicada's torture-point of song". The physicality of a very hot day in Australia reveals significance only under torture. And what it reveals is torture. Having no other in Brennan's poetry but its own non-recognition, its own lack of place, the spiritual manifests itself only by its absence, perhaps eliciting that dominant note of nostalgia.

Finally, Brennan and modernism. His close contemporary Yeats transformed his earlier Celtic Tweilight preoccupations into the political and existential substance of modernism; and the poets Stevens, Pound and Eliot were not very much younger than Brennan. Brennan's failure to extend his poetry to the point where it had to encounter, if not embark on, modernism could be explained partly by isolation, by the absence within literary culture in Australia of factors enabling that major development which took place in Europe and the United States. Such, in effect, would be my argument. But I do not mean by this that Australia's isolation from Europe caused Brennan to be ignorant of the new developments overseas. On the contrary, Brennan knew Yeats's later poetry but thought little of it. Why?

Modernism can be read as the response to, and an attempted solution to, a profound disappointment. Born before the last decade of the nineteenth century, the great American modernist poets were reared within the orderly cosmos of the Christian church (as was Brennan) and nurtured on the optimism of Emerson's translation of a Wordsworthian pantheism. But the events of the first two decades of this century seemed to make it unavoidably clear that not only was the "still, sad music of humanity" becoming altogether too harsh and too grating, but that "all thinking things, all objects of all thought" were no longer impelled by a "presence" capable of disturbing "with the joy / Of elevated thoughts". All objects of all thought — which meant not only all objects such as the natural world, the cities and their people, but also the economic and political realities — displayed an accelerating reification to which alienation was only the modernists' first response. Their answer to this sense of chaos, as Eliot called it, was an assertion of the symbolic and myth-making power of the imagination: an ability to create fictions whose value lies precisely in the fact that they did not accord with the chaos and reification of reality, but instead harmonized with the human need for order and meaning. These fictions were validated by their ability to accord with prior cultural manifestations of the same need for order, rather than by their approximation to a transcendental, or ideal, reality. Eliot's and Pound's concern with tradition stems from this.

Brennan's poetry grew up in a space devoid of these capacities for disappointment. The modernists' acute sense of disinheritance was never his, for the simple reason that he never had their inheritance. The objects of his world were never the vehicles of a spiritual force in the way younger poets in America felt theirs had been, or should have been. The chaos of objects, the reified world, with which his European and American contemporaries somehow had to make sense, excited a different problematic because to Brennan the sensible world was important primarily as a signifier of an "upper" (that is, more "spiritually pure") world. If "the things above are as the things below'' (*Prose* p. 397) then it followed that the things below were as the things above: neither chaotic nor, in fact, particularly tangible. For Brennan to have developed, after "Poems 1913", into a modernist poet would have required as radical and massive a reassessment and reorientation as Yeats achieved. But as the development of the Vitalists and the *Vision* poets shortly after the war demonstrated, there was nothing in Australian culture at that time to sustain such a rigorous reassessment. What little poetry Brennan continued to write became increasingly irrelevant — a fact of which he seems to have become aware — and the task of creating modernism in Australia fell to Kenneth Slessor.

5

Kenneth Slessor's Approach to Modernism

The literary movement which began in England, Europe and the United States at the end of the nineteenth century is generally considered to have developed to a point by the end of the 1920s at which it could no longer be usefully or accurately described as modernist. Despite a certain time-lag in the replication or reflection of overseas literary developments in Australia, it is both historically inaccurate and unprofitable to call recent Australian poetry modernist as, for example, John Tranter does in his introduction to *The New Australian Poetry*.[1] In fact, any writer whose work has been published mostly in the 1940s and later would fall within the period labelled generally, and rather vaguely, post-modern or post-modernist. Furthermore, one aspect of modernism's (and post-modernism's) historicity is that it represents a particular evolution of romanticism, as well as occupying a particular place in time. In Australia, only Kenneth Slessor filled this particular dual space — that is, both temporal and intellectual — in our poetry, though his achievement mediated European and American modernism to other poets, most notably Judith Wright, A.D. Hope and, possibly, Francis Webb. These latter, while clearly not post-modern in temper, are not actually modernist either. If, therefore, I start here by claiming that Kenneth Slessor is the only genuine modernist poet that Australia has produced, certain problems immediately spring up.

As I argued in my third chapter, modernism can no longer be considered a revolutionary phase of artistic development early in this century, a clean break with a Victorian past, but must be considered as the fate either of classical realism or of romanticism, depending to some extent on whether the critic's attention is on fiction or on poetry. In fact, any attempt at an account of modernism which does not read it in relation to its precursors is not only shortsighted. It also fails to take into account the fact that almost all literature in Britain and in the United States, since the middle of the last century, has been post-romantic not only in the simple historical sense, but also in the sense that it has been a series of necessary revisionary acts. Modernism and post-modernism are points on the trajectory of romanticism (now properly labelled post-romanticism) as it moves through time, constantly conserving and re-presenting an originary romanticism by its acts of displacing and destroying it.

But, as I have also pointed out, Australian soil failed to nourish romanticism, this child of the Old World, and its offspring, and Christopher Brennan's belated attempt to draw succour from a romantic symbolism led him away from, rather than towards, a poetic discourse which could say anything much about the world itself. Whatever the reasons, the fact remains that the profound family relationship with romanticism in England and the United States, which gave rise to what we now call modernism, had no exact equivalent in Australia. We are therefore faced with the problem of determining how Slessor can be described as a modernist poet.

It should be clear that there are several matters I am not talking about. For example, I am not talking about modernism simply as "a reaction to the growing chaos of modern life". Such a simple-minded notion of poetry ignores the fact that poetry exists not only in relation to society and history but also in relation to other poetry and other forms of discourse. This is why Fredric Jameson can claim that "a given style [is] a projected solution, on the aesthetic or imaginary level, to a genuinely contradictory situation in the concrete world of everyday social life".[2] What Jameson says of style (in fact he is discussing the novel) can be said equally of poetry. Poetry is not simply passive and secondary (a reaction) but also active, "a projected *solution*"; it is not simply social, but also speaks its solution "on an aesthetic or imaginary level" where other texts are to be found. The absence of a firm romanticism on that "aesthetic or imaginary level" presents a problem for any poetry which can be claimed modernist, irrespective of the social and historical conditions attendant on its making.

Furthermore, I am not talking here of some form of literary "influence" — as that term is usually deployed. In fact, I would claim that it was impossible for Slessor to "learn" to be a modernist simply by reading T.S. Eliot, Ezra Pound and other modernist writers whose works then "influenced" him to write similarly. In fact, Slessor writes most dissimilarly from these two, so that any notion of his imitating them is out of the question. This whole notion of literary influence is, as I have suggested in my second chapter, following Harold Bloom in this, a mis-formulation of the matter when it comes to a "strong" poet. It is not simply a matter of bad artists imitating, good artists stealing. It is, rather, a matter of the status of the arche-text. For the bad (in Bloom's terms, "weak") poet, the arche-text, the parental figure, the source of influence — call it what you will — is an aid, something to be borrowed from, something to be looted. It provides techniques, stylistic characteristics, turns of phrase, and so forth, and always, at the critical moment, claims back what has been taken from it, leaving the borrower exposed in the poverty of his or her own resources. For the strong poet, on the other hand, the arche-text is an obstacle occupying the place that the poet must himself or herself occupy. He or she must wrestle with it as Jacob wrestled with his angel, in order to displace it, in order to take its place while according it all due honour as the ultimate challenge. Slessor was such a strong poet, the first in Australia. His unique problem was that this dominating parent, this arche-text which he had to wrestle with, wrest askew, rewrite in his own handwriting, did not exist.

If my claim that Slessor is Australia's first strong poet is accepted (and there is little doubt that today his critical reputation is considerably steadier than Brennan's, the only earlier possible contender) then it should be clear that a lot is at stake here. We are dealing with more than the development of an important poet. We are, in fact, dealing with a moment of mythic integrity, the moment at which Australian poetry becomes itself. Haltingly, perhaps — and certainly with several false starts. But those false starts were essential to what eventuated, and the eyes of all subsequent Australian poets are on Slessor in his dilemma. To put that in a somewhat less dramatic fashion, subsequent poets have been influenced by Slessor in the obvious sense: for example, they deal with Australian material like he did, openly and unashamedly; they admire and try to emulate the rich materiality of his description; and they respond deeply to the emotional qualities of some of his best poems. But also all subsequent Australian poetry is read (and by that I also mean written) in relation to Slessor. His is the first inescapable Australian text that all subsequent texts must engage in discourse with. This is not to claim that Slessor is the "father of Australian poetry", because the father is prior, elsewhere, or nowhere at all, and I shall discuss this presently.

Originary moments appropriate narrative to themselves in the form of myth, in a strategy whose ultimate objective is to signify the birth of Time, without which narrative cannot exist. Slessor himself, as numerous critics have pointed out, is preoccupied with time. So it is not surprising to find in one of his poems, "Five Visions of Captain Cook", an account of the two-faced nature of time ("Two chronometers the captain had . . ." (a rudimentary account which will be considerably revised in "Five Bells") and a narrative account of the origin of Australian poetry which concludes "So Cook made choice, so Cook sailed westabout, / So men write poems in Australia".[3] I shall be looking at this poem with some care soon. For the moment, our purpose is better served if we follow the example of the epic poets and start *in medias res*. I will examine one of Slessor's apparently more simple but, in reality, most complex and revealing poems in the hope that this will shed some light not only on what followed it but also on what came before.

"Elegy in a Botanic Gardens" narrates, retrospectively, the course of a romance and its apparent termination. No cause is given for the death of the romance, but its effect has been to relocate the subject's consciousness from Wagner and memories of his springtime romance to Latin and botany:

> Never before
> Had I assented to the hateful name
> *Meryta Macrophylla*, on a tin tag.
> That was no time for botany. But now the schools,
> The horticulturalists, come forth
> Triumphantly with Latin. So be it now,
> *Meryta Macrophylla* . . . (P. 55)

Latin is a "dead" language, corresponding to the now "dead grove" which had been, in the springtime of the lover's romance, the Tristania tree where they had "kissed so awkwardly". The name "Tristania" has obvious allusions to the great romance of Tristan and Isolde (originally Celtic, then Wagnerian), to tryst (a pledged secret meeting between lovers) and to *tristis* meaning sad. This latter signification indicates that just as Tristan's and Isolde's romance was doomed, so this romance was already sadly inscribed by the Latin which triumphantly marked its end. In its dry objectivity, so unromantic and thus so hateful to the lover, Latin even informs the English language when it comes to the naming of scientific institutions:

> THE NATIONAL HERBARIUM
> Repeated dryly in Roman capitals,
> THE NATIONAL HERBARIUM.

This phrase, uttered twice at the end of the poem, ironically annuls the lovers' fantasies by asserting the unromantic reality within which they were played out. Following this line of interpretation, therefore, Latin is seen as the language of science; and science is seen as that passionless, taxonomic objectivity, the antithesis of the lovers' romance which might, in the spring, have given a concentricity to those "thousands of white circles drifting past, / Cold suns in water".

Such an interpretation however, gives us only part of the picture. Because, most interestingly, science in itself is not portrayed ultimately as the antagonist of romance. This is made clear in the delineation of an imaginary "Headlong Hall", usually interpreted as a lovers' fantasy, a place of cheerfully profuse romantic confusion[4] now replaced by the barren realism of "THE NATIONAL HERBARIUM". But the poem's depiction of it intimately links science with music (and thus, by implication, with art in general), love and enjoyment. In the time of the springtime romance, the "old house" used to be a

> Georgian Headlong Hall
> With glass-eye windows winking candles forth,
> Stuffed with French horns, globes, air-pumps, telescopes
> And Cupid in a wig, playing the flute. . . .

The instrument of science, "globes, air-pumps, telescopes" are things that children, or people with a certain youthful innocence, love to play with. They get pleasure from playing with them in a way in which they get pleasure from love and from art. The poem here thus harks back to a "spring" condition prior to the poem's present "autumn" — a "spring" in which science, art and love are not separated from each other. In terms of the poem's romance narrative, this is indicated by the fact that that happy wedding of nature and science (the Botanic Gardens) was intimately hospitable to the poet's romance and its musical (Wagnerian) and imaginative undertones. Inescapably, the contrast with the poet's present situation is pointed up — now science, art and love are all separated, bereft of each other's intimate companionship. It is only in this divorce from the emotional and the artistic that science takes on the quality of dry objectivity so hateful to the lover. This is the condition of multiplying specialization, differentiation, fragmentation, and hence alienation associated with late capitalist society and, without doubt, a condition traditionally seen as articulated in modernist writing. In this poem, Latin is therefore not simply the language of science; it is the language of reification, of alienation, translating nature into botany (transporting the lover to Botany Bay) and the lovers' fantasy English country house into a joyless, even minatory, scientific institute.

Having come thus far, however, we perhaps need to remind ourselves that while the phrase "THE NATIONAL HERBARIUM", even in Roman capitals, is an English phrase, two of its words are clearly of Latin origin, something which is by no means uncharacteristic of phrases in the English language. Although Slessor's language in "Elegy" is remarkably Anglo-Saxon in origin, there are still at least thirty-four words in it of Latin extraction. It is hard to imagine a poem of comparable length with fewer Latinate words in it; it is impossible to imagine one in the English language with none. English, the living language, can only go about its business of signifying because of its complicity with this dead other which it carries within it. Without it, English is not English: it only *is* English because it is partly constituted of what it is not. Without this Latin, the English of Slessor's "Elegy" could signify neither the ironic and hateful "NATIONAL HERBARIUM" nor, significantly, the "Tristania tree" on which all the poem's romance is grounded. (Nor, indeed, could the poem itself be called an "Elegy".) Therefore, just as Slessor's poem carries within its narrative the death of a romance, his language can signify romance and also the unified state which is the opposite of reification only because it is already inscribed by Latin, the language of reification, disunity, that which is isolated and de-naturalized, that which is alienated. The fact that the words "romance" and "romantic" are themselves of Latin origin should not escape notice, even though they do not actually appear in Slessor's poem.

One could possibly, at this stage in the discussion, make some claim for Slessor's modernism on the grounds of what has been shown above. Some such claim, I feel, could validly — though tenuously — be sustained. But it would be very much to oversimplify, and would involve us in getting somewhat ahead of ourselves. Instead, I want to follow the trail suggested by my claim that "Elegy" elegizes a dead romance. Many critics have pointed to the unsatisfactory nature of Slessor's early poems. Vincent Buckley, for example, claimed that "These early poems are in a very real sense Romantic — showing the strong attraction felt by their author towards the grotesque and exaggerated elements of experience, and towards a raffish sensuousness. These qualities stand behind the typically romantic attitude to expression which has just been mentioned".[5] Such a characterization of romanticism is clearly unsatisfactory for the present discourse, even though Buckley's depiction of Slessor is close to the point. For a description of that curious world produced by the *Vision* group and apparent in Slessor's early poetry, a description every bit as zestful as Slessor's own, we should turn to A.D. Hope in his essay *Slessor Twenty Years After*:

> A very odd layer-cake it turned out to be. On a foundation of minor classical mythology — Pan, the satyrs and the centaurs and the nymphs engaged in perpetual games of sexual hide-and-seek, Venus and Cupid, Aristophanes and Petronius — they erected a Middle Ages compounded of Boccaccio, Provencal courts of love, the thieves' kitchens and willing wenches of Villon's Paris and a pantomime version of the Arabian

> Nights. The Renascence supplied them with Rabelais and Brantome's *Femmes Galantes,* Marlowe's brawling taverns and Shakespeare's Bawdy, the seventeenth century with periwigs and trollops and buccaneers, the eighteenth with Chinoiserie, the spice islands, nabobbery and Macheathery and Hogarthery, and an aristocratic society of the 'sblud and stap-my-vitals school, and ending with the bucks, bruisers and dandies of the Regency and a touch of Baroness Orczy to show that the French Revolution had arrived.
>
> But by now, of course, Australia had been settled and the whole of this curious civilization was transported to Botany Bay where all its inhabitants rubbed shoulders with Currency Lads and Lasses, rum-rebels and bushrangers, while Pan and the satyrs continued to tumble a juicy nymph or two under the eucalypts. Later immigrants continued to arrive from the Paris of Murger, Columbine and Pierrot, set up their stage and the Australian Vie de Boheme was complete. Norman Lindsay painted it and the poets versified what he painted.[6]

And Hope goes on to make the important point that despite all this theatricality and play-acting, what was happening "represented something important, the first conscious movement of immaturity towards a mature literature, the first movement of provincialism towards autonomy".

There is no doubt that many of Slessor's early poems display that "strong attraction . . . towards the grotesque elements of experience" that Buckley noted, and which Hope lists. There is also no doubt that many of these early poems accomplish in no satisfying way whatever any real movement towards an unprovincial autonomy. But the early poems are by no means all immature pastiche. "Earth-Visitors", in particular, is a strikingly coherent poem which, from the point of view of the present discourse, warrants attention. The visual world created in this poem is familiar to us today from the rich fantasy illustrations of many children's books and also, of course, from the paintings of Norman Lindsay, to whom the poem is dedicated and whose house, Springwood, is mentioned in it. It is a world part Medieval, part semi-Asian, part magical:

> they were strangers —
> Princes gone feasting, barons with gipsy eyes
> And names that rang like viols — perchance, who knows,
> Kings of old Tartary, forgotten, swept from Asia,
> Blown on raven chargers across the world,
> Forever smiling sadly in their beards
> And stamping abruptly into courtyards at midnight. (P. 1)

These ancient gods came down from wherever they lived to leave "only a confusion of sharp dreams / To vex a farm-girl — that, and perhaps a feather, / Some thread of the Cloth of Gold, a scale of metal, / Caught in her hair". But now "The unpastured Gods have gone". All except one, that is. Venus still appears, on wintry nights when "Springwood steams with dew", to inaugurate a springtime renewal in which "A thousand birds cry 'Venus!' " Thus at one level of interpretation "Earth-Visitors" can be read as a nostalgic evocation of a (non-existent) past in which heaven and earth, the gods and humanity, were more accessible to each other than they are today. It is also a celebration of love and sensuality as being all that can open up for us that fuller sense of wonder and awe which we rarely experience but can still dream about.

Another way to read the poem is in the light of what Northrop Frye has to say of romance, in particular: "The perennially childlike quality of romance is marked by its extraordinarily persistent nostalgia, its search for some kind of imaginative golden age in time or space."[7] The applicability of such a statement to Slessor's poem hardly needs pointing to, except that perhaps it should also be noted that for Slessor the humans are cast in the role of children, addressed as "child", and run or tumble obediently to the whims of the gods. Leaving to one side, for the moment, the matter of "quest", Fry's further comments are equally applicable:

> Translated into dream terms, the quest–romance is the search of the libido or desiring self for a fulfilment that will deliver it from the anxieties of reality but will still contain that reality . . . Translated into ritual terms, the quest-romance is the victory of fertility over the waste land. Fertility means food and drink, bread and wine, body and blood, the union of male and female.[8]

Such a description fits the *Vision* world well. It fits "Earth-Visitors" exactly. Even the "strange tongue" spoken by the gods is nourishing as well as exotic, "sweet as pineapple", and the "union of male and female" is central both to the poem's evocation of the past and its depiction of the present.

However, Frye also claims that "the element that gives literary form to the romance (is) the quest" and that "A quest involving conflict assumes two main characters, a protagonist or hero, and an antagonist or enemy".[9] Although such a line of discourse seems less immediately applicable to "Earth Visitors" than others, it is instructive to push it closer. Frye continues:

> The central form of romance is dialectical: everything is focussed on a conflict between the hero and his enemy, and all the reader's values are bound up with the hero. Hence the hero of romance is analogous to the mythical Messiah or deliverer who comes from an upper world, and his enemy is analogous to the demonic powers of a lower world. The conflict takes place in, or at any rate primarily concerns, *our* world, which is in the middle, and which is characterized by the cyclical movement of nature. Hence the opposite poles of the cycles of nature are assimilated to the opposition of the hero and his enemy. The enemy is associated with winter, darkness, confusion, sterility, moribund life, and old age, and the hero with spring, dawn, order, fertility, vigor, and youth.

Turning back to the poem, then, it could be suggested that the hero makes two appearances: once in the form of the gods of old (Mercury and his fellows) and once in the form of Venus, who is an avatar of the former. The hero comes from "the upper world" down to the level of the human and, as Venus, the Morning Star, inaugurates dawn as well as vigor, youth, fertility and, in the cry of the birds, spring. (Significantly, order, that persistent obsession of modernist poets, does not yet figure in Slessor's poetry, perhaps for the simple reason that it is not yet problematical for him, he is not yet a modernist.) These qualities are the object of her quest, the fruits of her journey that eventuate with her arrival at Springwood. The antagonist, the enemy, therefore, must be sought in all that hinders the hero in her attempt to gain these qualities and confer them on "*our* world". Concealed in the poem, in fact, there is a narrative in which the hero's first avatar is vanquished by the antagonist, a defeat which is reversed in the last two stanzas with the triumph of the second avatar, Venus. In so far as the poem points to the nature of the antagonist at all, the stress on past tense, past action ("There were strange riders once . . .". "It is long now since . . .", "The unpastured Gods have gone . . .") leads me to suggest that it is Time itself which has ejected the old gods from our world; and it is Time which Venus — love, sensuality, youth — defeats in order to inaugurate spring in Springwood. She has, in effect, reversed the passage of Time which marked the end of the earlier "golden age" so as to reinstitute a new one.

It is possible, however, to sustain an alternative interpretation of the poem's last three lines. In all of the above, I have interpreted the phrase "Your name, child?" as being uttered by the visiting hero, the goddess, just as it was uttered by Mercury earlier in the poem. But if that is so, why is the question answered by her own name as "A thousand birds cry 'Venus!' "? It could be that the birds are not answering the question, but announcing the name of the questioner: at which point it should be noted in passing that even where the name of the goddess is the voice of nature, it speaks in Latin. But if we take the cry of the birds to be the answer to the question, then the questioner is not the goddess but the inhabitant of Springwood, addressing the female as "child" just as Mercury had. Such an interpretation reads just as naturally from the grammar of the last stanza as the earlier did, but it gives us a different dramatis personae. Time is still the antagonist, having (temporarily) swept away the object of quest. But now it is the artist who is the romance hero, interrogating nature in such a way as to identify and welcome Venus and thus successfully complete his quest, which is to find her and bring her, with the benefits she entails, into our world by defeating (reversing) Time.

Thus "Earth-Visitors" is inhabited by two romance heros, each active and questing, but also — as the object (Venus) of the other's quest, or as the recipient (the artist) of the other's bounty — passive. For even at her most active, Venus is also passive: "Her breasts are berries broken in snow". And the questing, interrogating artist does his questing at home, apparently passively, waiting for Venus to visit him.

It should be clear now how the romance elegized in "Elegy in a Botanic Gardens" is not simply a love affair, but romance itself. Venus, as hero, fails to accomplish her tryst any longer; the poet, as questor, is no longer able to find her. Instead of a thousand birds crying "Venus!" he encounters "The smell of birds' nests faintly burning" which "Is autumn". It must be stressed that one essential of romance is the ultimate success of the quest. What has occurred between "Earth-Visitors" and "Elegy" is that the quest has foundered. Given the medieval trappings of Slessor's earlier version of it, it is not surprising that it should be seen to do so in that most un-medieval, industrial means of transport, the train.

It would seem difficult to get lost on a train, but in "The Night-Ride" (p. 31) the subject of Slessor's poem does so most convincingly. Anyone who has done much country train travel at night will recognize in this poem an acutely observed mimetic realism. But where elements of the grotesque enter the poem (for example, "Black, sinister travellers", "mysterious ends", "private Fates") they do so as unhoused ghosts of the now dispersed realm of romance, and their effect is to question the adequacy of mimetic realism as a means of accounting for experience, by posing questions that realism cannot answer. Slessor has been constantly praised for the immediacy of his observation of physical detail, a quality as apparent in "The Night-Ride" as anywhere else. But here the detail fails to ground in an empirical world the subject's quest for coherence, for a demystification of the sinister mystery of what he observes. Instead, the accumulated detail denies any possibility of a successful coherence by insisting on and highlighting its own discreteness. Romance and realism join hands here to frustrate the demands which the journeying questor should be able legitimately to make of each of them. The situation is one which looks forward to such fiction as Thomas Pynchon's or, at another cultural level, to the mystery story or thriller, where "facts" multiply but pattern is suppressed. The poet's only solution offered in "The Night-Ride" is to obliterate perception and consciousness: "Pull down the blind. Sleep. Sleep."

If, as he claims, "Of Rapptown I recall nothing else" he has, none the less, told us a lot. Romance quest, hence the romance model, has foundered in a mechanical, reified world where the questor can join T.S. Eliot's figure in "The Waste Land" in declaring "I can connect / Nothing with nothing". The romance model has collapsed under the pressure of the demands Slessor put on it. But the journey, the journeying artist, still continues. He will still seek a triumph but it will now have to be, in Brennan's phrase, "a triumph won in defeat".

"Five Visions of Captain Cook" presents us really with only one vision of Cook — seen though from four different points of view — and one (double) vision of time. The double vision of time is located most clearly in section III, though it is also operative in section V. We need not be much detained by it at the moment, except to note its presence and to observe how time, being the element in which Cook's fate is inscribed, is not only his antagonist, "Dragging Captain Cook to the Sandwich Isles" and to his death, but inevitably the victor. Yet Cook is also envisioned as a victor, not only temporarily (for the time being), but permanently (for all time). Thus his victory, like his fate, is inscribed in what vanquishes him, it is written in the characters of its own negative. As T.S. Eliot put it in "Burnt Norton", "Only through time time is conquered".

The nature of Cook's triumph is more problematic. The most forthright characterization of it is found in these lines from section I:

> So, too, Cook made choice,
> Over the brink, into the devil's mouth,
> With four months' food, and sailors wild with dreams
> Of English beer, the smoking barns of home.
> So Cook made choice, so Cook sailed westabout,
> So men write poems in Australia. (P. 58)

Cook rejected the prudence that had recalled Tasman and Bougainville with "The voice of God", in favour of the daemonic, "the devil's mouth"; and this choice is causally linked with the fact that men (Slessor included) write poems in Australia. Cook is depicted as one of those "Daemons in periwigs, doling magic out", "more like warlocks than a humble man", as a "mesmerist" with a "spell", as "Caesar", even as a "god". His daemonic power can be set aside voluntarily (section IV) in moments of simple human enjoyment, and involuntarily, violently, in his death (section V), which, while apparently so accidental, is yet also a result of his daemonism:

"Vengeance in a cocked hat", "carried on a sailor's back". Cook's powers are deployed, and thus apparent, partly in his ability to bend others to his will, and partly in his ability to guide his boat, unscathed, against the tides and winds, and between the murderous coral reefs. (The poem makes no mention of the damage actually done to the historical Cook's boat by coral.) Slessor's Cook is humanity in its "larger than life", more than "mere mortal" aspect, and has rightly been seen as having a Nietzschean, superman, character.

It is more than tempting to see in this vision of Cook an embodiment of those qualities which enable men — and, of course, women — to "write poems in Australia". His daemonic power to defy chaos, to engage with "mystery", to choose "a passage into the dark" and to charm order across the face of disorder — all is linked causally with poetry in such a way that it insists in being read as metaphoric of it. If indeed "men write poems in Australia" today it is because — the poem suggests — they deploy those qualities celebrated in Slessor's portrait of Cook. Thus we have here Slessor's attempt at defining a second model of the artist following the displacement of the romance model. This new one has clear affinities with Moses (who leads his flock to, but does not himself enter, the Promised Land) or Beowulf (whose triumph for his people is won at the cost of his own life). Because this protagonist accomplishes his quest only at the cost of his own life, we need to distinguish him from the romance model and call him, a little loosely, heroic — heroic as, for example, in the pre-romance, Heroic Age of Anglo-Saxon and old Germanic literature.

But the same poem which proposes this model also withdraws it, negates it. At the most obvious level, Cook is never credited with the one attribute which, since the end of the eighteenth century, has been deemed essential to the creation of poetry — imagination. We are told that modernist writing from England and the United States was well known in Australia in the twenties and thirties, and there is no reason to doubt this. But the fact that Slessor's poem could advance, even metaphorically, a model of the artist which lacked that "shaping spirit of imagination" indicates more clearly that any argument of mine the enormous non-existence of romanticism in the Australian artistic consciousness of that time. In Slessor's poem, Cook's daemon is will, not imagination; his forté is action, not thought. Where angels fear to tread, (for example, that "necessary angel" which, for Wallace Stevens, is the figure of the imagination) Cook, being a god or a Caesar, wades in and is killed by "a knife of English iron, / Forged aboard ship, that had been changed for pigs". Such irony fails to strike down Joseph Banks, or the humbler Alexander Home.

Captain Alexander Home's blindness is due to the fact, or

emblematic of the fact, that "he lived like this / In one place, and gazed elsewhere". He is not an empiricist any more than he is a rationalist and his will, unlike Cook's, is totally at the service of the past. His one — and unavoidable — act of realism, since he is not insane, is in that pathetic moment at the end of the poem when

> putting out one hand
> Tremulously in the direction of the beach,
> He felt a chair in Scotland. And sat down.

His dreams — the only sight he has — are vexed and obsessed, and his guests are bored, by Cook's death. The tropical luxuriance of Home's obsessions however is not Cook's creation but Cook's nemesis, the ultimate chaos over which Will cannot triumph. But at one level of interpretation that chaos and its triumph are preserved, presented, represented by Home's imagination; at another, by Slessor's text. Home's imagination subverts Time and displaces the present by inscribing Cook's absence, his disappearance in the South Seas, as a "presence" within the world of discourse. Home's Homeric blindness is impelled by his hero's absence into that compulsion to repeat which is, like poetry, both a denial of Time and the despair of his wife. The result is an avatar of Cook from which Cook's mortality has been erased by virtue of its repeatability, and in which it has been permanently inscribed by the facts of its occurrence. Only by death has Cook become immortal, just as it is only in Home, or in Home's absent listeners, or in ourselves, the absent readers of the (dead) Slessor's poem — all that is not Cook — that Cook lives, that Cook finds a home. Cook, at one level the figure of the artist of will and activity, can live only by virtue of the imagination of another who is an artist of imagination and inactivity, who occupies the space left by the failure of Cook's will to achieve in itself imagination and order, and who achieves them for him.

And where, all this time, is Joseph Banks, custodian of Latin and "the horrid Gorgon squint / Of horticulture" which turns flowers to stone? Articulate in the language of the other, Banks can speak the Latin that transforms the living into the dead. But "hung pensive in a porthole" Banks is also the "passive" other of Cook's will to action, he is the consciousness which can penetrate the looking glass of the sea's surface and observe "stone turned to flowers", the inanimate transforming itself into the animate, the deathly ("a reef that would have knifed / Their boards to mash, and murdered every man") into the fragilely mortal and back again:

> you'd snap a crystal twig,
> One petal even of the water-garden,
> And have it dying like a cherry-bough.

Latin, the dead tongue, is also the password to the underworld, the language in which the dead come alive. But there came a time, of course, when the dead refused to come back to life in Slessor's poetry. The romance hero had failed in his quest: poetry could not be romance. And already in "Five Visions of Captain Cook" the heroic figure which is a model of poetry is triumphant only in defeat.

Thus we have to move on to "Five Bells", generally considered Slessor's masterpiece. It is a powerfully moving poem, in which the sharp note of anguish is unmistakably audible. But the poem's significance depends as much on how it came to be said as on any emotions that might be generated by it. In "Five Bells" the subject's Homeric descent into the Underworld in order to interrorage his dead friend Joe Lynch furnishes him with little but his own memory ("The flood that does not flow") and the inescapable failure of two earlier models of poetry. The poem's questing consciousness finds neither romance success nor a heroic triumph won in defeat. The questor discovers that any "way of controlling, of ordering, of giving a shape and a significance to the immense panorama of futility and anarchy which is contemporary history" comes from the symbolic power of imagination itself or not at all.

The poem's search for meaning is equated with the subject's desire to hear again the voice of his dead friend:

> If I could find an answer, could only find
> Your meaning, or could say why you were here
> Who now are gone, what purpose gave you breath
> Or seized it back, might I not hear your voice?

Interestingly, the dead friend's "voice" is anything but absent from the poem, which in fact retells much of what Joe had said to the subject. In one section Joe is even nothing *but* voice:

> So dark you bore no body, had no face,
> But a sheer voice that rattled out of air
> (As now you'd cry if I could break the glass),
> A voice that spoke beside me in the bush.

But this voice resides in memory, "the flood that does not flow". It is, when all is said and done, the contents of the subject's mind, not the living speech of another, from whom he is separated by death as though by a pane of glass through which he can see but not hear:

> Are you shouting at me, dead man, squeezing your face
> In agonies of speech on speechless panes?
> Cry louder, beat the windows, bawl your name!

But I hear nothing, nothing . . . only bells,
Five bells, the bumpkin calculus of Time.
Your echoes die, your voice is dowsed by Life . . .

The voice of memory is not original but a repetition of what has passed; it is mimesis, an echo of truth but not truth, not meaning, not presence itself.[10] Yet if he is to recover that originary speech, that language of presence, the subject acknowledges that he must "find an answer . . . find / Your meaning". But that meaning is spoken only in that originary speech, that voice which cannot be heard. To put that in a slightly different way: the subject expresses the wish to bring his dead friend back to life by finding the meaning of life and death. But that meaning can be conveyed to him only in the actual, as distinct from the remembered, speech of the man who died. Trapped in that circularity, and acknowledging the futility of his desire, the poem ends with the subject watching the harbour in which his friend drowned, and listening to the sound of Time (the bells) and of the life which "dowsed" the voice of presence:

all I heard
Was a boat's whistle, and the scraping squeal
Of seabirds' voices far away, and bells,
Five bells. Five bells ringing coldly out.
Five bells

In the world that the poem's subject now observes, there is no immanent meaning, not even in heroic action, and the voice of presence is inaudible. This is, indeed, the world of the modernist, in which the only instrument for order and meaning is the imagination speaking its own failure as it struggles "to idealize and to unify" in the very words which, failing to recreate Joe Lynch as man, create that failure as text, which create one of our finest poems.[11]

Australian poetry, therefore, came with Slessor to modernism somewhat by default. As a result of the absence of a firm romantic and particularly a Wordsworthian presence in our tradition, geographical and historical circumstances furnished Slessor with models of poetry which led him only by a roundabout path to the mainstream of contemporary literature in his time. With hindsight, it is tempting to see his early infatuation with romance as youthful folly and the result of the influence of a powerful but aberrant father figure, Norman Lindsay. Nonetheless, it occupies a place in Slessor's development which is far more meaningful than such a description would suggest. It marks his embarkation on a quest which, initially promising fair success, led him beyond the meaningfulness of heroic defeat to a confrontation with meaninglessness itself. This quest led him, in fact, even further, to a final confrontation with language, after which he ceased writing poetry altogether. But at this point it is perhaps worth emphasizing that if the models Slessor adopted and discarded were debased or anachronistic, it was nonetheless the relentless demands that he made of them that forced them to reveal their inadequacies and made him displace them, eventually replacing them with nothing but the energy of his own imagination. This double parricide left him an orphan, the true role of the modernist who can expect meaning, order, significance neither from nature (see, for example, Slessor's "South Country") nor from society (for example, his Baudelairean "Last Trams") — much less from God. If Australian poetry came into being, therefore, as an orphan, that is how all strong poetry comes into being; and it is because Slessor found anything less than that — or anything more — inadequate.

But, as I have just said, Slessor's journey did not end with "Five Bells", but with the final confrontation with language which is "Beach Burial". In the earlier "Elegy" as we have seen, Latin was the language of reification — of alienation, disunity — inscribed within English, the other of English without which English could not be itself. This duplicitous quality of language enables Latin, in "Five Visions of Captain Cook", in the guise of its custodian Joseph Banks, to penetrate the otherworld beneath the sea, to watch life transform itself into death ("Flowers turned to stone") and death transform itself into life ("Stone turned to flowers"). However in "Five Bells" such a transformation is no longer possible. The surface of the water in which Joe Lynch drowned has hardened into a pane of glass, the barrier of death across which no language can pass. Meaning is sought only in the living speech of "presence", and that is inaudible to the living since those who speak it are not present, are not at all except in a replication of non-presence, in the faltering language of memory which is the only language available to the living and whose only certainties are its contingent, provisional nature, and the fact that as a repetition it is not "the thing itself".

Finally, in "Beach Burial", language confesses its ultimate powerlessness, its defining duplicity, its inability to name:

> And each cross, the driven stake of tidewood,
> Bears the last signature of men,
> Written with such perplexity, with such bewildered pity,
> The words choke as they begin —
>
> *"Unknown seaman"*. . .

"Perplexity" and "bewildered pity" characterize the mood of both "Five Bells" and "Beach Burial" itself. There came a time to many people in the 1940s when history became unspeakable, when language became incommensurate with the enormity of empirical reality. This happens with Slessor in this poem. Pressing language — any language — to be meaningful, even to gesture towards meaning, in the face of such pointless death, the poem finds

> the ghostly pencil
> Wavers and fades, the purple drips,
> The breath of the wet season has washed their inscriptions
> As blue as drowned men's lips.

The inscription of death, of silence, language's other, of non-signification, of *insignificance* — this is what language has become. Yet it is only in language that language can signify its insignificance.

This is the modernist impasse. After the harsh irony of the nursery rhythms of "The Hollow Men", Eliot embraced Christianity, immanent meaning. Pound pinned his faith on politics and culture, broadcast for Mussolini and watched his Cantos peter out, incomplete, uncompletable. Stevens, who at one stage had claimed that "the gaiety of language/ is our seigneur", had none the less forged a concept of the imagination which he consciously deployed against the faults of his time: "It is a violence from within that protects us from a violence without. It is the imagination pressing back against the pressure of reality."[12] But Slessor rejected religion and politics. Notions of culture and tradition available to Eliot and Pound in Europe simply were not available to him in the Australia of his time. And because he had come to modernism in his own way, by default, he had no coherent theory of the imagination deriving from romanticism which could deploy language's manifest meaninglessness in a meaningful way. His response was to quit poetry altogether, and "Beach Burial" is his *vale* to it. For a poet of Slessor's stature, it is only fitting that his obituary to language — in which he reveals its inability to signify and thus, in the face of history as he knew it, its insignificance — is eloquent in its simplicity.

6

A.D. Hope: The Double Tongue of Harmony

An insistence on metrical formality, stanza forms and rhyme is in no way peculiar to A.D. Hope. It was shared by most of his contemporaries, both overseas and within Australia. However, unlike Robert Lowell and most younger poets, Hope has never relaxed the metrical formality of his verse, and has consistently and conscientiously refrained from those experiments with non-metrical form that characterize both an earlier and a later generation. Iambic pentameter and rhyme are so naturalized in Hope's language that it is hard, even perverse, to imagine it any other way. They are as integral a part of his own "noble, candid speech" as they were of Yeats's, and despite their anachronism today (it is difficult to think of any other comparable poet except Larkin or Wilbur who has so scrupulously resisted Pound's injunction to "break the pentameter") one could not wish it otherwise.

This measure of formality, this formal measure, it not a historical accident; nor is it a matter of provincialism or strict conservatism, since Hope has always been exceedingly well-informed in contemporary poetry, not only in English but in other languages as well. He defends his practice in an essay entitled "Free Verse: A Post-Mortem":

> The effects of poetry are not mysterious, though they may not be capable of minute analysis or reduction to formulas. If they produce an effect of greater tension, a higher excitement, and a richer texture and harmony, it is because poetry is different in structure from prose, and it is therefore foolish to expect the more limited and different resources of prose to produce these effects. I have already pointed out what these extra resources are. The immense resources of variety within regular verse come from the basic expectation of a regular pattern, which, constantly varying, never disappoints that expectation of regular points of return within the line, of rhyme, of alternation of line with line in the stanza. It is this which gives good poetry its tension, its elasticity, its feeling of grace and vigour, of purposeful and delightful movement.[1]

As a refutation of the principles and practice of free verse, Hope's essay is misguided. For example, his attempt to demonstrate that the rhythms and cadences of a passage of T.S. Eliot lose nothing if typographically rearranged merely demonstrates the unbridgeable gap between his own position and that of others. But as an explication of traditional metrical practice, Hope's essay is as lucid and as precise as one would want. It is, however, only part of the story. Formal metrics and regular rhyme do not occur in conversational speech, but inhabit a discourse which they themselves have traditionally marked out as poetry or verse. Verse is thus artefact (poetry is made, as its etymology reminds us) and cultural, in a way that conversational language is not. Metrics and rhyme thus serve to frame discourse as poetry, to separate it from "natural language" and inscribe it within culture, where it will be read in relation to the great poetry of the past rather than in relation to the chatter in the laundromat. The fact that Hope has been able to deploy these cultural formalities within a language which can sound, when he wants it to, so unforcedly conversational is one of his great achievements. That metrics and rhyme have proved to be accidental rather than essential to verse (few people today would seriously contest that "The Waste Land" is not poetry) is less significant here. Even free verse has its ways of inscribing itself within cultural discourse, an activity which is at the very heart of Pound's endeavour in *The Cantos*. One could say simply that Hope's adherence to traditional formalities was a critical act: an expression of allegiance to certain traditions of poetry, and a reading of the corpus of poetry in such a way as to erase certain forms and developments of poetic discourse with which he felt little sympathy. It was his way of reading Eliot out of poetry and inscribing himself into it as the continuer of a tradition whose more recent exponent had been Yeats.

But we can go still further than that. R.F. Brissenden draws attention to Hope's claim that poetry is "an act of celebration" performed by "a man who has continually before him a vision of the world as a whole, whose mind naturally dwells on and seeks to grasp the complexity, the variety and the mystery of the world of man as a whole".[2] To establish his point, Brissenden quotes from Hope's poem "Vivaldi, Bird and Angel", and since the lines are relevant to my own argument as well as to his I shall quote some of them here:

> Somewhere beyond this frame of natural laws,
> Moving in time on its predestined grooves,
> I hear another music to which it moves.
> Wherever I go, whatever I do, I seem
> To step in time to that resistless stream . . .
>
> I only know I hear it and, as well
> That when I hear them humbly, as I do,
> I know with pride, the masters heard it too.[3]

Brissenden says of these lines:

> The music to which the poet is here referring is what in classical and renaissance times was called the music of the spheres. To hear the music of the spheres is to become aware of the underlying harmony of the universe, to have an almost physically intense and overpoweringly joyful vision of the natural order. True art, Hope would maintain, necessarily reflects this universal harmony — music perhaps more faithfully than any other form. Man's apprehension of the fundamentally coherent nature of things also manifests itself in poetry.[4]

As Brissenden claims, Hope is a poet attentive to an immanent order. He is thus akin to those post-modernists who see order as being found by the imagination within experience and the phenomenal world rather than created by the imagination to supplement a lack. Poetry, music, culture, the products of "the masters", utter this immanent order or universal harmony, a harmony which transcends the merely natural but which also informs it. Yet for Hope poetry can do so only by a reformation, a re-forming, of "natural" language, which renders it an "unnatural" language, one from which conversational formlessness has been excluded and replaced by metrical form and rhyme. These artefactual features, therefore, on the one hand articulate that music of the spheres to which the poet steps in time; their characteristic repetition and variation within a unity of orderly recurrence — in other words, their *musical* quality — signify that natural order *par excellence*, that other music to which "this frame of natural laws" moves. On the other hand, by separating Hope's discourse off from natural language, they inscribe it as culture, that which is not given, nor simply apprehended, but made.

Although at one level of analysis it is something of a truism to say that verse is artefact and cultural (in a way that conversational language is not), it is of course a gross oversimplification. It can be pointed out, for example, that in novels and plays conversation is pure artefact, and is inscribed within culture while still remaining conversational. Just as importantly, it can be shown that although we engage in conversation "naturally", we do so in much the same way as we use grammar generally, more or less unconsciously or automatically conforming to a series of rules of conversation which govern the possibility of our discourse. The fact that these rules of conversation can be consciously transgressed and are therefore not inalienably inherent, indicates their conventional nature and makes possible a whole range of comic dialogues based on misunderstandings, misappropriations and misappropriateness.

What is really at question here is whether there is a "natural" language at all, or only degrees of conscious conventionality. Hope privileges a language which employs conventions obviously not found in the conversational speech which I called, for the sake of convenience, "natural". But as we have seen, this speech is itself conventional: the conventions are merely naturalized, rendered largely unconscious, by daily use. Furthermore, as a consequence of Saussure's demonstration that virtually all linguistic signs are unmotivated — that meaning does not inhabit the word in some theological way, but that words signify only in terms of the differential system within which they exist — we can say that all language is inscribed with arbitrariness and convention.[5] In his famous attempt to locate a language free of contingency (one in which the *eidos* was lucidly present, unmediated and whole), Plato distanced himself from the sophists and poets by privileging the spoken word or, more precisely, the word spoken in dialectics, the ostensible vehicle of the (written) dialogues of Socrates.[6] But in his analysis of this part of the *Phaedrus*,[7] Derrida has shown how even such speech is a transcendental illusion. As he writes elsewhere, "Immediacy is derived . . . all begins through the intermediary".[8]

Hope's attempt to make his language sound unlike the conversational dialectics of the Socratic dialogues is a poet's revenge on Plato who, as we all know, banished poets from his republic. Whereas Plato's dialogues utter truth by sounding like conversation, Hope deploys non-conversational conventions within his language to ensure that no matter how conversatinal his tone may be his language is distinguishable as poetry, not so much conversation as "versation", a turning towards verse. But he does this in order to fulfil the project of Platonic speech: to realize that dream of a language of transparent immediacy, of pure presence, where even the elements furthermost from conversation render themselves invisible in the act of articulating a truth, a musical harmony, which no conversation — not even Socrates' — can achieve. But the music of the spheres is no more present in the music of poetry than any other truth is present in its signifier. Seen in this light, Hope's deployment of rhyme and metre is not in any essential way a registering of the transcendent order that he hears, but a way of inscribing his discourse within a poetry in which affirmations of the kind he makes are traditional, and traditionally signified by them.

I approach Hope's poetry in this somewhat roundabout way so as to say something about the nature of traditional poetic language and metrical form, of which Hope is our foremost exponent. On the one hand, traditional metrics (and to a lesser extent, rhyme) clearly proclaim themselves as conventions in relation to "natural" or conversational speech. But on the other hand they have so long been considered the signature of verse and indispensable to the sounding of its "music" — that quality which is so difficult to understand and yet so profoundly rewarding for the poet — that their role has been mystified. Yet that valorization of music (Pater's dictum that "all poetry aspires to the condition of music" is only the most famous example) is really another attempt to claim poetry's intimacy with the sublime by effacing or bypassing the signifier in the deployment of signs that constitutes all discourse, poetry included. But the conventional nature of rhyme and metre, their essential arbitrariness, points to the fact that they themselves are also signifiers, albeit paralexical and to some extent parasyntactic. These latter qualities have helped to obscure the fact that a discussion of the "music of poetry" merely marks a move from one system of signs (lexical) to another (paralexical), and in no way constitutes an escape from or a transcendence of the conditions of signification. Brissenden does not, in fact, make any such claims in drawing the conclusion that among the foremost of Hope's "great and distinctive qualities as a poet"

> is his eloquence. In one of his poems he praises Yeats for having found "that noble candid speech In which all things worth saying may be said", and his own poetry at its finest is distinguished by the same nobility and candour. His work is above all civilized: it both embodies and endorses the central values of our culture, values which can be sustained and defended only through the humane exercise of the intellect and the imagination.[9]

Some questions about culture are begged here. For example, if we ask more pressingly whose culture it is, the values of which are endorsed by Hope's poetry, the answer is likely to be the culture of people who read Hope's poetry: the educated, liberal, artistically-aware middle class. And when Brissenden argues his claim that Hope is intimately concerned with "that rational, joyful and ordered way of living to which man continually aspires", we may doubt — as Hope himself appears to — whether man actually does so aspire or quite so continually.

A short and comparatively late poem such as "The Sacred Way" concludes:

> Whatever we learned, the heroes were what we *knew*.
> We were fortunate indeed.
>
> We have lost that world. How shall my son go on
> To form his archetypal image of man?
> Frankenstein? Faust? Dracula? Don Juan?
> O Absolom, my Son![10]

The sacred way of the poet's own youth, marked out for him by such heroes as "Hercules, Samson, Roland, Robin Hood", has been lost to the monsters and perversions he names in the final stanza, monsters of duplicity and dissimulation, and in permitting this to happen the father/subject, like King David, has squandered his birthright and betrayed his son. In contrast to the present, the poet's youthful "unripe soul" had been fed on these wholesome legends, whose characteristic it was to "Stand firm, stand fast!" The "sacred way" is thus defined in terms of univocality, unequivocality: "Whatever we learned, the heroes were what we *knew*" (Hope's emphasis). Concerned as it is with locating the "image" and the "names" to "fix our heritage" (the word "fix" here clearly signifying not only "remedy" but even more importantly "fix in place", "locate with stability"), the poem valorizes the names of his childhood heroes. It does so not simply because those heroes themselves stood firm and fast — thus exemplifying moral qualities notably lacking, the poem suggests, in the modern world — but also because the names themselves stood firm: we knew what they stood for, they did not lie.

Nonetheless the motivating fact of the poem is that "the sacred way" marked out by the heroes has indeed been lost: "We have lost that world". Leaving their names behind them as empty and treacherous simulacra to hide their absence, the heroes of steadfastness and unequivocality have crept away, and "what we knew" is known no longer. Their place has been taken by Frankenstein, Faust, Dracula, and Don Juan, and the thought that the younger generation's "archetypal image of man" would be formed by such figures fills the poem's subject with abhorrence. However it is not clear how Goethe's Faust rather than Marlowe's, or Byron's Don Juan rather than Mozart's, should be read out of the poem in order to justify that uncharacteristic note of abhorrence, even despair. And indeed, if we take these apparently irrelevant allusions seriously — irrelevant only if we ignore the treachery of the subject's youthful heroes — we find that the poem constitutes itself in a somewhat different way. Faust is not only the overreacher whose hubris results in a mere trivializing of knowledge and his eternal damnation (this is how he is depicted by Marlowe, and even more significantly in Hope's own poem "Faustus") but also the hero of Goethe's great drama of redemption. Don Juan is the monstrous despoiler of women, crushed to death by a statue in Mozart's opera: destroyed by a work of art he is also immortalized by one. And he is also that figure of youthful vitality, sexual exuberance and resilient honesty at the centre of Byron's satirical masterpiece, which Hope has described as one of "the last two great narrative poems".[11] The despairing note of the poem's last line, when read with this in mind, may not result from the father's sense of having betrayed his son and bequeathed him a world of monstrosity and perversion. It may result, rather, from the subject's inability to comprehend damnation and redemption, sexual predation and sexual vitality, inscribed in the same figures. He deplores the loss of a world of unequivocal images and names. Yet as we have seen, the delusory and duplicitous nature of this world is actually the occasion of the poem, since permanence and impermanence are also inscribed within the same figures. My first interpretation of the poem is predicated on the assertion (articulated in the poem itself) that there is a clear distinction between the heroes of the second stanza and the "monsters" of the fourth, and that whereas the father can see this and deplore it, the world of the son cannot, and has thus lost "the sacred way". But this interpretation depends on the poem's concealing what my second reading reveals: that this distinction is itself a delusion. By thinking otherwise it is the father himself who has lost the way and its sacredness, both of which, moreover, are also revealed to be delusions.

This second interpretation may seem perverse in itself. Particularly, it goes against that candour of language which Hope praised in Yeats. But language, as we have seen, is not candid in the sense of "clear, pure, immaculate" (*Webster's Dictionary*) or "frank, ingenuous, sincere" (*Oxford*), although those adjectives may well describe its user. Language is duplicitous, marked with its other, and subversive. As Hope himself writes in his "An Epistle: Edward Sackville to Venetia Digby":

> Nature, which makes each member to one end,
>   May give it powers which transcend
> Its first and fruitful purpose. When she made
>   The Tongue for taste, who in the shade
> Of summer vines, what speechless manlike brute,
>   Biting sharp rind or sweeter fruit,
> Could have conceived the improbable tale, the long
>   Strange fable of the Speaking Tongue?[12]

That tale is now even longer and, for some, even more improbable than when Hope wrote those lines in 1959; so it seems like a judicious foresight that led him to write in the same poem that it is Love, not speech, which "grows to be / The language of the mystery". However, a poet cannot inscribe in love alone, and any recourse to speech is fraught with contradictions.

A fairly late poem, "What the Serpent Really Said", written in 1971, can serve as our text here.[13] Hope has frequently had recourse to the great myths which have both reflected and structured western thought from its earliest times, and has not hesitated to rearrange and reinterpret them where he felt necessary. In this way his poetry is inscribed within a powerful tradition which receives further vitality from his rewriting of it, while at the same time animating ways in which his own poetry is to be interpreted. "What the Serpent Really Said" is a rewriting of the Genesis story of the temptation and fall of Eve at the instigation of the serpent, and in such a way that the biblical and Miltonic priority of man over women is apparently reversed.[14] The serpent's words tempt Eve with an account of the relation between male and female in which her biblical role as "fitting helper" is transformed into a maternal and genetic one, while Adam's genetic role (Genesis tells us that Eve was fashioned out of one of his spare ribs) is transformed into that of the child, for whom Eve's otherness is an image of Eden:

> Before you bite, pause, listen, look around
> This natural world of which you are a part,
> Though Adam forget it as he breaks the ground,
> You will always keep virgin in your heart . . .

and

> Your nakedness will always be the dim
> Image of this paradise as it was;
> The act of love, within its joy, for him
> Echo the re-enactment of its loss.

Eve is the Eternal Mother, the Eden from which we are all by the act of birth expelled, and to which we all long to return. She is that ground of ultimate knowledge which forever exposes our ignorance yet lovingly protects us within it, that passive ground of power whose force is knowledge ("For you and for your daughters, each in turn, / Only to eat this apple will be to know"). All this will be Eve's if she will

> Take now this apple and eat! That you may live,
> Take death into your mouth and learn to die.
> Till it know loss, no heart can learn to give,
> Nor know truth till it prove it by a lie.

Like Christ, whose death also rendered him immortal and whose words Hope echoes, Eve loses all to gain all:

> This is your body broken for his reprieve;
> This is your sacrament; take, eat and die!

As a consequence of her initial act of accepting the Serpent's persuasion, therefore, Eve is passive but knowing, the dim embodiment of that Eden which is lost through her action yet saved by her being. She is the transcendental maternal for whom the male is always lover and child.

In contrast to Eve's passivity, her inactivity, Hope's poem portrays man as active, frustrated, seeking vainly to overcome frustration by his action:

> Painfully, step by step, his sons must learn;
> Their Babel of words, their tower of science will grow:
> For you and for your daughters, each in turn,
> Only to eat this apple will be to know.

"For you he will make history", the poem continues, and "He is your means to change the universe". But this relentless activity is doomed to a failure which is contrasted with the clear, Madonna-like gaze of Eve:

> For in your fruitful belly you must bear
> His future worlds and in your heart his past,
> Foreknowing the next he gropes towards, aware
> Of what decreed the ruin of his last.

The pattern is not an unfamiliar one. Even from within Australian poetry alone there are echoes of Brennan's Lilith. And this poem is the culmination of a long line of poems by Hope exploring the relation between woman and man, the natural and the human, which includes such significant achievements as "Standardization", "Chorale", "Lot and his Daughters", "Imperial Adam", "An Epistle: Edward Sackville to Venetia Digby", "The Double Looking Glass", "The Countess of Pembroke's Dream", and "On an Engraving by Casserius".

"What the Serpent Really Said" explicitly claims that while knowledge of Good and Evil is Adam's curse, the knowledge of all that lies beyond is Eve's, is woman's. We should look a little more closely at the poem to discover what she might discern there. Would she be pleased to discover, right at this point, that she has, apparently, no knowledge of Good and Evil? Would she be pleased to find that while Adam is invested with "thought or skill", she is "The naked animal hid in human dress", not human after all, it seems, but an animal masquerading as one? Would she be pleased to learn that science will be made exclusively by Adam's (apparently not Eve's) sons, while she and her daughters eat fruit? Or that he will make not only history but also "Gods, civilizations, systems, law and art" which she passively "will accept"? And that as a culmination of this supreme passivity she will, "in the hour of passion"

> Cry out: "Now take, possess me as a god;
> Do with me what you will; think not of me;
> Master me; crush me; break me with your rod"?

In a moment of prescience, she may be reminded of the famous desire to be destroyed expressed in Donne's sonnet "Batter my heart, three-personned God . . .", which ends with the Christian paradox that spiritual life results from the destruction of that same human and unredeemed, animal nature which Hope's poem attributes to Eve. But would she be pleased to learn that in addition to being mastered, crushed and broken she will at the same moment proclaim: "Only if I am nothing shall I be free"? She may well conclude that the serpent is offering her a bad bargain if she can exist (for man) only by being less than human, totally without an active part in the achievement of culture, and most real (for man) to the degree to which she is "nothing" (that is, "nothing" to his "something"). Even her "fruitful belly" bears, as it turns out, not her own children but "His future worlds": her own maternity is stolen from her, in the name of the Father. Julia Kristeva writes:

> if we suppose that a *mother* is a subject of gestation, in other words the *master* of a process that science, despite its effective devices, acknowledges it cannot now and perhaps never will be able to take away from her; if we suppose her to be *master* of a process that is prior to the social-symbolic-linguistic contract of the group, then we acknowledge the risk of losing identity at the same time as we ward it off.[15]

By ascribing the mastery of science and the social-symbolic-linguistic contract (the son's "Babel of words") entirely to the male, and by effectively taking away the products of the maternal process by identifying them as this Adam's "future worlds", the serpent robs Eve of the mastery of everything except, perhaps, her own nothingness, and averts the risk of the male losing his identity (his role as subject) by depriving the female of hers. This does not mean though that she ceases to figure in the male universe, the Fallen World which — apparently as a result of the serpent's enticing speech — she brings about. Kristeva continues:

> We recognize on the one hand that biology jolts us by means of unsymbolized instinctual drives and that this phenomenon eludes social intercourse, the representation of pre-existing objects, and the contract of desire. On the other hand, we immediately deny it; we say there can be no escape, for mamma is there, she embodies this phenomenon; she warrants that *everything is*, and that it is representable. In a double-barreled move, psychotic tendencies are acknowledged, but at the same time they are settled, quieted, and bestowed upon the mother in order to maintain the ultimate guarantee: symbolic coherence.

The serpent assures Eve that she will jolt Adam's sense of his own being, for she will be "the doubt his mind explores" and a continuing reminder of his primal expulsion: "The act of love, within its joy, [will] for him / Echo the re-enactment of its loss". But at the same time she will represent for him what he has lost by offering him "symbolic coherence"; she "will always be the dim / Image of this paradise as it was". In other words, Eve figures in the male (fallen) world as signifier: not as that which she is (and not, certainly, signifying herself) but as that whose nothingness, whose self-effacement, is the condition of something other. By annulling herself, by accepting her nothingness, she assures the male that "*everything is*": "mamma is there".

The King James version of Genesis tells us this:

> Now the serpent was more subtil than any beast of the field which the Lord God had made. And he said unto the woman, Yea, hath God said, Ye shall not eat of every tree of the garden?

> And the woman said unto the serpent, We may eat of the fruit of the trees of the garden:
>
> But of the fruit of the tree which is in the midst of the garden, God hath said, Ye shall not eat of it, neither shall ye touch it, lest ye die.
>
> And the serpent said unto the woman, Ye shall not surely die:
>
> For God doth know that in the day ye eat thereof, then your eyes shall be opened, and ye shall be as gods, knowing good and evil.
>
> (Gen. 3: 1-5)

It seems to me that not only is the biblical serpent more succinct than Milton's, but he is also more logical than Hope's. By offering Eve the power to "be as gods" he offers her the one thing she does not have in Eden that she could conceivably want. In comparison, the offer he makes her in Hope's poem seems infinitely less persuasive, though such an arrangement would obviously be more attractive to Adam. But this implausible situation could have come about simply because the biblical Eve tried to dress up her position, so to speak, for Adam by trying to make her fall seem more logical for his male mind than it really was. For as the first stanza of Hope's poem assures us, the Genesis account is actually a lie on Eve's part, "What Eve told Adam", as distinct from "what the Serpent really said to Eve". Thus Eve's fall from person to signifier is associated with another fall, that from truth to falsehood. By opening the gap between signifier and signified in that moment of original sin, language can now signify falsely. No longer able to face God walking in the Garden, to exist in the living and unavoidable presence of the Logos, our original parents conceal even their own present nakedness from each other behind a screen of fig leaves. They fall thus into the duplicity of language, which is symbolized not only by the serpent's double tongue and by Eve's mendacity but even, it seems, by the Bible's ability to reproduce her lie. If even the Word of God does not unerringly signify the truth, but can faithfully (even truthfully) duplicate falsehood, can mere mortals expect to achieve unerring veracity in language? Even the most candid speech is inscribed with its other.

To be reminded of the ineradicable duplicity of language is particularly significant in the case of Hope's poetry. Of all Australian poets, Hope is the one most concerned to replace duplicity by candour, the contradictory by reason, disorder by order or orderliness, discord by harmony. Sometimes, as in early poems like "The Pleasure of Princess" and "Pyramis *or* The House of Ascent", this is done by an assertion of will usually and loosely described as Nietzschean: an affirmation of "Intemperate will and incorruptible pride". Elsewhere, as in "The Death of the Bird", it is love which "pricks the course in lights across the chart"; and when this "guiding spark of instinct winks and dies" (as indeed it must one day for everybody), the "vast design" of things nevertheless "receives the tiny burden" of death with a balanced equanimity, "with neither grief nor malice". It is this latter sense, a sense of an immanent order, which motivates most of Hope's poetry, whether he is castigating our neglect of it (as in his more satirical works) or celebrating its evanescent manifestations (as in, for example, "Chorale" or "An Epistle: Edward Sackville to Venetia Digby"). The "mystery", as he more than once calls it, is a mystery of harmony, and the opposite of harmony is not diversity or plurality (in music, harmony depends on the simultaneous sounding of more than one note) but discord. Yet because of the duplicity of language even — or especially — harmony is inscribed with discord, inscribed by what it is not. Hope's whole vision highlights and underscores the poignancy of its own endeavour.

One of his most renowned later poems is "On an Engraving by Casserius" (1967).[16] It presents itself as a major — perhaps the major — statement of Hope's views on questions of continuing and vital centrality to his poetry: the scope of the intellect and the imagination, the relation of the present to the past, the place of humanity within a frame of universal harmony, and the significance of maternal creativity. The poem is a celebration of those great spirits

who stare
Into the night of nescience and death,
And, whirled about with their terrestrial ball,
Ask of all being its motion and its frame.

And in particular it celebrates the great anatomist, "the foremost surgeon of Italy, / Giulio Casserio of Padua" whose skill combined the analytic precision of science and the imaginative (synthesizing) comprehension of great art. This harmony of science and art has produced that ikon of a universal harmony which the poem also celebrates and which, in its own way, it aspires to emulate: the anatomical engraving of a pregnant woman and child.

Here in its singularity he has shown
The image of an individual soul;
Bodied in this one woman, he makes us see
The shadow of his anatomical laws.
An artist's vision animates the whole,
Shines through the scientist's detailed scrutiny
And links the person and the abstract cause.

"This one engraving", we read, "reaches towards the central mystery / Of whence our being draws and what we are". Its blend or fusion of scientific and artistic vision epitomizes the opposite of

An age in which all sense of the unique,
And singular dissolves, like ours today,
In diagrams, statistics, tables, maps.

The ikon itself, the anatomical engraving which apparently occasioned the poem and which is described (inscribed) within it, is essentially a harmonizing of singularity and the plural: mother with unborn child within her. And in the poem's final three stanzas it is suggested that this is as far as "all man's intellectual quest" can as yet go:

Who knows, but to the age to come they speak
Words that our own is still unapt to hear:
"These are the limits of all you sought and seek;
More our yet unborn nature cannot bear."

If in the past this ikon or image has served "to show / The mask behind the mask behind the mask", similarly in this poem there is a kind of nesting effect. In the centre is perhaps the child, surrounded by the body of the mother, engraved within Eden just before the fall. The engraving is executed by Casserius, whose skill and vision are also inscribed within the poem which, in celebrating this unifying vision, gives verbal expression, even a verbal form, to it. Much of the poem's force derives from the apparent seamlessness with which this nesting is accomplished. Unless we search for a reproduction of it in a library, we do not have the engraving before us when reading the poem. But by inscribing within itself the vision engraved by the earlier artist/scientist, and by displaying considerable historical and scientific erudition in the poem's second, third, fourth, and fifth stanzas, Hope's poem harmonizes the subject's own first person singularity with the great scientist/artists of the Renaissance. It forges a bond between our own time and that of Casserius, and presents a reading of one vision of "the mystery" which is not only articulated in the poem but also endorsed by its procedures.

In the light of such an accomplishment, it may seem perverse to seek for a loose thread with which to unravel this apparent seamlessness. But even the most coherent poems — those in which New Criticism found an organic unity — are constituted by what Barbara Johnson calls "warring forces of signification within the text itself".[17] There are several threads we can tease loose, but one will do. The woman, "Dragged from the river, found in some alley at dawn" — one of the unknown, unclaimed poor — is described as appearing in the engraving thus:

the sublime
Shaft of her body opens like a flower
Whose petals, folded back expose the womb,
Cord and placenta and the sleeping child,

Like instruments of music in a room
Left when her grieving Orpheus left his tower
Forever, for the desert and the wild.

It is clear, in one reading, how these terms of praise are a way of rendering the woman's delicacy and beauty, as well as her connection with the world of nature and her transcendent link with mythic and sublime art. Another reading might suggest that she is less than human, in so far as her biological ability to reproduce links her with the vegetable world and renders her a passive instrument for the male to play upon. After all, Orpheus was famed not for the quality of his lyre but for the art he practised on it, which exercised considerable power over the vegetable kingdom but aroused the wrath of the Thracian women. This may seem a quibbling and ungenerous misreading. But two stanzas later we are told that

She too was overshadowed by the Word,
Was chosen, and by her humble gift of death
The lowly and the poor in heart give tongue.

For all her miraculous ability to bear children, the woman is passive before the male logos which "questioned her with his knife". Mary was similarly passive — chosen, not choosing, her only option being (as with the nameless woman in the engraving) deathly and sacrificial,

Offering . . . her child in death to be
Love's victim and her flesh its mystic rose.

The tradition to which this vision of women belongs is an ancient one and so radical a part of our culture that it needs little discussion. It is enough to point out — as indeed, numerous others have in recent years — that the notion of harmony it enshrines is one which elevates women only by positing them as inferior. The second Eve can exist only as a positive duplicate of "the first Eve" who "tasted, of the Fatal Tree". Yet even the second Eve is passive since, as the poem implies, a "figure with wings of fire and back-swept hair / Swoops with his: Blessed among Women!" to rescue her from her fallen status, within which she would be doomed to stay forever but for his male intervention. Eve's weakness caused man to be expelled from Eden. So Mary's maternity, the product of the logos (she is *made* pregnant, we recall, as a result of an Annunciation) gives birth to salvation or redemption for mankind by placing in scripture (in Scripture) women's sacrificial and passive roles. Woman is the vehicle for male action. In Hope's poem, this third Eve does not even give birth to a child of her own maternity but

stands among the monuments of time
And with a feminine delicacy displays
His elegant dissection.

In this tradition, harmony depends on the maintenance of a duality in which one term (the male) is privileged over the other (the female). Seen from the male point of view this is harmony; seen from the female, it may well look like something else. Certainly, in Hope's poem the mother and child became an ikon of something transcending "The universals we thought to conjure with", but they achieve that status only by being drowned or by dying at night in an alley, by being cut open before an audience of men and described as vegetable. "Tortured into song", her body utters a "magnificat" for "the vile", enabling "The lowly and the poor of heart" to "give tongue". In other words, by forcibly ravishing her of all but the functions of a signifier, the male can revere her because no matter what he has done in his attempts to erase her, "mamma is there" signifying, despite it all, "symbolic coherence".

Although none of this may be immediately apparent, and is certainly not explicit in Hope's poem, it is indubitably there, just as it is in the tradition to which the poem so powerfully subscribes. If I have dramatized things a little, it is simply to highlight the way this poem (inevitably, it seems) has to have recourse to the other of harmony in order to invoke, extol and — can it now be said? — *impose* harmony in a world which is simultaneously proclaimed immanently harmonious. Thus a reading of Hope's inscription of his own poetic project within such a tradition of harmony stirs up the disharmony of which both poem and tradition are constituted. As Kristeva said, maternal woman will indeed offer "symbolic coherence". But she also "warrants that *everything is*, and that it is representable". When the Fall from presence into language is mediated by woman, and when all active functions except that of signifier are taken from her, it should not surprise us therefore that in signifying, speaking out, she will say some things which the male had possibly not expected.

7

Always the Other Half: The Poetry of Judith Wright

The desire to annul or to transcend duality seems to be as old as Western civlization, if Jacques Derrida is right in his analysis of the logocentrism of Western metaphysics. His analysis of Plato's privileging the spoken over the written word suggests that the reason for this is the irreducible duality of language, the signifying system which permits us to know whatever it is we know both about ourselves and about all that is not ourselves.[1] The lure of the transcendental signified, the logos existing of and for itself in a self-sufficiency which requires no signifier to make it manifest, would thus be the metaphysical equivalent of the attraction of Lacan's pre-linguistic phase of childhood prior to the birth of desire, which I discussed in my chapter on Christopher Brennan. A return to this pre-symbolic state would thus be not simply to transcend the dualities, divisions and conflicts of everyday life. It would also be to remove the subject from involvement in that alienating system of differences (language) with which it articulates and manages experience, and which is radical to its own constitution. For a poet, this would entail the invocation of the logos as the other of language, as the transcendental silence of self-presence which renders all poetry — even, and especially, that poetry which invokes it — secondary, marked by failure. It is the problematic of this common, and contradictory, impulse which I wish to examine in relation to Judith Wright, in whose work a striking and recurring sense of duality, of internal otherness, is accompanied by a recurring urge towards a corresponding singleness which must be uttered, signified, by the Word itself.[2]

A comparatively late poem, "Naked Girl and Mirror" (*C.P.* p. 241) which first appeared in her volume *The Other Half* provides us with a striking example of Wright's sense of doubleness in its complex interplay of multiple dualities. The subject of the poem is a pubescent girl, and the first duality one can perceive is that of the poem's subject and her own reflection in the mirror, which she addresses as "you". Moreover what she sees in the mirror is both herself and the other of herself. Her first words are, in fact, a disclaimer: "This is not I". The difference between her own self and the "mirror self"[3] is adumbrated in terms of the child's absence of body and the adolescent's and mature woman's bodiliness: "I had no body once" the girl claims, contrasting her elusive freedom from the claims of the body with the "dark brimming eyes" and the "new body's grace" of the mirror self which, betraying her to a lover, will culminate in the grown woman's "dumb and fruitful years". Thus the child's bodilessness, her sprite-like quality, is contrasted with the woman's mature physicality which is just starting to manifest itself in the mirror self. And the child's elusiveness — her marginality "on the fringe of foam and wave and sand and sun" — is contrasted with the mature woman's domestic stability: when the lover comes, "he will be your home". The introduction — or premonition, more accurately — of the lover thus introduces a further duality, that of female to male, within which the mirror self may find stability and fruitfulness: as the subject says to her image,

> You are half of some other who may never come.
> Why should I tend you? You are not my own;
> you seek that other — he will be your own.

Thus we also have a contrast between the already accomplished fulfilment of the child, and the uncertainty of future fulfilment; and this possible future fulfilment in turn contrasts with the child's solipsistic self-sufficiency by being dependent on someone else, on another. And lest we should be tempted to interpret the poem as treating the end of childhood as a moment when childishness disappears to make place for something else, the poem itself reminds us that the subject will remain even when the emergent mirror self goes:

> Some day we may love. I may miss your going, some day,
> though I shall always resent your dumb and fruitful years.
> Your lovers shall learn better, and bitterly too,
> if their arrogance dares to think I am part of you.

Thus in the further duality of permanence and transience, it is the childish subject which is permanent, and the emergent maturity and sexuality which is transient.

To summarize then, these dualities line up to produce a moving and powerful dramatization of the moment of puberty. The physically innocent, almost bodiless child — sexless, sprite-like, marginal, self-absorbed, free and self-fulfilling — apprehends her own image in the mirror and discovers that it is different. What she apprehends there is the other of herself, the other within herself. It will have sexual identity defined as difference, female in relation to male; it will not be autonomous or self-fulfilling but will be bound to, living in, dependent on another; and it will be still incomplete without the complicity of the poem's subject who will outlive it, despite its apparent permanence. The poem thus dramatizes a move from completeness to incompleteness, wholeness to multiplicity (it is really more than doubleness), independence to dependence, innocence to a knowledge of betrayal and duplicity: "shut out here / from my own self . . . I am betrayed by someone lovely". In other words, a move from an unmediated self-presence uncontaminated by signs — a transcendental signified, in fact — to the very condition of the sign.[4]

But such an account of the poem still simplifies it. First of all, although the subject claims that she had "no body once", she is forced to concede that this is not quite right:

> only what served my need to laugh and run
> and stare at stars and tentatively dance
> on the fringe of foam and wave and sand and sun.
> Eyes loved, hands reached for me, but I was gone
> on my own currents, quicksilver, thistledown.

We may be reminded of Wordsworth's image of his own childhood in "Tintern Abbey" "when like a roe [he] bounded o'er the mountains". More precisely, though, the child in Wright's poem has enough body to maintain her own marginality, to evade entrapment. Her evasion of the body, in other words, depends on her having body enough to serve her need, temporarily to avoid or avert its own complex and duplicitous self. And if we notice how that body is described in the second stanza we discover that it was "once hermaphrodite". In other words, the androgynous child body is not sexless but contains both sexes, is not single but already and always double. The onset of puberty is not the moment of origin of a doubleness where previously there had been only singleness. It is the ejection of the male half and its projection onto a male partner in such a way as to enable the "single" female half's development to sexual maturity in relation to an external male other. Seen in this light, the child's self-sufficiency is neither bodiless nor sexless, nor is it a condition of indivisible unity. On the contrary, it is physical and determined by internal sexual difference. Finally, when we ask where this childhood state comes from, we find that it comes from the other, from the mirror self: from the "dumb and fruitful years" of the mother and her lover, the child's father. The child's mirror self may seem to threaten and betray her, but it is furnishing her the condition of her own genesis and of her own continuity within the chain of creativity. Difference breeds difference; but it is also inescapable that only difference is capable of breeding.

"Naked Girl and Mirror" is a striking, complex and powerful example of radical otherness, but it is by no means alone among Wright's poems in expressing it. Less a theme than a condition of her awareness, a sense of doubleness or otherness manifests itself in many of her poems, most notably of course in the poems of maternity in *Woman to Man*. But rather than look at these yet, I wish first to examine a poem which has not, perhaps, received as much attention as it merits. In one sense, "The Killer" (*C.P.* p. 53) is a poem about fear, much as D.H. Lawrence's more famous poem, "Snake" is. In Australia, common sense requires one to be wary of snakes as many of them are, or can be, quite literally killers. But with a reflexive irony as moving as it is dramatic, Wright's poem reverses the expected roles of snake and person, making us realize that "the killer" in this case is not the snake, since it is the snake which is killed. The killer is the poem's subject herself. Springing "from the dark / in a violent birth", a horror of the snake suffused her with a compulsion to kill, so that she "struck again and again", destroying her apparent adversary only to realize that the real adversary "has slipped from his death aside" and gone back where it came from. It is this "nimble enemy" which has transformed her (as D.H. Lawrence was also almost transformed) into a killer. Therefore the poem is an articulation of guilt — not so much simply guilt at having killed something presumed innocent, but guilt at having failed to recognize the "nimble enemy" as being within herself, and thus having killed.

One question to ask here is just what is it that elicits such "black horror" as the poem expresses? It is normal to be scared of snakes, but this reaction is unusually violent, even though it is associated with a sudden awareness of mortality:

> Black horror sprang from the dark
> in a violent birth,
> and through its cloth of grass
> I felt the clutch of earth.
>
> O beat him into the ground.
> O strike him till he dies,
> or else your life itself
> drains through those colourless eyes.

The phrase "black horror sprang from the dark" initially reads as metaphoric of the snake, particularly since the following two lines are also metaphoric, and we learn shortly that the snake actually is black in colour. But already such a reading is unsettled by the poem itself. We have been told that "the day was clear as fire" and it is thus difficult, even impossible, to locate any equivalent to "the dark" in the physical landscape. This unsettling prepares us, therefore, for the later equation of darkness — not with anything physically in the landscape — but with the subject's mind, the origin and refuge of her own "nimble enemy" which survives the snake's destruction. But it was that crucial moment of more than metaphoric equation of internal darkness and external object, that actual fusion or *con*fusion of them into singleness, which caused the snake's death and the subject's guilt.

Any situation which brings together snake, guilt and death asks to be read in the light of its earlier figurations. To do anything less with such a literate and sophisticated poet as Judith Wright would be to deny her own inscription on a tradition which is clearly a powerful enabling factor in her poetry. At the genesis of this tradition, we are told that the serpent was expelled from the company of upright and other right-walking creatures — branded with two-dimensionality, in fact — because of his success in tempting Eve to eat of the fateful tree:

> Because thou hast done this, thou art cursed above all cattle, and above every beast of the field; upon thy belly shalt thou go, and dust shalt thou eat all the days of thy life:
>
> And I will put enmity between thee and the woman, and between thy seed and her seed; it shall bruise thy head, and thou shalt bruise his heel.
> (Gen. 3.14-15.)

In this Genesis account, as we have already seen, there is no real reason given for the serpent's action. He is not the devil in disguise, as he is for Milton, but merely "more subtil than any beast of the field", a kind of Loki-like prankster which the humourless Old Testament God would have found particularly tiresome. It is clear of course that our mortal and less than perfect state was in no way caused by the presence of serpents in Eden. Instead, the serpent is a symbol of our ability to rebel against the Father, transgress the law, suffer guilt, and die. The serpent signifies our freedom in its least acceptable aspect, as that which we would rather not have, what we dearly wish we did not contain within us; and it signifies it in such a way as to externalize it, to expell it from within. It is, therefore, a particular kind of signifier: in fact, a scapegoat. By suffering expulsion, it serves to rid us of the evil within us which it signifies.

Writing of ancient Athens, Jacques Derrida says

> The ceremony of the *pharmakos* [scapegoat] is . . . played out on the boundary line between inside and outside, which it has as its function ceaselessly to trace and retrace. *Intra muros/extra muros*. The origin of difference and division, the *pharmakos* represents evil both introjected and projected.[5]

The scapegoat is simultaneously within us and without. It is within, in so far as it signifies that of which we desire to be purged, in so far as what it signifies is significant to us as something we wish to be other than ourselves and thus rid of. It is without, in so far as we succeed in purging ourselves of what it signifies, in so far, in other words, as we continue to sustain it as signifier, as something which is not unmediated self-presence. It is therefore possible to consider Wright's poem "The Killer" as the account of what occurs when that particular form of signification represented by the scapegoat is destroyed. Surprised into confusing signifier with signified, the symbol with what it symbolizes, the subject literally destroys it. The result is that "black horror" — an acute sense of mortality and guilt — returns to her mind, unmediated by the symbol whose function it was to keep it out, to hold it at a distance.

I have chosen to discuss "The Killer" here because it dramatizes in a particularly striking way a characteristic of all language: that is, its role as a source of power, as that alienating structure with which we create and maintain the space within which we live. "Thus the symbol manifests itself first of all as the murder of the thing" Lacan writes, "and this death constitutes in the subject the eternalization of his desire", clearly pointing to both the positive and the negative aspects of this structure.[6] But when the symbol is employed in a scapegoating situation, we can see in a particularly clear way how it confers power on us, power to place at a distance, to project and expel that within us which we fear or which threatens us. Destroying the symbol destroys our own power, reinvoking that which it is the symbol's role to subdue. So when the subject, in "The Killer", destroys that duplicitous symbol, that double-tongued snake, she discovers that she is powerless to control what it symbolized — that is, the fearful power to transgress the law, to kill, to suffer guilt. Only by being at the mercy of the signifier's duplicity, it seems, can we avoid being at the mercy of what it signifies.

A somewhat later poem, "Snakeskin on a Gate" (*C.P.* p. 245) provides further commentary on this. As with many Australian poems, "Snakeskin on a Gate" is a meditative narrative bordering on parable. It is a poem about change and, explicitly, renewal. Finding a cast-off snakeskin in January, (the month of Janus, "double-faced month of change"), the subject hangs it on a gate, that traditional image of transition, "thinking it emblem . . . of a time of life"

> that looking backward sighs for the dedication's innocence,
> then turns too many pages, to find the end of the book.

This time, this stage, seems to be, as I understand it, one in which the subject is infused by a kind of weary impatience to be through with life now that it has lost its innocence and even its dedication. It is a time of tedium. But the snakeskin, which up to the end of the second stanza has been so literary — even verbal — in its association with books and their pages, surrenders its function of emblem or "omen" within the subject's reverie on the nature of her own life when she touches it. Immediate physical contact apparently bypasses any ratiocinative or semiotic process. Apprehended in this "gut" way, the snakeskin reminds her of death, being "neither alive nor decayed", its "life withdrawn". It also reminds her that where there is a freshly cast snakeskin there is also likely to be a snake:

> and I went uneasily, watching, for my life's sake,
> for a coil of poisonous dark in the pools of shade.

However when the woman in fact sees the snake, she sees that it has been transformed by the act of casting the old skin. It thus comes to represent for her the possibility of renewal within her own life: "Like this from our change, my soul, let us drink renewal". The poem celebrates the natural process by means of which death, emblematic in that which has died, can be cast off in a positive act of renewal, thus ridding the soul of the fear which causes it to be dangerous or venemous:

> Set free of its dim shell, his glinting eye
> saw only movement and light and had no fear of me.

Since, by shedding its dead carapace the snake can now see clearly, it has no fear of the woman and is not dangerous to her. Likewise she, for her part, has no cause to fear the snake, which becomes an image of the possibility of her own renewal.

The poem is structured around several dualities which give it a dramatic tension. The lifeless, empty snakeskin is contrasted with the living creature "stretching warm in the sun". The woman tediously adrift *nel mezzo del cammin* is contrasted with the woman who can "drink renewal". These dualities for example, can be added to the two ways of acquiring knowledge predicated by the poem: by "emblem", that is, by sign, semiotically and verbally; and by touch, a process which brings knowledge "closer than omens" and which seems to short-circuit the semiotic process. Together these dualities serve to give the poem dramatic tension, a sense of internal difference which is finally classically resolved as the three privileged terms — life, renewal, the non-verbal — combine in affirmation. But if we look beneath this fairly simple level of interpretation we find another patterning which resists resolution while at the same time adding a further flavour of poignancy.

The snakeskin which "blew in the wind on the closed gate" "between two realities", is our clue to this other pattern. Wright's phrasing strikingly reminds us of Derrida's description of the *pharmakos*, the scapegoat, which within the context of Derrida's whole argument is, in fact, a description of language itself, "on the boundary line between inside and outside, which it has as its function ceaselessly to trace and retrace". And when we look carefully at Wright's poem, it readily becomes clear that even if the snakeskin can convey knowledge by touch rather than by words, it none the less continues to signify. And so too, as the poem continues, does the snake. The fact that each signifies several contradictory things (skin: tedium, death, and the shedding of these; snake: death, threat, renewal) is relevant; but what is more to my purpose here is that each signifies only in relation to the other, only by means of what the other is. For example, the skin signifies tedium, hollowness — the woman's own condition when it "speaks to her" in the first stanza — only by being a hollow, dessicated simulacrum of the living creature. It signifies, later, death by signifying, literally, "life withdrawn", the withdrawal of the living creature, whose actual absence enables the empty skin's condition of being and signification. Without that absence the skin could not signify what it does: presence elsewhere. By the same token, the living snake erases fear by signifying renewal, but only by virtue of what it is not, of what is separated from it: its other, its empty mockery, the empty, dead space which it has ceased to inhabit and which it cast, as a scapegoat, from itself. The poem's celebration, at a thematic level, its shedding of the deathly and tedious, is accomplished within the poem's narrative by a one-way move from death to renewal. But it is enabled by a system of signification, by a language, which ceaselessly traces and retraces that borderline, "strange, between two realities, neither alive nor decayed".[7]

Despite its affirmative conclusion, "Snakeskin on a Gate" clearly indicates thematically that doubleness, otherness, while being the precondition for renewal (at a non-thematic level, the actual condition of renewal) is nonetheless troublesome. Psychologically or existentially a problem rather than a problematic, doubleness threatens with alienation or simply with itself. That this is so not only for the subject of "Naked Girl and Mirror", but also possibly for Wright herself, is indicated by a number of other poems which attempt to resolve it. The ambition of these poems is to transcend doubleness, reaching beyond it to a transcendental unity. An early poem, for example, declares that pain, even death, can be transcended by a kind of heroic upsurge of natural effort:

Out of the torn earth's mouth
comes the old cry of praise.
Still is the song made flesh
though the singer dies —

flesh of the world's delight,
voice of the world's desire . . .

('Flametree in a Quarry", *C.P.* p. 62)

In a much later poem, the feeling seems to be more orthodoxly religious:

> Every path and life leads one way only,
> out of continual miracle, through creation's fable,
> over and over repeated but never yet understood,
> as every word leads back to the blinding original Word.
>
> ("To Hafir of Shiraz", *C.P.* p. 217)

Both early and late quotations suggest that unity is not achieved through a process of dialectic, but by an act of transcendence which cannot be dissociated from song, voice, words, and indeed, the Word — that transcendental unity of signifier and signified in which the signifier is elided in order that the transcendental signified be manifest in its own immaculate self-presence — what Emmanual Kant would call a transcendental illusion.[8]

"The Other Half" (*C.P.* p. 217) is the title poem of Judith Wright's 1966 collection, and at one obvious level of interpretation deals with the relation of the conscious mind and the unconscious, "The self that night undrowns when I'm asleep", and which "beats in anger on the things I love". But this second quotation already indicates that to see this "other half" as unquestionably the unconscious is misleading. The unconscious is not necessarily antagonistic to consciousness or to what one consciously loves.[9] Rather, what we have in Wright's poem is more simply the internal other of consciousness, in a dramatization distinctly reminiscent of the Renaissance dialogues of self and soul in which two radically conflicting interpretations of life are collided. Thus the mutual antagonism within the first stanza of Wright's poem is one aspect of this radical alterity: "I am the cross it bears, and it the tears I weep". However, this process of collision, with which the first stanza is concerned, gives way as the poem progresses to an attempt at reconciliation and finally at unification. The first step is reconciliation. This takes place at the end of the second stanza where "the other half" takes on the dramatic role of a lover, and antagonism makes place for a somewhat clandestine harmony: "My silent answer and my other half, / we meet at midnight and by music only". But the initial force of the alterity in the first stanza impels the poem beyond mere harmony towards an annihilation of duality in oneness:

> Yet there's a word that I would give to you:
> the truth you tell in your dumb images
> my daylight self goes stumbling after too.
> So we may meet at last, and meeting bless,
> and turn into one truth in singleness.

The two halves, it seems, may finally meet and merge in "truth". But despite the Renaissance echoes of the poem, there is little suggestion that this "one truth in singleness", is achieved in death in the Elizabethan metaphorical sense. In fact, nothing in the poem locates a site for it — unless it be in actual death, or unless it be thoroughly mystical and hence beyond discussion.

There is an interesting entangling of dumbness, words and truth here which sustains unravelling. Dumbness is associated with both "halves": "the other half" tells, in its "dumb images", the truth which the "daylight self goes stumbling after" in its "dumb days". The implication is that the "days" (in the first stanza) are dumb because they do not utter the truth (hence the "stumbling"). And the "images" are dumb because the truth they contain is not expressed in words, which are the property of the "daylight self". Unity can only be achieved when the "word" belonging to the "daylight self" is united with the "truth" embodied in the other self's dumb images: that is, when signifier is inseparable from, single with, the signified. Thus the poem in one sense affirms that impossible "candid speech" in which truth and language are identical — an identity which renders language, the signifier, unnecessary and accidental and hence, incidentally, other than, non-identical to, the truth. But it does so by means of revealing a deep sense of unbridgeable division within the self, and within the very self of language — between word and "truth", between signifier and signified — which not only motivates the poem but which is the constitution of the sign, the actual condition of language. Even the language of affirmation, or the language of singleness. It is no accident, therefore, that this affirmation has a ring of death about it. Just as a physical union of lovers is inconceivable unless it both depends on and preserves the lovers' separateness, (anything else would cause more than Elizabethan "death"), so such a transcendent singleness as the poem affirms will always occur just beyond the border of the possible, achieved by the death of language which is rendered redundant before the transcendental signified, "the blinding original Word". Furthermore this transcendent singleness is duplicitous in another way too. It can be achieved only by positing a further duality which defines it, a duality of singleness/multiplicity, in which singleness is now the privileged term — but still one of two. The transcendence of doubleness (it makes no difference whether we talk of two wholes or two halves) to "one truth in singleness" is achieved only by shifting the discourse to another level of duplicity, and this regress is infinite. There is always "the other half".

If I have chosen to centre this discussion of Wright mainly on poems which have received little attention from other critics, that is not because of a perverse desire for novelty on my part. As befits her achievement, Judith Wright's poetry has received a great deal of critical attention. Her major preoccupations (a word which she herself made popular) have been listed and examined, the outlines of her career traced and retraced. I have chosen the path I followed, therefore, partly to avoid trampling over the ground of others and obscuring their work, and partly because it provided me with a way into her poetry at a point where certain aspects of it which have not been much discussed could now become clearer.

We have seen, for example, how a sense of the other, of doubleness, reveals itself in her work. The poetry does not attempt a a resolution of this doubleness in terms of harmony as, for example, A.D. Hope's does; in particular her poetry is not a verbal attempt at registering a harmony somehow inherent in the universe, in the way things are. Rather, its attempts to resolve doubleness move towards transcendence. But such a move only establishes another duality; and when one term of that new duality is privileged as Love or Truth or the Word, it reveals its duplicity in the fact that the word is never the Word, but is always other than what it signifies. Yet when, in "The Killer", the signifier itself is destroyed, the subject discovers that she is without defence against what it signified. By way of conclusion, I want to make a few brief comments on two of Wright's best-known poems in order to show how the preceding remarks apply to them too.

"Bullocky", from Wright's first book *The Moving Image*, and "Woman to Man", the title poem of her second, are both poems of origin. The first poem accounts movingly the origins of Australia's fruitfulness in the privations and endurance of the pioneers. The second, and slightly later, poem deals with the origin of a new life, that of a child, within the woman's body and within the love that exists between the woman and the child's father. But where, in fact, is origin itself to be located? If we look for a moment of origin in "Bullocky" all we find is a vertiginous regression of perspectives. Privation drives the old bullocky mad till the years "ran widdershins in his brain". As he grows older, he lives earlier, to the point where he thinks that he is Moses leading the Children of Israel, ("the slaves") into "the Promised Land". Taking as a cue the bullocky's mad delusion as to his own identity, the poem makes Moses a metaphor for those whose suffering helped to make Australia fruitful. But it also makes it clear that it is patently not true that the bullocky was Moses, or even much like him. This falsehood, the bullocky's delusion, is being offered as conclusive, clinching truth. The fact that this does not outrage us is due to our familiarity with the conventions of reading metaphors; we know to bracket their obvious untruthfulness (without which, of course, they would not be metaphors) in order to see how else they signify. This particular metaphor is in a crucial, key position in the poem, in that it ties together the hardships endured in an unsettled land, the crazed bullocky, the prophet Moses, and the Promised Land which is now fruitful. This should be where the moment of the fruitful land's origin is. But when we look closely at the words, we discover that that moment of origin resides in, but cannot be found in, the gap between metaphorical "truth" and its obvious lie, in metaphor's method of signifying by necessarily signifying awry. To put that another way, by locating the moment of origin within a metaphor, it becomes something non-originary, doubly deferred through language.

Turning now to "Woman to Man" we find that the language of the whole poem is intensely metaphorical: "The eyeless labourer in the night . . . builds for its resurrection day", "This is our hunter and our chase", and

> This is the strength that your arm knows,
> the arc of flesh that is my breast,
> the precise crystals of our eyes.
> This is the blood's wild tree that grows
> the intricate and folded rose.

(*S.P.* p. 25)

This metaphoric quality accounts greatly for the poem's passionate appeal: one senses here that language is being wrought out of its normal channels, twisted aside from its normal procedures, in order to perform a more than normal task. The poem's final exclamation, "Oh hold me, for I am afraid", provides a moving culmination for this sense of urgency, while at the same time casting the reader into the dramatic role of the man, the child's father, who is being addressed. The poem is justly famous for the strength yet delicacy with which it deals with the mysterious process of maternity. Yet its power is, as I said, largely attributable to its pervasive metaphoric language, and metaphor signifies by signifying awry, by declaring something by declaring it something else.

If, as we have seen, even the pubescent girl in "Naked Girl and Mirror" is already — and always already — double, then Wright's search for Oneness beyond all duplicity or plurality is more than an attempt at transcending the condition of language which marks us as human. It is an attempted return to origin — to that condition of presence in and for itself which is primal non-self-recognition or, in Kristeva's terms, to the pre-symbolic condition of narcissism, the semiotic. Being both "the maker and the made", both "the question and reply", the unborn child would seem to epitomize this condition. Like the Egyptian god-king, Thoth, in Plato's parable of the origin of writing in the *Phaedrus*, the child "does not know how to write [or speak], but that ignorance or incapacity only testifies to his sovereign independence."[10] But when "Woman to Man" says that "this has no name to name it by" it is not simply attempting to defer the inevitable. It is true that the moment the child is named it is signified by what it is not, even by such a simple, innocent, or magical thing as a name. Born into language, into a world constituted by discourse, every child is a twin of its other, to which it must have recourse in every act of knowing itself or of knowing anything else. But the poem's explicit disavowal of naming is actually part of a more complex strategy, because of course the poem names all the time — by metaphor. With something so fragile, so primally significant, as the origin of a human life, its recourse to metaphor is perhaps a wise precaution, erecting as it does a double wall of language around the conception, a double duplicity to preserve its integrity. The fact that the unborn child in "Woman to Man" (and, indeed, in "Woman to Child" and "The Unborn") is wrapped so protectively in layer upon layer of language, that it is disclosed only by an act of massive concealment, contrasts markedly with the male "elegant dissection" which reveals the unborn child in A.D. Hope's poem "On an Engraving by Casserius".

The intense sense of otherness, of doubleness, discernible in Judith Wright's poetry leads, it seems inevitably, to an attempt to evade it, to elide it, to erase it. But to long for the Word alone, the Logos alone, is to long to escape from language entirely, which means to escape from the whole constitution of human knowledge. Taken to an extreme, such a longing for "one truth in singleness" would entail either a pathological regression to a prenatal preconsciousness or a move beyond language into a mysticism which would brook no discussion. In either case it would be a regressive move toward origin. But the direction of this move, in Wright's case, involves her poetry in a revelation of the power of language to resist, to protect its own nature, to protect its own, to evade all attempts to alter it and abort its processes. "The intricate and folded rose" which is Judith Wright's poetry — flowers from the very impossibility of realizing the dream which it nurtures of its own annihilation.[11] In "Woman to Man", as in so many of Wright's poems, the place of the Word, the male Logos aspired to, is taken by a powerfully female and maternal language, revealing by protecting, bodying forth by concealing, disclosing by enclosing, being itself always the locus and the matrix of the other. Swaddled in metaphor, the origin of the child and the origin of origin — the origin of creativity — are clearly there yet, if we look closely enough, clearly unseen.

8

The Spilled Cruet of Innocence: Subject in Francis Webb's Poetry

Any collection of essays dealing with Australian poetry that does not make some mention of Francis Webb is clearly going to be seen as deficient, no matter how little the writer aims at being comprehensive. Whether Webb's reputation is as large today as it was when *Poetry Australia* issued its special Francis Webb number in September 1975 is open to doubt.[1] David Campbell's perceptive and original brief essay on him in the revised edition of *The Literature of Australia*[2] praises him highly, and Vivian Smith, in *The Oxford History of Australian Literature* writes that Webb

> has continued to exert influence on succeeding younger generations. Webb has in recent years through the tragic relationship between his art and his life become something of a cult figure and he may well exert for succeeding generations the kind of influence that Hart Crane exerted in America or even Gordon in Australia at an earlier stage.[3]

The Oxford Companion to Australian Literature makes a similar claim: "Something of a cult-figure since his death, Webb exercised considerable influence in the development of some of the new attitudes that spread through Australian poetry in the late 1960s and 1970s."[4] Still, it would be hard to find any Australian poet writing today whose work bears even a superficial resemblance to Webb's, with the possible exception of Bruce Beaver who is himself a deeply original poet and of the same generation as Webb. In fact if one were to look for a figure of that generation who has exercised an influence on "succeeding generations" one would turn to Beaver rather than to Webb. Webb's influence — if, in fact there actually was one — would be found more in the example he set of someone who resolutely ignored fashions of poetry current in the nineteen fifties and nineteen sixties, than in his actual poetic.

The reason for this may well be the obscurity, the difficulty of much of his poetry. *The Oxford Companion* mentions this:

> In the later, extremely complex, poetry the obsessively religious nature of his personal response to experience, the brilliance of his language and

> intensity of imagery have combined to categorize him as an extraordinarily gifted, though esoteric and somewhat inaccessible poet. (P. 734)

And there is no denying that Webb's poetry is difficult: its frequent religious preoccupations set it aside from much contemporary poetry, while the language is often obscure, involving a private rhetoric which eschews the colloquialism so favoured by poets of the last several decades. It might be fair to claim that today Webb's reputation is high among those who care for Australian poetry, but his actual poetry is not read very much. In his introduction to the *Collected Poems*[5] Herbert Read points to a single-minded pursuit of his own preoccupations which to some extent isolated Webb from contemporary trends, claiming that "From the beginning Francis Webb has sought that 'so tender voyaging line of truth', single-mindedly, and with a somewhat disconcerting unawareness of the fashionable poetry of his time". And he further claims, I think rightly, that Webb's prosody "is not 'modern' except in its psychological and metaphysical intensity".[6] Prosody aside, what Read means by modernness in relation to Webb is in fact close to what I have been calling modernism. Read, in fact, places Webb in the context of Rilke, Eliot and Pasternak, and concludes that he "cannot, after long meditation on his verse, place his achievement on a level lower than that suggested by these names".[7]

Read expands on his analysis of the mood of Webb's poetry by means of a quotation from Kierkegaard's *The Sickness unto Death* which deserves to be quoted in full.[8] Claiming that in "Eyre All Alone" Webb returns to "his earlier epical manner", Read says that the myth articulated in that poem is

> the journey of the soul, through the wilderness of despair: the despair of aloneness, of abandonment, which is also the despair of the self — of the many forms of despair perhaps the one described by Kierkegaard as the despairing self that "is constantly building nothing but castles in the air, it fights only in the air."

Read then continues the quotation from Kierkegaard:

> All these experimented virtues make a brilliant showing: for an instant they are enchanting, like an oriental poem: such self-control, such firmness, such ataraxia, etc., border almost on the fabulous. Yes, they do to be sure; and also at the bottom of it all there is nothing. The self wants to enjoy the entire satisfaction of making itself into itself, of developing itself, of being itself; it wants to have the honour of this poetic, this masterly plan according to which it has understood itself. And yet in the last resort it is a riddle how it understands itself; just at the instant when it seems to be nearest to having the fabric finished it can arbitrarily resolve the whole thing into nothing.

It is not my intention here to embark on a lengthy analysis of Kierkegaard — nor, for that matter, of Francis Webb. Both writers could amply justify a far larger and more rigorous discussion that I can provide here; the linguistic density and complex referential and self-referential qualities of Webb's poetry could readily be the subject of a book-length study, and the absence of one to date perhaps backs me up in my hunch that he is a poet more respected than read. But the passage from Kierkegaard points to another aspect of modernism, one which has been running as an undercurrent through the present study, and which I would like to discuss in relation to several of Webb's poems. It has to do with the constitution of the subject, not simply the subject in poetry but the subject as it is found in our biological and psychological selves — the subject as Ourself/Myself, and its relation to language.

But first I must say a little about Webb in relation to modernism. In my earlier discussion of Kenneth Slessor I claimed that Slessor was perhaps the only true modernist poet that Australia had produced, a claim which I would still maintain but which must be qualified. To start with, it has become conventional to agree that the classical period of modernism ended roughly at the end of the 1920s, just as it is now largely agreed that tendencies in poetry and other arts after the Second World War can more accurately be described as post-modern or post-modernist. Of course the classical modernists such as Pound and Eliot continued to write well after the end of the 1920s, and it would be absurd to claim that elements of classical modernism failed to persist, even to the present. After all, the history of poetry involves as much a carrying on of the past as a rejection of it or a reaction to it: the rejection/reaction involves a taking on board of what now becomes the invisible other of the new, and its invisible presence helps to determine and shape the new as surely as a stone in a field will leave its empty impress on a potato growing beside it. Thus my claim that modernism was, to a large part, the product of a profound disappointment with romanticism, and my argument that without a prior Australian romanticism Kenneth Slessor could come to modernism only by a highly individual and circuitous route. Francis Webb, who was born in 1925, began writing poetry long after the historical period considered to be classical modernism had ended; and like other Australian poets, he lacked the prior Australian romanticism which would have been an enabling condition of an indigenous modernism.

None the less, traces of modernism existed in Australian poetry, as in poetry elsewhere, long after the 1920s had ended. A.D. Hope's "Australia" displays an *Angst* and a disgust with contemporary culture (most particularly in the poem's first five stanzas) that place it closer to Eliot than to Arnold. And although his claim to hear a universal harmony would answer more to a post-modernist poetic, the depth of his concern with harmony — and culture — is itself less a throwback to the eighteenth century than a reshaping of concerns thoroughly central to Pound, Eliot and Stevens. In the poetry of Judith Wright, the characteristic tropism towards unity, towards an annulment of duality or division, could not be imagined without the impact of modernism: duality simply would not have been a matter of concern in her poetry. One could look at other aspects of modernism which continued to make their presence felt in the 1940s, 50s and even 60s of Australian poetry: for example, R.D. FitzGerald's interest in history as the *tabula* on which the pattern of human significance is written or James McAuley's concern with the "heroic" aspect of Captain Quiros. Finally, John Tranter, in his introduction to *The New Australian Poetry* claims — rather confusingly — that the poetry of the "Generation of 68" is in some sense modernist.[9]

At first glance, the central role played by figures of heroic or mythic significance within a number of Francis Webb's poems seems also clearly related to the modernism of Kenneth Slessor. As I have shown in my discussion of the earlier poet's work, the figures of Cook and Home in "Five Visions of Captain Cook" mark a crucial passage from romance through the heroic in a trajectory which will eventually arrive at modernism. But this arrival is not achieved until "Five Bells", which then articulates the classic modernist position. Briefly, by opposing its own "blessed rage for order"[10] against the intractable and meaningless disorder of reality, the subject of that poem — like that of "The Waste Land" — learns that the chaos of modern life cannot be assimilated to a mythic or archetypal pattern of order such that the chaos ceases to exist (or ceases to matter).[11]

When we turn, at last, to Francis Webb's poetry, the figure of the bushranger Mad Dog Morgan in "Morgan's Country" (*C.P.* p. 46) in his own desperate and unlikely way appears to be a similarly modernist protagonist. Caught between the devouring "Cave, his mother" and the threatening "stone Look-out, his towering father" as the troopers close in for the kill, Morgan seems to be the figure of total alienation, alienated even from his humanity. He is "The grey wolf" for whom "their eyes / Are poison at every well where he might drink". And yet the power of his desperation transfers to the country around him qualities which previously had been his own: "This country looks grey, hunted and murderous". Morgan's ability to recreate the country ("Morgan's Country") in his own image is a perverse manifestation of Cook's in "Five Visions of Captain Cook". Like Morgan le Fay, the Morgan of the Webb poem transforms what is normal into what is perverse; but such a transformation testifies, none the less, to human power, not to powerlessness at the hands of fate or of a chaotic universe. Thus "Morgan's Country" adumbrates a role closer to what I have called the heroic; and in according it a perverse efficacy, it sets itself aside from the main thrust of the modernists' sense of the intractability of the world.

Equally, but for slightly different reasons, one would hesitate to call Webb's sequence "Eyre All Alone" (*C.P.* p. 181) a modernist poem. There are simply too many non-modernist elements in it, quite apart from the date of its composition (it was published in *Socrates* in 1961). The poem has at its centre a heroic questing figure, loosely based, as a note on the poem tells us, on the historical figure Edward John Eyre, who succeeded in crossing the Australian continent from east to west in 1841, but only after considerable hardship and the murder by two black members of his party of his European companion, Baxter. Webb's note tells us that his use of this historical figure is essentially to fulfill an ahistorical or anti-historical purpose:

> Eyre's personal journal is infinitely more dramatic than this poem can pretend to be. My insistence upon Eyre's aloneness is not an overlooking of Wylie [Eyre's third black companion], but comes from my seeing such a journey of discovery as suggestive of another which is common to us all. (*C.P.* p. 251)

Eyre's journey is the acting out, or writing out, of a myth of personal suffering and redemption, a successful journey through what, in Patrick White's *Voss*, is called "death by torture in the country of the mind". That such a coincidence of the temporal (historical) and the atemporal (mythic) can ever have taken the form that it did in "Eyre All Alone" indicates that it is not a modernist text. Webb's poem affirms a coherence of pattern and correspondence going far beyond the manifold linguistic improvisations and variations, the linguistic bravura even, of James Joyce's deployment of myth in *Ulysses*, or Eliot's essentially static image of chaos in "The Waste Land". These modernist texts subdue the chaos of "contemporary history" by "manipulating a continuous parallel between contemporaneity and antiquity" (notice the force here of Eliot's word "manipulating") as a way "of controlling, of ordering, of giving a shape and a significance" where otherwise there would be none.[12] But Webb's poem locates within one realm of experience the pattern of another. By divesting itself of accidents, or rather by being forcibly, even brutally, divested of them, the subject finds within its narrative penetration of the natural world the paradigm of its own redemption. In a way that would please Northrop Frye or a structuralist interpreter of Webb's poetry, and in a way which harkens back to the symbolism of Christopher Brennan, the narrative of Eyre's journey acts out in a series of lyric moments a pattern of regeneration which informs both the non-human and the spiritual worlds.

That this correspondence of pattern is not a disguised version of modernism can be demonstrated by the progression from section 8, "Aboriginals" to section 10, "Banksia". After the murder of his white companion, Wylie, in section 3, and his rejection by a female sea which, by being undrinkable, is unsustaining (section 7), section 8 sees Eyre in a familiar modernist impasse:

> Innumerable times the great Expedition of my thought
> Has gone to pieces,
> Frightened horses galloping in all directions.
>
> You are everywhere at once.
>
> My instinct is to shudder away from you.
> Love? It is for dry bread like a stone in my mouth,
> For petty concentric days stemming from me . . .

The imagery here is very close to the desert landscape of "The Waste Land" above which, in Eliot's poem, the thunder utters its injunctions only to be greeted, ominiously, by admissions of human inadequacy.[13] But it perhaps needs to be pointed out that the anguish and longing of the subject in "What the Thunder said" serves to distinguish it from the barren landscape which signifies its spiritual condition and which offers it so little solace ("If there were water / And no rock / If there were rock / And also water . . ."). It is precisely this disjunction which is an index of the subject's alienation: not only is it alienated, but it feels it, it knows it. In the event of the subject's impotence to change its condition, Eliot's line "These fragments I have shored against my ruins" thus utters the modernist imagination's imperative. But the lines from Webb's poem make it clear that Eyre's physical duress and his spiritual purgation cannot be separated in this way: the "great Expedition" is both thoroughly external and thoroughly internal, the "frightened horses" are inextricably both animals and thoughts. Furthermore, after the repetition of the refrain in section 9, Webb's poem moves beyond this admission of defeat to acknowledge an epiphany:

> Turn the horses loose. Out of earth a power:
> Banksia, honeysuckle, forked-lightening-fruit of pain.
> Motive pierces the cloud-scrub once again.

"Motive", or meaning, significance, is manifest in this physical/spiritual identity by means of the symbolic power of the banksia which is a "fruit of pain" as much as of the earth. As with all epiphanies, we have here a curious elision of the signifier in the name of religious immediacy. Precisely because of the poem's identification of human and non-human in a tortured approach toward a post-Wordsworthian romanticism, the banksia "is" "motive" itself, "present" without any mediation within the poem's subject — it grows there in a most un-modernist fashion. But within the linguistic act which is the poem itself, the banksia continues, as it inevitably must, to signify. Not only does it signify "motive" (and we need not dwell here on just what *that* word signifies); it also signifies this mystical elision of the signifier, its own self-erasure in the plenitude of presence. Interestingly enough, its nature as signifier, akin to that of the burning bush observed by Moses,[14] is subsequently emphasized when Eyre enjoins it to "carry fire, like the thurifer / Over my sandy tongue-tied barren ground". The movement of the poem from this point on is towards a spiritual redemption which can be achieved precisely because "motive" or meaning, whether human or divine, inheres in both the natural and the human/spiritual. One could say then that in this way, and at this point (from section 8 to section 10) "Eyre All Alone" passes thoroughly beyond modernism to a religious version of post-modernism.

It is at this moment that we should remind ourselves of Herbert Read's comments in the introduction, and in particular of the Kierkegaard passage he quotes from *The Sickness unto Death*. Is it really the case that the "self" in "Eyre All Alone" "is constantly building nothing but castles in the air, it fights only in the air"? And is it the case that "just at the instant when it seems to be nearest to having the fabric finished it can arbitrarily resolve the whole thing into nothing"? If this is the case, then "Eyre All Alone" is a modernist poem *par excellence*, an affirmation of the imagination's (or the "self's") power to create fictions whose fictionality it can then reveal in a powerful annulment which embraces both fiction and self simultaneously. But the foregoing account of the poem renders such an interpretation unacceptable. It is true that "Eyre All Alone" has a desperate quality to its tone and language, the tenseness that comes from playing for high stakes — and in this it is typical of a great deal of modernist poetry. And it is also true that it conveys very clearly a sense of the self under threat — under very great threat indeed. But there is a sense of the self none the less, and one which lacks the power to "arbitrarily resolve the whole thing into nothing". The self in Webb's poem participates in the larger pattern of meaning ("motive") apparent (though possibly only through divine grace) in the world at large, by means of which it arrives at a sense of personal redemption. At the same time this self can recognize itself as a historical entity within the larger ahistoricity. This does not result in the alienation manifest in "The Waste Land", however. On the contrary, it means that the historical Edward John Eyre is a particular manifestation of the mythic figuration, and thus one whose "journey of discovery is suggestive of another which is common to us all".

Yet there is something very attractive about the passage from Kierkegaard, something which tells us that it should not be lightly dismissed as inappropriate. And if we change the word "self" to "subject" we can perhaps begin to see more clearly where its appropriateness lies. It has been a long time since a poet has been able to proclaim, as W.E. Henley did, that "I am the master of my fate: / The captain of my soul".[15] And even this proud declaration elicits from us now something of a raised eyebrow, and the muttered aside that "Methinks he protesteth over much". What is in question here is not the power of the self to control its own fate, but something far more radical. In our post-Marxist and post-Freudian world, it is the actual constitution of the subject itself that is called into question. Who, or what, is that "I" that declares its authority so defiantly "Out of the night that covers me, / Black as the pit from pole to pole"? We can no longer think of it as unproblematically itself, a self distinct in nature and outline from all that is not itself. Ever since Freud convinced us of the existence of the unconscious, we have had to accept that the subject is constituted by internal difference; ever since Marx we have had to accept the subject as a construct, as being constituted in relation to what is not itself — provided that such a "self" can still be talked about. It is by means of Lacan's notion, however, of the subject constituted by language — a notion which I first raised in relation to Christopher Brennan — that we can most fruitfully further a discussion of the subject in relation to poetry.

In his brief account of Webb in *The Oxford History of Australian Literature* Vivian Smith has this to say:

> It is significant that Webb's central figures — Boyd, Leichhardt, Eyre, and St. Francis — are not dramatic presences. They are not *there* in the poems built around them in the way that Browning's Duke of Ferrara is present in "My Last Duchess". (P. 412)

It should be obvious from what I have written earlier that any notion of any figure being "*there* in the poem", being — in any sense whatever — "present" is problematic in the extreme. That such an innocent notion of presence still survives amongst critics and poets in Australia is perfectly exemplified by this recent comment in a review of poetry: "It's always hard to explain why a personal presence comes across as pressing and immediate . . .".[16] As long as critics continue to believe that they can find in poetry what has never been in it, they will indeed find it hard to explain how they find it. My discussion of Gwen Harwood and Dorothy Hewett in the following chapters will look at this question in further detail. Still, one can undoubtedly agree with Smith that even the illusion of a continuing dramatic entity that we might call an Eyre *persona*, or an "Eyre effect", seems tenuous, seems constantly on the point of vanishing, in "Eyre All Alone". (I imagine it is this quality that has reminded Herbert Read of Kierkegaard's comments on the vanishing self.) It is less easy, though, to agree with Smith's explanation:

> This is because Webb is less concerned with defining characters through word and deed than with showing what they have become — "myths", "legends", "monsters", "clowns". Webb's sense of the quest, his exploration in search of meaning, is ultimately metaphysical.

There are several obvious objections to be made to this explanation. One is to the easy conjuring up of what Webb is "concerned with". Even if one were to bypass the over-familiar arguments against the Intentional Fallacy, one would still have to ask just what is that "Webb" whose concerns Smith seems so sure about. The answer would have to be that it is a fiction, like a legal fiction, woven out of Smith's readings of a number of texts published with the name Francis Webb on the title page. As Michel Foucault has written,

> these aspects of an individual which we designate as making him an author are only a projection, in more or less psychologizing terms, of the operations that we force texts to undergo, the connections that we make, the traits that we establish as pertinent, the continuities that we recognize, or the exclusions that we practice.[17]

Smith's apparently casual "characterization" (and I use that word deliberately, with all its novelistic implications) of the "author" is traditional to a great deal of twentieth century literary criticism in English. An identical attitude underlies David Campbell's comment in *The Literature of Australia* that "Webb's poetry is a record of his revolt from and wavering acceptance of his genius and of a fate that was at times 'pitched past pitch of grief' ".[18] Whether the critic postulates Webb the poetic practitioner, as Smith does, or Webb the suffering psyche, as Campbell does, or even Eyre the poem's explorer-protagonist, the problem remains the same. In all cases the subject is a fictional construct, woven not by the "actual" Webb (who is, in any case, absent and, in fact, dead), but by an ongoing series of linguistic operations performed by the reader. The point here is not that the subject of every poem or body of poetic texts is mediated for us by language, which is assumed somehow to transmit it to us intact and inviolate — although even that would indeed be a strong argument against any simple notion of presence. Rather, it is that the subject in any text is ineluctably a linguistic creation, one wholly dependent upon the reader's reading of language. In his 1953 essay, "The function and field of speech and language in psychoanalysis",[19] Lacan takes this a logical step further. While discussing the unconscious and the place of language in what Freud himself called "the talking cure", Lacan argues persuasively that our own subjectivity is not immediate, manifestly self-present, but mediated to us (to itself) through language. In so far as we can be said to be aware of ourselves at all, it is by means of the mediating agency of a system of signifiers whose relation to their signified is arbitrary — as Saussure has shown — and not the expression of some metaphysical identity. The gap thus opened within the subject is the gap between the signifier and the signified: it is both the mark of language itself, and the mark of the normal human being's entry into the estate of desire and language which comes after the "mirror-stage".[20]

The tenuous existence of Eyre in Webb's sequence, which Vivian Smith correctly noted, can therefore be read in the light of the above. Most particularly, the identification of the subject with the landscape through which it moves has two effects. The most obvious, because the most traditional, is to establish the landscape as an external correlative of the internal (human) condition, to write the drama of the human "journey of discovery" in large across the face of the continent. The other effect is something close to the opposite of this. Eyre is constantly suffering the threat of being overwhelmed by landscape, of disappearing into it, like Voss, and not coming out again. By this I do not mean that the "persona" Eyre would die in the Australian continent like his European companion Baxter, but that the linguistic figuration of the subject of the poem is so much without boundaries of its own, so integral to the mythic pattern of suffering and redemption written within the landscape, that its continued existence *as subject* has to be achieved by a strenuous linguistic self-assertiveness which is, when all things are considered, a linguistic self-creation. The first person deployed throughout, the frequent exclamations, interjections and questions, the occasional address to another (to Wylie or to the dead Baxter) as well as the refrain with its repeated injunction, "walk, walk": these all serve to privilege the subject of this poem as that which speaks, and therefore that to which we (as well as Wylie, the dead Baxter, and the subject itself) listen. It is symptomatic of the crucial constitutive role of speech in this poem that when the speaking finally stops, we are at some loss to determine just who has stopped speaking:

> Looking down, or up, at the town from the brow of this hill
> I am truly alone. And hardly visible now
> The straight grey lines. I am coming, I am rainfall,
> And all doors are closed and stilled the merrymaking.
> One year on the march, an epoch, all of my life.
> But their faces will be golden when the doors open,
> Their dress shining. My torn stinking shirt, my boots,
> And hair a tangle of scrub; the long knotted absurd beard
> That is my conscience grown in the desert country.
> How shall I face their golden faces, pure voices?
> O my expedition: Baxter, Wylie!
>
> But the rain has stopped. On the main road Someone moves.

(*C.P.* p. 191)

With the exception of the refrain, all the characteristics of the verse I mentioned are apparent here, creating a disjunctive tension between the subject as speaker and the subject as landscape/spiritual condition ("I am rainfall", "hair a tangle of scrub" and "absurd beard / That is my conscience grown in the desert country"). Indeed, it is only by this tension of itself against itself that the subject exists at all. Yet just how readily that tension can be dispersed is shown by the uncertainties with which the poem's last line is fraught. At the simplest level one could ask who is speaking this line. Is it Eyre? And, if so, who is that "Someone" that he sees? Or is it "they", the inhabitants of the town with their shining dress and golden faces, that speak? And if so, has Eyre become "Someone", capitalized into a further dimension of significance? Our uncertainty is not resolved by reading this passage against its obvious pre-text, Christian's arrival at the Celestial City at the end of John Bunyan's *The Pilgrim's Progress*. Or is the "Someone" the Christ who appeared on the road to Emmaus?[21] Since there is nothing in the text to prevent us answering Yes to all these questions, one thing is clear: at this point that constitutive tension has disappeared, and the subject with it. It has disappeared — and there is absolutely nothing fortuituous about this — at a moment of epiphany, when someone becomes Someone, when the human cannot be distinguished from the divine, when speech ceases to signify, when language has gone as far as its divided nature can go and thus says no more. Inevitably, at this point the poem can do no more, and no less, than to achieve its close in the fullness of silence, which is the other of speech.

A theme that recurs through Webb's poetry is that speech, if not a curse in itself, is at least a sign of a curse, of our fallen (in the orthodox Christian sense) nature. As is traditional within so much of western thought, whether Christian or otherwise philosophical, "the Word unwritten" (*C.P.* p. 225) is the divine plenitude of self-presence whose sovereign lack of any need of mediation is the transcendental signified which Jacques Derrida has summed up in this way:

> God the king does not know how to write, but that ignorance or incapacity only testifies to his sovereign independence. He has no need to write. He speaks, he says, he dictates, and his word suffices. Whether a scribe from his secretarial staff then adds the supplement of a transcription or not, that consignment is always in essence secondary.[22]

But like the banksia bush, this transcendental signified also *signifies*: it signifies (symbolizes, you might say, or exemplifies, but signifies none the less) utter freedom from the desire which, according to Lacan, marks us as human subjects. This unalloyed freedom is the state of blessedness beyond discourse, or before language: the primal innocence which the human spirit enjoyed before its fall into the self-awareness of the normal child and adult.

A number of Webb's poems point to the innocence of those suffering from what we would call mental illness. One of his best known poems, "A Death at Winson Green" (*C.P.* p. 153), portrays the mental hospital as an island of innocence in a fallen world. When the visitors from that world leave ("The last of the heathens shuffles down the isle"), "we / Like early kings with book and word cast down / Realities from our squared electric shore" and "work / To cleanse our shore from limpet histories". The dying patient, refined by approaching death and borne upon the "tattered, powerful wing" of the hospital screen which is also that of the Holy Ghost, exceeds in innocence even the child-like subject:

> I sleep as a child, rouse up as a child might.
> I cannot pray; that fine lip prays for me
> With every gasp at breath.

This is a prayer which is performed without language, the ultimate prayer of the whole of humanity which achieves its culmination in silence, beyond life itself:

> He is all life, thrown on the gaping bed,
> Blind, silent, in a trance, and shortly, dead.

The sequence "Ward Two" also privileges the mental hospital as the sanctuary of innocence, particularly in two poems, "Harry" and "Wild Honey". The penultimate stanza of "Wild Honey" explicitly links "thought", "the prompted unnatural hunger" (Lacanian "desire" again) with the loss of Eden, an Eden which can momentarily be glimpsed in the actions of one of the patients:

> Down with the mind a moment, and let Eden
> Be fullness without the prompted unnatural hunger,
> Without the doomed shapely ersatz thought: see faith
> As all such essential gestures, unforbidden,
> Persisting through Fall and landslip.
>
> (*C.P.* p. 231)

Thought — language in the mind, preceding even speech — is "ersatz", literally a substitute. Added to what is essential, as a substitute for "essential gestures" which persist beyond the "Fall", the language of thought is "unnatural", opposed to "faith" which is timeless; and being temporal it is "doomed", no matter how "shapely" it may be. In this poem, thought, language itself, is Derrida's supplement as curse.[23]

The same theme occurs in one of the finest of Webb's poems, "Harry" (*C.P.* p. 224). Harry, one of the inmates of Ward Two, is a mongoloid "moron", an "imbecile": "because your children would scream at the sight / Of his mongol mouth stained with food" he has been put into the mental hospital where "His vestments [are] our giddy yarns of the firmament, / Women, gods, electric trains, and our remaking / Of all known worlds". His "vestments", the clothing added to (supplementing) the essential man, are secondary, "remakings" and not the real itself; they are "yarns", spun by the other inmates, of the world beyond the hospital. In other words, he is clothed in language, but the language of others by means of which they hoard "some shining loot" saved from the world outside the hospital: "Wife, mother, beach, fisticuffs, eloquence". But this language, with all its associations of the fallen world, has been transformed by Harry's innocence into "vestments" which he wears while he "weaves his sacrament" because "it is no goddess of ours guiding the fingers and the thumb" of the moron as he tries to write a letter.

The poem leaves us in no doubt that Harry is not only innocent of literacy, he is also innocent of the fallen condition of this world: "not yet / Has our giddy alphabet / Perplexed his priestcraft and spilled the cruet of innocence". The connection is clear: his innocence is intact, unspilled, because it is uncontaminated by the written language of the fallen world. This is why Harry "is filled with the Word unwritten", the divine logos which needs no writing, and "has resurrected / The spontaneous thought retarded and infantile Light". But as in "Wild Honey", it is not simply written language which retards the "infantile Light", that pristine innocence that precedes our fallen state, but thought itself – language unwritten, even unspoken. Only the Word does not contaminate, because it utters pure uncontamination, pure self-presence free of all shortcoming and desire. Just as a cruet contains wine for the sacrament, Harry contains the innocence which precedes the mind's fall from such divine self-presence: "Was it then at this altar-stone the mind was begun?" Harry shares the innocence that existed "*ab aeterno*", before even the earth took on, like Adam and Eve, the supplement of clothing. This was the condition in which the human and the divine could come together in an erotic union which was also a joyful unity or identity, the "Eden" of "Wild Honey":

> Before seasonal pelts and the thin
> Soft tactile underskin
> Of air were stretched across earth, they have sported and are one.

Harry's attempt to write a letter, his essay into language, is the result of a tropism towards what we would call normal human life. But the poem leaves us in no doubt that by failing to write it Harry has avoided a fall from primal innocence and communion with holiness. Despite the pathos of his failure to be a normal person, or even a normal psychiatric patient, he has averted a fall from the

Word and the Light with all their powerfully theological connotations.[24]

It is not surprising therefore that a poetry which privileges "the Word unwritten" so signally should also display a precariousness with regard to the subject. It is not the case, I would contend, that the subject "just at the instant when it seems to be nearest to having the fabric finished . . . can arbitrarily resolve the whole thing into nothing". Such a diagnosis, given the power implied by that word "arbitrarily", accords the subject in these poems too much freedom of choice, too much authority, too much potency. Rather, I would contend that these poems register the desire of the subject to rid itself of its own enabling and ineluctable desire, and to terminate its necessary condition of separation from itself, of internal difference — in effect, to be one with the transcendental signified and thus cease to be a subject at all. As with the somewhat different case of Judith Wright, this desire is expressed in language; but this expression in language, which is the poetry itself, is a triumphant testament to the temporary failure of the subject to realize its longing for annihilation. Strong, almost overwhelming though that longing may be, it is none the less a manifestation of the subject, whose condition it signifies. The elision of the subject would be the elision of human life itself in the sleep of death. But between infancy and death there is the waking, the knowing itself which is the life of the subject, and the utterance of the poetry — no matter how painful or reluctant that may be. It was fortunate for Australian poetry that the truncation of that waking, the running together of the innocence of infancy and the salvation of death, expressed in "Nessun Dorma" — one of Webb's last poems — should have been postponed for as long as it was:

No one, no one shall sleep
Till the cry of the infant emergent, lost and lame,
Is the cry of death gone towering towards the Flame.

(*C.P.* p. 247)

9

Gwen Harwood: The Golden Child Aloft on Discourse

Those of us who recall that time in the late 1950s, when Gwen Harwood's poetry was first starting to appear in Australian journals, will remember a period of excitement and also of bewilderment. It was not simply that a new poet of unexpected virtuoso technical accomplishment, wit and insight had appeared; rather, there seemed to be two of them, or possibly more. Guessing which poems, over different names, in the *Bulletin* were actually written by Gwen Harwood became a regular game. Moreover, her deployment of two further personae in two significant groups of her poems — Professor Eisenbart the physicist, and Professor Kröte the alcoholic suburban Orpheus — served to multiply the range of talents and personalities which appeared in the poetry. Would the real Gwen Harwood, people could be imagined muttering, please stand up and make herself known.[1]

She has, of course, done that today. With a small, but substantial, body of poetry published now, her reputation in this country is firmly established. One suspects that it would be even higher if she would consent to leave her home in Tasmania and appear on platforms and in readings on the mainland. To our regret, the tangible, physical Gwen Harwood is even less visible than she was when she first started publishing: in her absence, it is left to her works to speak for her. But there is no longer any mystery surrounding the authorial origin of the poetry and libretti published under her name. To the best of my knowledge, the pseudonyms have been abandoned, having served whatever psychological or social need they were designed to serve. The personae, by and large, have also gone, although Professor Kröte still puts in an occasional but ageing appearance. With the advantage of hindsight, we can see thematic and stylistic continuities between the Professor Eisenbart poems, the Kröte poems (originally published under the pen-name of Francis Geyer), other poems originally published under the pen-name of Miriam Stone, and Gwen Harwood's other, and more recent work. With a body of work spanning more than twenty years now spread before us we can talk, I suppose, meaningfully about the poet's development: though that is not what I propose to do here. The deliberate mystification has gone, our sense of who the poet is and just what "a Gwen Harwood poem" is, has strengthened. But are we any closer to grasping that tantalizing and elusive object of so many people's desire: a sense of the identity of the poet herself? Can we, in fact, ever grasp it?

It should not be necessary at this late stage, I hope, to present here a detailed theoretical case to back the claim that identity in literature — as, indeed, in life itself — is a fictional or textual construct.[2] Nonetheless a "commonsense" reading of poetry, even today, seems unable to avoid searching for something like "the true voice of the poet"[3] which will give focus and a point of resolution to the multiplicity of texts or personae which constitute the poetic discourse. It was at the source of our search, in the 1960s, for "the true Gwen Harwood" amid the welter of pseudonyms and personae. But the search was then, and is now, for an ideal rather than for something which actually exists; the search is actually the product of the inescapable condition which it seeks to deny. "Reading between the lines" for the true identity of a poet is still an act of reading; and what is being read — if it is, indeed, "between the lines" — is determined by the lines on either side, as surely as the unplayed space between the grooves of a gramophone disc are. And the outcome of this process, no matter what the illusion generated or what commonsense might claim, is constituted textually.

My aim here is not to present a detailed account of Harwood's development as a poet: from the comments above it should be clear that this way of describing one traditional critical task, if not the task itself, is problematical. Nor do I wish to give yet another assessment of her role and value within Australian poetry, except — perhaps — implicitly in my having chosen her for detailed discussion. After all, it is the most complex and subtle texts, texts in which language is working with greatest subtlety and provocativeness, that are the most rewarding. Least of all do I wish to give a thematic analysis of her poetry: that is a task which any sensitive reader can do unaided. Instead, I want to discuss Gwen Harwood's poetry in relation to the questions of Identity which it both poses and attempts to conceal — through the strategies her discourse adopts.

"In the Park" (*S.P.* p. 27) is a conveniently simple starting point.[4] An unnamed woman (could it be the poet herself?)

> sits in the park. Her clothes are out of date.
> Two children whine and bicker, tug her skirt.
> A third draws aimless patterns in the dirt.

Suburban monotony and tedium, the niggardly penny-pinching that often comes from having children, the disharmony, the aimlessness: they are all economically conveyed. Into this depressing scene enters a former lover/beloved, surprising the woman before she can "feign indifference". While the two adults chat brightly about "the children's names and birthdays" — those topics close to the stereotyped image of a suburban mother's sense of fulfillment — another, "silent", conversation is taking place. The woman apprehends the man's sense of a lucky escape written cartoon-style in "a small balloon" above "his neat head". And her own sense of being trapped and destroyed by domesticity and child-rearing is spoken to the wind which, as we know, cares for and preserves words entrusted to it as faithfully as does sand:

> Then, nursing
> the youngest child, sits staring at her feet.
> To the wind she says, "They have eaten me alive."

The fact that when we read the poem we unquestioningly assume that the "they" in the final line refers to the woman's children rather than, as it could, to the woman's feet, is not fortuitous. (After all, feet are commonly said to be "killing" people.) Rather, the poem sets up deliberate strategies to make us interpret the "they" as the woman's children. The most obvious is the dramatic situation. The woman's final utterance is in quotation marks, thus signalling us to read it as a continuation of her words to the man that "It's so sweet / to hear their chatter, watch them grow and thrive" where "their" and "them" can refer to nothing else but the children whose "names and birthdays" were discussed immediately before. Having heard her speak last about her children, the poem's employment of direct speech predisposes us to a continuity which suggests that the woman will still be speaking about the children the next time she uses the word "they". It does this by establishing the woman as someone who has a continuity of existence in her own right: it creates for her a fictional identity.

And yet this is precisely what the woman herself, in the poem's final lines, is denying. Having been "eaten . . . alive" by her children, whatever independent existence she might have had has been dispersed among her offspring. As an orthodox reading of the poem would suggest, this is her problem. Her life has been sacrified for her offspring: she has been broken, eaten, made part of them, made less part of/less herself. And without any of the Christian consolation that she will be enriched by her sacrifice, or that her immolation is in some Eucharistic way enriching to them. But if we look at the earlier part of the poem, we discover that she — as we constituted her in our reading — was already dispersed among her children. It is they who "whine and bicker", while the "aimless patterns in the dirt" we are asked to identify with the woman's conception of her own life are drawn by her third child.

My point is simply that there never was such a thing as an identity of this woman within this poem — let alone beyond it. The poem has constructed the woman's "identity" by systematically revealing its dispersal. It exists only in what is not herself. Perhaps a more accurate formulation of this would be the following. The fictional construct which we apprehend as the woman's identity is constituted by its non-existence as identity, by its character of dispersal. The woman's "identity" is actually the other of identity, if, by that word, we mean "The quality or condition of being the same; absolute or essential sameness; oneness . . . Individuality, personality" (*N.E.D.*). And yet our response to the poem, the pathos generated, depends on our sense that the woman has individuality, personality, an identity which can comprehend its own non-existence.

What we have here is not a muddled poem, but a subtle demonstration of the textuality of identity, its characteristic, if you like, of not being itself. We have, of course, only been looking at the identity of a fictional character, the "woman in the poem", and not at that of the poet herself. And with a poem such as "In the Park" there is little danger of confusing the two. To start with, the poem refers to the woman in the third person, thus requiring a strenuous act of interpretation on our part to equate woman with poet. Second, the poem is a sonnet. Its (fairly loose) iambic pentameter and strict rhyme inscribe the discourse within literature as distinct from non-literary language, despite the poem's conversational quality. The poem displays the badges of its poetic regiment, so to speak, clearly, guiding and shaping the intonations of our reading so as to emphasize the qualities of wit, incisive phrasing, deft modulation, and so on, which we conventionally associate with good poetry. These are qualities we ascribe to the poet, and are not those associated with the woman in the poem. But it should go without saying that they are qualities generated by our reading of the text, not qualities mysteriously present which the text somehow enables to appear.

"In the Park" is a comparatively simple poem, and there is little temptation to equate the woman in the poem with the poet herself, despite the frequent references throughout Harwood's poetry to her children and the role of mother which delayed, one can only assume, her emergence as a poet. But other poems present a more complex picture, for example those which employ personae and, perhaps surprisingly, particularly those which appear to abandon all artifice and disguise, and which appear to reveal most directly the poet's identity.

By way of characterizing how a sense of the poet's identity is generated in the poetry, I would describe the process rather loosely as akin to a masque. A masque, as we know, was a highly ritualized kind of stage presentation. One would hesitate to call it dramatic, and it is precisely its almost-but-not-quite dramatic nature, distinguishing it from drama proper, that suits the term for my purpose. It has a quality of ritual, of elaborate management, of deliberate artifice, in contrast to the greater sense of naturalness, even naturalism, we more frequently associate with drama. Masque also has connotations of mask, of disguise, of impersonation, of duplicity: all of which are relevant to the process I am examining. But I would want to make it clear that in using this term (rather loosely, let me stress again) in a discussion of Gwen Harwood, I am not accusing her poetry of displaying any of the artificiality or effeteness often associated with courtly masques. Rather, I am attempting to draw attention to the complex and highly conscious way certain rules are adhered to and roles adopted in order that a (necessarily fictive) identity may be constituted. And it should be clear from what I have already said that the term "fictive identity" does not mean a false one, a deliberate disguise, but the only kind there can be.

But Harwood has adopted, or created, false identities too: all of which must somehow be accounted for within the over-all economy of her poetry. It is hard to reconcile the arrogant Professor Eisenbart with the lonely, frequently drunk but engaging music teacher, Professor Kröte, whose German name means toad. Eisenbart, on the other hand, means iron beard; it also perhaps suggests "Eisenbahn" or railway; certainly there is a hardness and a directness about Eisenbart, a kind of steely efficiency on which he prides himself. But there is considerably more to him than that, as the poems in which he figures make clear.

The Eisenbart poems are, largely, poems of reversal. For example, in "Prizegiving" (*S.P.* p. 29) the "honoured guest" who has come "to lend distinction" to a school prizegiving recognizes himself in the poem's final stanza as "a sage fool". Age, scholarly excellence, science, maleness — all qualities which in Eisenbart's world and, it appears, in the girls' school too, are held to be preeminent — are subverted by youth, intuitive brilliance, art, that is, music, femaleness. In "Professor Eisenbart's Evening" (*S.P.* p. 32) a mind capable of comprehending the formulae of a bomb which might destroy the moon is powerless before the menstrual cycle of his mistress. Sexual need is more powerful than intellect; yet it is also clear how intellect applied to nuclear physics is also more powerful than sexuality. "Panther and Peacock" (*S.P.* p. 33) is a particularly dizzying series of reversals and subversions. Power displays itself as vulnerability, civilization as the other side of barbarism or bestiality, conscious intellect as the obverse of the unconscious's vertiginous dreams, pride as weakness. Yet throughout all these poems the reversals seem to be presided over, in fact presented by, something which itself suffers no reversal: the organizing activities of the poet herself which manifest themselves as a kind of "presence" for her, Gwen Harwood's "voice", call it what you will. We could say that, in these poems, reversal is inseparable from continuity, (a formulation which might point towards an interesting theoretical approach to the notion of "imitative form"). But is this authorial identity — in the sense of a unified, coherent point of orientation of the discourse, one possessing "The quality or condition of being the same, absolute or essential sameness" — actual? Or is it rather a chimera, something not there whose apparent presence is actually its absence artfully disguised?

"Ganymede" (*S.P.* p. 36) is one of the most interesting of the Eisenbart poems, and strikingly demonstrates the series' preoccupation with reversal. As in other poems, Eisenbart is prey to his own sexual needs. Apparently on holiday (though with his intellectual work, as usual, with him) and separated from "his mistress and her tiresome sweetness", he is attracted by the "wealth / of beauty" of a young boy staying at the same hotel. (There are reminiscences here, clearly, of Thomas Mann's story, "Death in Venice".) The physicist leaves "his magic / formulae", which are powerless against the demands of sexuality, and brings the boy into his room. But at the point of seducing him, Eisenbart is shocked to see that "Corruption, dumb, / winked, a sour beggar, through his perfect eyes / miming its own deceit in flesh and feature". He abandons his planned seduction, the boy leaves, mocking him crudely, and the professor "turned to live, / to work in his own world, where symbols might / speak to him their sublime affirmative".

Children occur frequently in Harwood's poetry. We have seen their destructive aspect in "In the Park", a role they assume in several other poems, for example "Suburban Sonnet". And in "Monday" a vicious child causes Kröte to lose his wine. In other poems, most notably "Fever", and "An Impromptu for Ann Jennings" (*S.P.* p. 76) children signify something quite different. In the latter poem, they are

> our new lords whose beautiful
> tyrannic kingdom might restore the earth to
> that fullness we thought lost beyond recall.

Children are innocent and vicious, the uncorrupted future and our own uncorrupted selves in the past, remorseless consumers and dispersers of their mothers' vitality and identity, possible redeemers of a fallen world. Harwood is robustly unsentimental in the picture of children which her poetry creates, and nowhere more so than in "Ganymede". The beauty of the boy already contains the corruption of the man. What Professor Eisenbart recognizes with horror is a grotesquely physical exemplum of the contradiction which is both the child and the mature man because it is the point at which they meet, the point at which each is defined as being not the other, but also not simply itself. It is not just that we are not what we seem, or that, in adolescence, childhood innocence starts to make way for a more unsavoury adult sexuality, though perhaps the poem is saying that too. The boy's physical beauty signifies childhood innocence and perfection precisely by signifying that these are not corrupt; yet the boy's corruption signifies the adult world by its being neither innocent nor perfect. Both acts of signification are located inextricably within the one signifier, which signifies each condition simultaneously in terms of its opposite. The boy's identity, as signifier, consists in this internal contradiction, in this negation of identity.

We can perhaps understand now the otherwise puzzling comment, earlier in the poem, that Eisenbart "feared the lift's steel cage": the physical (and all signifiers are physical) is duplicitous, and can become a snare, a cage, a trap — as, in fact, Eisenbart's sexuality and the boy's beauty had almost become for him. The boy's "graceful ivory body, bared, / spoke of itself alone," thus signifying the physical in both its perfection and its narcissistic corruption. So Professor Eisenbart returns to his world of physics (physics, we note, replaces the physical) "where symbols might / speak to him their sublime affirmative". Only in some world of "pure" or utterly abstract signifiers, it seems, can a non-duplicitous "sublime" and a non-ambiguous "affirmative" be sought. Yet, as we know, and as this poem has demonstrated, few things are as duplicitous as a signifier. Furthermore, the "sublime affirmative" to which Eisenbart turns is achieved at the cost of any involvement in the physical, it is affirmative by an act of exclusion, by an act of denial.

Within this slippery realm of duplicity, there is nonetheless an apparent unity serving as a point of orientation, even as a principle of organization within the poem. This is, of course, what is loosely described as "the poet's voice". Certain characteristics are instantly recognizable. The poem is written in more or less regular four-line stanzas and regularly rhymed. The effect of this is to fix the poem not only within a continuing practice of Harwood herself (i.e., most of her poems are like this) but also to inscribe it within a long tradition of "personal" lyric or meditation within English and Australian poetry. Within this tradition, which dates back to the Renaissance and thus far pre-dates Freud, the identity of the poet's voice is assumed to be virtual, and various strategies are employed to create the illusion that it is.[5] Without going into the details of this, one can see here how Harwood's rhythm and metre generate expectations of regularity which are, in fact, fulfilled: although Eisenbart's seduction goes awry, the poem does not. A coherence of tone is also imposed upon the slightly mandarin language as the regularities of traditional metre tether our reading of it to accepted norms of tonal variation. Thus the elevated language of the poem's first stanza, undercut by the mundane phrase, "Light poking past his nose" in stanza two, is assimilated into this coherence as an instance of irony. And, of course, the poem displays a narrative coherence: the "events" are seen from an apparently consistent point of view located outside the actors in this little drama, and this omniscient narrator tells us all we need to know to understand it.

Harwood's employment of the traditional strategies for the generation of this fictional narratorial identity works because it inscribes her poetry within a tradition (essentially non-modernist) which predisposes us to allow those effects to be produced, which activates our search for a unitary subject of enunciation and prompts us to create one in our reading of the text. But to claim that the poet is thus somehow present in her poem, that the coherent, unified point of orientation in all this duplicity is actually her identity as heard in her "true voice", would be to make the same mistake that Professor Eisenbart made to his peril. That is, we would be mistaking signifier for signified, duplicity for simplicity.

A reader skeptical of the theoretical background of this discussion — one who feels, for example, that the identity of the poet is unproblematic, since it is "there in the language of the poetry" in a commonsense way since it is the poet who writes the poetry — might raise two objections at this point. First, such a reader might claim that what I have pointed to above is the way poetry always works; that it is simply the way the poet becomes present. There are two answers to this objection. On the one hand, this is not the way all poetry works. There is a large and traditional body of poetry, loosely called "dramatic", which has never aimed at the presentation of the poet's voice at all, but which seeks to make audible the voice of some *dramatis persona*. Furthermore, a great deal of poetry since the beginning of the modernist period has worked to negate or call into question the nature of identity in poetry. And on the other hand, this objection overlooks the fact that these procedures do not enable the poet's identity somehow mysteriously to be "present", to be manifest to the passive reader in something of the way that light is manifest in a room when we turn on the switch. Rather, the identity which appears to be present is a fictional construct, created by the reader in the act of reading.

The second objection the skeptical reader might well raise at this point is that if what I have pointed to is true, then it is simply another example of a brilliant and protean poet being hard to pin down. In one sense, of course, this is true. And my choice of "Ganymede" as the poem to discuss would seem to back this up, since the poem lacks any obvious pointers to, or point of reference to, the poet herself. But my argument is that what I have claimed for "Ganymede" holds for all her poetry. It will therefore be necessary to look at a poem in which the poet seems to speak openly, directly, unequivocally in the first person.

Poems of this kind seem to become more prevalent after her first volume. Certainly *Poems Volume Two* contains a number of poems in which the poet seems to have dropped some of the impersonality of her first book. A commonsense critic could plausibly claim that Harwood's career as a poet demonstrates a growing willingness to emerge from behind the masks she had once adopted, and "to speak about herself in her own voice", a process which has culminated so far in such poems in *The Lion's Bride* as "Mappings of the Plane", "Oyster Cove Pastorals", "A Quartet for Dorothy Hewett", "Dialogue", and "Mother Who Gave Me Life". Such a way of putting things, however, unavoidably lays one open for confusing persona with reality, as could be done with "Father and Child" (*S.P.* p. 109) which, while appearing to be autobiographical, is claimed by the poet herself not to be. A more accurate way of describing what has happened can be obtained by employing the terms of the present discussion. In Harwood's more recent poetry, a fictive identity of the poet herself has been created and located at the centre of the poetry as part of its subjectmatter. The effect of this is to create the illusion that the subject of enunciation and the subject of the enounced are one and inseparable: that is, that the "woman in the poem" is actually the poet herself somehow "present" in her work, and that the gap between signifier and signified has been magically annulled.

One brief poem in which this effect is clearly evident is "An Illumination" (*Lion's Bride* p. 38). It is not one of the more complex poems in this volume, but its apparent simplicity, its air of straightforward candour, makes it an appropriate poem to discuss in this context. The title suggests enlightenment and clarification, with perhaps a shade of revelation as well: an illumination is something which comes usually unexpectedly, or in unlikely circumstances, or through an unlikely agent. And, of course, this is precisely what happens within the poem's narrative. All in all, the title suggests a sudden and unexpected access to truth, and it is deliberately and discreetly ambiguous as to whether this is what the poem is about, or whether this is what the poem is, and offers us. The point of this ambiguity is that we are thus predisposed to read the poem as both "about" illumination and as itself an act of, a moment of, illumination. However an illumination is also an artful and decorative embellishment of a text, as anyone familiar with medieval manuscripts knows.

A straightforward thematic interpretation of "An Illumination" is easily accomplished. The poet – well, at least the first person speaker of the poem – is walking "in a poor part of town" in winter, troubled by the memory of a dream which has prompted thoughts of her own death and insubstantiality. Depressed by these thoughts and also by the bleakness of the neighbourhood, which fills her with "neurotic angst", she comes across a child playing in one of the gardens who asks her, "Are you a lady or a bear?" The question is apparently prompted by the "warm coat of yellow wool" which she is wearing. When asked for his own opinion, the child replies that he thinks that she is a bear, and smiles at her in response to his own joke. After wiping his nose on her coat, he runs inside, leaving her with the illumination of that smile as a "useful" memory to set against her earlier thoughts of insubstantiality and "the flux of time".

As in the two other poems I have looked at, in this one the figure of the child is prominent. In "In the Park", the children were the agents for the woman's dispersal of identity, they were the scattered constituents of her identity as dispersal, as non-identity. In "Ganymede" the boy is the duplicitous signifier, signifying both perfection and corruption; being the point of contact of youth and adulthood, he signifies both, but only each as being not the other. "An Illumination", by contrast, seems to present the child in a positive aspect, as that which confers solidity and identity to one who has, temporarily, lost them. It can thus be seen as having close affinities with "An Impromptu for Ann Jennings" (*S.P.* p. 76) and "Matinee" (*S.P.* p. 77). Still, the child is not as unequivocal as might appear at first sight. It is against the apparent solidity of her own daughter that the speaker/subject appears so insubstantial: "I put my arm round my daughter's waist / and it curled through her like a mist." (Even here, it seems, we can find echoes of "In the Park".) Yet this so substantial daughter is, within the poem's narrative, actually a dream, a mere image signifying the substantiality which is the other of the speaker/subject's wraith-like withdrawal. Already we have a significant reversal: within the primary narrative of the poem we have a secondary narrative which concerns a dream by the substantial figure who is the primary narrator. Within that dream narrative, the substantiality of the dreamer is negated in relation to the apparent solidity of one of her own dream images.

In contrast to the dreamed daughter, however, the boy in the poem appears to be not only solid but also real. He figures in the primary narrative and, it seems, gives it its point. But he does so by not telling the truth. When asked by the woman whether he thinks she is a lady or a bear, he answers that she is a bear. Of course they both know that he is playing a game, or making a joke. Hence the smile which, emerging from such angst-laden surroundings, illuminates the woman. The boy is, in fact, engaging in metaphor. In her coat, which is "fuzzy with a thick golden pile", the woman is clearly bear-like and embraceable. (In general, children look upon bears as a cuddly — which they usually are not.) The boy is enchanted by her appearance, rapt from the mean reality surrounding them into a world of fantasy, different in mood but not wholly unlike the world of the woman's dream, which is also a world of fantasy. Under the influence of this fantasy he consciously misnames her. Yet by naming her as what she is not — neither human nor female — he restores her substantiality, re-establishes her identity.

But the question to ask at this point is, of course, just whose is this identity which has been re-established by such a contradictory activity — re-established, it appears, by being denied? It is, obviously, that of the "I" who is the narrator of the poem. Does this mean that she is Gwen Harwood? Naturally, only a very rash critic would hasten to say yes, particularly given Harwood's history of masquerade. Yet certain features of this poem actively encourage us to equate the woman in the poem with the woman who wrote it: the poem deliberately adopts strategies aimed at encouraging us to elide the signifier and to take the signified, (the woman in the poem, the subject of the enounced) as the person who has written the poem, and thus as a manifestation of the poet's self-presence.

The first of these strategies is a simple one: the use of the first person narrator, a powerful inducement to compound speaker with writer in poetry (though rarely in fiction). Then there is compliance with whatever we might have been told in other poems, or have otherwise known, about the poet herself. The "I" in the poem is a woman, and has at least one daughter. She is also vexed by thoughts of death: many other poems in *The Lion's Bride* are similarly concerned with death. Furthermore, the "I" who narrates her story does so with the economy, the humour, and the deft editorial sense that characterize other Harwood poems, leading us to assume that since she shares these qualities with her creator she is thus the same person. (In this respect, "An Illumination" differs markedly from "Suburban Sonnet".)

Other strategies at work within the poem's formal elements serve to re-inforce this impression. The most obvious is the marked loosening of the rhyme scheme. There is still some rhyme in the poem, but it is not regular, and closer to consonance — for example, "afternoon / town", "wool / pile", "had / dead", "waist / mist". Even this fairly minimal half-rhyme becomes less apparent as the poem progresses, though "hair / bear" and "nose / glows" underscore the poem's crucial lines. Similarly, the formal metricality of the lines is far more relaxed than in many earlier poems. "An Illumination" is written in a four stress line which generally contains eight, sometimes nine, and on one occasion ten, syllables. The stresses are distributed within the lines in such a way as to be closer to syllabic verse than to iambic tetrameter. Also, Harwood has eschewed the quatrains characteristic of much of her poetry, the poetry being organized instead into four stanzas of nine, eleven, four, and three lines respectively. The first stanza consists of a single sentence, the second of four, the third of five, and the fourth of one. This disposition of sentence structure across line grid results in a flexible cadence far closer to "normal" or conversational speech than that of "Ganymede" or "In the Park".

Earlier, I argued that the employment of certain formal conventions served to inscribe Harwood's poetry within a tradition of poetic discourse which activates our search for a unitary subject of enunciation and prompts us to create one in our reading of the text. Enough of these elements remain in "An Illumination" to activate that search, and the coherence of the narrative line is the thread that holds it together. But the poem's suppression of the more obvious formal elements which signal that what we are reading is poetry, rather than normal talk,[6] has the effect of rendering minimal, almost inoperative, our awareness that the text we are concerned with is written rather than spoken. We "hear" the voice speaking within the poem and are led to identify it with the subject creating that voice. In other words, the "I" of the poem, the subject of the enounced, the brooding woman in her yellow coat, superimposes itself upon the subject of enunciation and hides it from view. "An Illumination" is then not written by Gwen Harwood but spoken by the woman who met the boy in that "poor part of town". But since the poem appears in a book of her poems, and in the first person, it must follow that the woman who met the boy and speaks the poem is *ipso facto* Gwen Harwood. Signifier (in this case the linguistic fictionality of the text) is elided by signified (the narrative fiction which is the "woman's" story told in her "voice".) The result is an access of truth apparently authenticated by the "fact" that the woman in the yellow coat speaks to us with the poet's true voice: an illumination indeed.

That such an illumination is apparent rather than real, fictional rather than transcendental, should be clear, I hope, from my argument. It is an embellishment of a text, rather than an access of enlightenment to or by the poet. For when we look to find the identity of the poet, we find the identity of a fictional figure obscuring it — a fictional character whose identity is, moreover, constituted of contradictions, defined as being what it is not, what she is not.[7] I hope it is clear, however, that this is neither a fault in Harwood's poetry, nor something peculiar to her characteristic protean evasiveness. It is a characteristic of all poetry which — as "An Illumination" does — purports to "speak directly" from poet to reader, to eliminate the intervention of a persona, and which seeks to minimize our awareness of the necessary mediating activity of language, of any signifying system, of any textual intermediary. Contrary to commonsense expectations, it is not that the fictional is elided by the originary, which was the motivation, I suppose, behind the practice of "confessional" poetry (a contradiction, obviously, of terms). Always, and inevitably, because of the textual nature not only of poetry but of the subject itself, the originary subject constitutes itself as text, is available — not only to us but to itself as well — only in fictional form, and works to be elided by, obscured by, its own fictional construct.

I wrote earlier that the process which establishes Harwood's sense of identity as a poet — within the texts which constitute her as a poet — is akin, rather loosely, to masque. By this I meant that it is artful rather than natural, being conducted according to certain agreed rules and procedures, and has unmistakeable associations with dissimulation. I should also have said that whatever identity as a poet Harwood has is established only by our reading of the texts she makes available to us. (I know nothing, and can know nothing, of her own sense of herself in her own reading of her texts, except what she tells me — which is, inescapably, yet another text.) For her masque to make any sense to us, we must also understand the rules. This is made easy for us by the fact that the rules governing her masque have been operative within poetry in English since the Renaissance, when the masque originated. We react to them automatically — so much so, usually, that we are unaware that what we react to is artificial, artifice, and not an ineradicable human trait. To do this is to undervalue the power of the human mind to devise fictions, and the power of human society not only to perpetuate them but, often to our peril, to naturalize them.

Harwood's poetry does not explicitly question the enabling rules of her masque. By this I mean that her poetry evades the modernist's conscious foregrounding of the fictionality of poetry, attempting characteristically to naturalize her discourse. This is done either through enlisting our support for her procedures by inscribing them within a pre-modernist tradition, or by attempting to erase her artfulness by superimposing a fictional figure, a subject of the enounced, which occupies her authorial space. But her complex adoption of masks, personae and pseudonyms works as it does because of the fictional space poetry opened to her and which she understands so well. When she starts to sound most like "herself" and least like a "fabulous artificer" (who, we must remember, was also confined, though involuntarily, to an island), then we should most be on our guard. It is one thing to make truth sound like poetry, and that is the goal of all poetasters. It is an entirely different thing — and one which she can do so consummately — to make poetry sound like truth.

10

The Labyrinth of Dorothy Hewett

Although in recent years Dorothy Hewett has become most widely known as a playwright, she has also succeeded in building a firm reputation as a poet. Her first collection, *Windmill Country*, was published in 1968, and her two succeeding volumes have consolidated her reputation as a writer of powerful, vivid and direct poetry.[1] So direct has some of it seemed, in fact, that due to legal action her second collection, *Rapunzel in Suburbia*, was withdrawn from circulation and reissued only after several poems had been deleted.

Whatever one might think of such legal suppression of poetry (it would be hard to imagine Dryden or Pope surviving unscathed for long in Australia today) this incident points to the fact that a number of Hewett's poems seem to bear directly and openly upon personal, sexual and political relationships existing in the world outside poetry. In fact, in a time when the term "confessional poetry" was still seen as having some meaning, some of Hewett's poems seemed very confessional indeed. "Legend of the Green Country" (*Windmill Country*), "Memoirs of a Protestant Girlhood" (*Rapunzel*) and "Father & Daughter" (*Greenhouse*), for example, deal with adult child/ageing parent relations in a way which has since become familiar in Australian poetry:

> I can still see you reading the rain gauge
> under the almond trees
> where we buried the wax doll that winter.
>
> We played at horses whinnying down the lawn
> lay in the Willys Knight by the cubby-house
> re-enacting Death & the Maiden.
>
> When we dug up the wax doll with her melted face
> she had pride of place in the empty playroom
> victim of an acid attack.

(*Greenhouse* p. 69)

The model for "Father & Daughter" is to be found in Robert Lowell's *Life Studies*, which had a large impact on a number of Australian poets in addition to Hewett.[2] The poem consists of a series of apparently random memories, flash-backs in which the past is seized with the vividness of photographs in an album. The resultant collage serves to define the subject's attitude towards her childhood and those adults who figured in it, while simultaneously recreating it in its historical context.

Even more "confessional" in the Lowellian mould are poems such as "This Time" (*Rapunzel*) and "Winter Solstice" and "Summer Solstice" (*Greenhouse*) in which Hewett recounts the rhapsodies, the loneliness and the suffering of an adulterous love affair:

> It's over now,
> the waking up to pain,
> the compensatory eating's almost stopped.
> On a diet I'm even interested in other men.
> My calendar measures months.
> My capacity for faithfulness was always limited.
> Yet there's a dreariness, not visionary at all,
> old flicks, old times,
> the sepia snapshots in my family album.
>
> (*Rapunzel* p. 52)

Poems of this kind, addressed as they are to a "you" who is clearly the other partner in the relationship, seem to approach the condition of letters. This effect is furthered by the colloquiality of language, which strips it of any foregrounding effect in a free verse that moves with the natural rhythms of speech. The result is a poetry which hardly seems to be poetry at all: the "art part", as John Ashbery calls it, seems to have been eradicated. In its absence we seem to have virtually unmediated access to the thoughts and emotions of the poet herself, before which the language discreetly effaces itself, rendering itself invisible so that the "reality" of the poet's situation can shine through all the more immediately.

If the term "confessional poetry" is to have any meaning, then it must refer to poetry which produces this effect.[3] It is a poetry which appears to provide us with as close as we can get to the unmediated presence of the poet's personality, no matter how complex it might be, in its act of undergoing experience: in other words, the experience of reality itself, which is the same as the reality of experience. In such poetry, the effect is not so much that reality has been transformed into language, and far less that it is reality signified by language. Rather, it is as though language has been transformed into reality: it has surrendered its linguistic nature as a system of signifiers to become concrete, immediate, the very thing itself, real life.[4]

An example might be found in the opening of "Living Dangerously":

O to live dangerously again,
meeting clandestinely in Moore Park
the underground funds tucked up between our bras,
the baby's pram stuffed with illegal lit.
We hung head down for slogans on The Bridge,
the flatbed in the shed ran ink at night.

(*Rapunzel* p. 42)

There is a breathless rush about this evocation of the excitement of youthful idealism and commitment tinged with danger, accentuated by the fact that the past tense does not enter the poem until its fifth line. But as the poem progresses — because it is, after all, a poem — it becomes clear that the Revolution actually was constituted by words and has become a story: "WOW! WHAT A STORY! . . . guerrilla fighters / wear cardigans and watch it on The Box." Even Mrs Petrov, wife of a Russian defector and the subject of a famous photograph showing her being hustled across Darwin airport by two burly Russians, is a "shorthand typist, / hiding from reporters". Not even sex can escape this invasion of the word: the bed is "the flatbed in the shed [which] ran ink at midnight", and the "pulling at the crutch" in the last line is done in the name of a brand of trousers:

But O O O to live
  so dangerously again,
their stamina trousers pulling at the crutch.

Stamina, it now appears, is an attribute of the trousers, not of the revolutionary men. The effect of this ending is precisely to put into question the dangerous life — not only its danger but its actual liveliness — which the poem began nostalgically to recall, and the revolution itself which, it appears, was always already words: "illegal lit." and "slogans". Thus a poem which seems to start with an instance of words subserving the reality they describe can be read as an exemplum of how words supplement and supplant what they signify. An engagement with reality is, in fact, nothing more than the manipulation of "mere words" for those who fail to understand that reality does not inhabit words in some magical way, to become present to the extent that words render themselves transparent. The only reality that words have is their own as signifiers within that system of differences which we call language: the only power they have is derived from their not being what they signify. To ignore or forget this is to remain passive to the power of words, and of reality, not to wield it.

I have no argument whatever with the kind of poems once labelled "confessional". In fact, a number of these, by Hewett and others, are important contributions to Australian poetry, just as works by

Lowell and Ginsberg are to American.[5] My argument is with the notion of "confessional poetry" as a critical term. Unfortunately, the fact that the term itself has largely dropped out of use has not rendered the notion itself obsolete: it underlies virtually all the current practice of the teaching of poetry writing in schools, and elsewhere, in Australia. In so far as the term signifies only a poetry which takes as its subjectmatter material traditionally reserved for the confession — sexual infidelity, drunkenness or other lack of control over appetite, and similar transgressions — it can be a convenient but not a very illuminating term. However any attempt to take it further is fraught with problems. On a practical level, a confusion of poetry with confession is evidenced by the thousands of spiritless outpourings of thought and feeling received by magazine editors every month. Practitioners of this enterprise are guided by the notion that sincerity is the ultimate test and, in most cases, the only one. Yet it is a commonplace that virtually all bad poetry is sincere. However in the best poetry of a "confessional" strain — and some of it can be very good indeed — the "art part" is not absent, as aspiring poetasters might think, but concealed. It consists precisely in its own self-effacement, a self-effacement which simultaneously conceals the fictionality, the textuality, of the poem's subject. This carefully sustained illusion produces a poetry which is actually a version of realism.

Australian criticism has traditionally favoured realism, so it is not surprising that Hewett's poetry in this mode was warmly received. It directly broached subjectmatter hitherto largely untouched in our poetry, in particular that of female sexuality, sexual need and its extra-marital fulfilment. It was also refreshingly frank in its picture of childhood and parent-daughter relationships. This, together with its abandonment of most of the trappings of an earlier generation's formalism, and its deployment of a free verse which appeared to convey not only the cadences of a direct and emotionally frank speech but also something like the movement of thought itself, gave the impression of a poetry springing directly from the emotional and intellectual core of someone with a wide and adventurous grasp of what it meant to live in Australia at the moment. Readers seemed to be in the powerful presence of such a person, whose thoughts and feelings flowed through the language of the poetry like water through a pipe. What must not be overlooked or misunderstood, however, is that this presence is not virtual but textual, produced by the reader in the act of reading and responding to the poetry. No matter how much the realist text disguises its textuality or attempts to efface its fictionality, the "speaker" of the poem — its speaking subject, the "Dorothy Hewett we hear" in the poem — is ineluctably textual and fictional.

❧ ❧

In using some of Dorothy Hewett's poems in this discussion of "confessional poetry" I do not want to give the false impression that this style is characteristic of all her work. Like her friend, Gwen Harwood, Hewett is a protean figure as a writer with a wide capacity for experiment, who has written a novel and numerous plays in addition to her poetry. Any reading of her poetry will immediately reveal a wide range of literary reference, ranging from Tennyson to Robert Lowell, from Lewis Carroll to Faulkner and T.S. Eliot. Also the various sections of *Rapunzel in Suburbia* are introduced by quotations from Tennyson's "The Lady of Shalott" while the book's title refers to the folktale figure. In fact folktale and mythic elements are frequent in her writing. Thus while some poems work to disguise their textuality in the way I have suggested above, all these other elements serve to emphasize it, drawing a necessary distinction between poetry and life. The poet herself seems to be warning us of our need to remember this distinction in the title of her poem, "Miss Hewett's Shenanigans", where a rococo series of adventures could serve as a parody of what some unsophisticated readers and colleagues might think of as her private life.

It is quite possible, of course, that this poem is an allegory of real events, a kind of private joke, having as its pre-text a crypto-narrative available only to the poet and those with whom she chooses to share it. If this is the case — and for all I know it may well be — it is nonetheless of little help to the reader who lacks the secret thread. It is, quite simply, for that reader a different poem, and the aim of any allegorical interpretation of his would have to be a decoding of the cryptic text in order to produce something like the hidden pre-text which, in its turn, might then reveal something about the reality of the poet's situation. Rather than approaching the poem in this way, (that is, as disguised or cryptic confession), I intend to look at the structures of power, of dominance and subordination, which it puts into place. In this way we approach a grasp of what the poem is saying in its own condition as a text.

Seen in this light, "Miss Hewett's Shenanigans" makes it clear that the Prince is the dominant one, the female subject subordinate — his subject in the political sense as well as being the subject in the poem. When at the start of the poem she "swans down" to meet the Prince, it is nonetheless a movement down, no matter how graceful or glamorous; while it is he who mounts, who mounts her. She can be his princess only by being his whore: and whichever she is it is by virtue of being his. This hierarchy is continued throughout the poem: the subject's career might be exciting, but it is so principally by association. The Prince can move apparently effortlessly through the drab world of political power where "the lights all fail" and where "Brehznev has cancer" without the drabness infecting him; he can even spirit them over the Berlin Wall unscathed. Perhaps his capacity to do this is due to his friendship with Nabokov, and to the fact that he has the autographs of "Picasso, Ghandi, Garbo, Pasternak", all workers of miracles in their various ways. The Prince thus signifies a Romanovian accretion of political and imaginative power untroubled by middleclass moral scruples: "Next morning he leaves, / taking all my roubles".

Yet the female subject is not powerless either; rather, her power is eclipsed or annulled by his, and is reasserted in his absence, in fact to annul his absence. It is she whose necromancy, calling up the dead in memory, brings him back after his death while "the dust settles from the chandelier / on his bald head". Better a live subject, it seems, than a dead object. The female may lack political power, may be only an accessory to the Prince's; yet she replaces him, and not only in the sense of taking his place — like Derrida's supplement — within the poem's narrative after his death. She also reinserts him, puts him back into place, not only within herself ("each night we couple") but within the poem's overall economy. It is thus her desire, which obtains from both his presence and his absence, which authorizes his dominance in the poem. Thus it can be said that her power is inseparable from her being a subject — in both senses of the word.

Read in this way, the poem tells us nothing about Dorothy Hewett, the "real person". Nor should we expect it to, as this would be to court the mistake that a naive theory of "confessional poetry" encourages, and to fall into the trap so flagrantly set by the poem's title. But it does tell us quite a lot about sexuality, desire, power and discourse.

I wish to turn now to two poems which seem far from the "confessional" mode: "Grave Fairytale" (*Rapunzel*) and "Psyche's Husband" (*Greenhouse*). Neither of these poems offers much promise of allegorical decoding in terms of a secret pre-text; and their folktale elements reinforce the strong quality of myth which they display, inscribing them within a mode of reading which generates a general (communal/common) rather than an individual provenance and descriptiveness. Both are concerned with sexuality and power, and both centre on a female subject.

"Grave Fairytale" (p. 90) is a reworking or revision of the Grimm folktale, but with a number of major changes.[6] In fact, change appears to be a major element in the poem, which begins by stressing it:

> I sat in my tower, the seasons whirled,
> the sky changed, the river grew
> and dwindled to a pool.

Whether this change also encompasses the subject however is not yet determined, though her passivity of the first five lines suggests that she is more static than all around her. It appears that only with the entry of the "black Witch" and, later, the Prince into the poem (into her tower) does her passivity leave her. Her activeness is found largely in her hair, which is the ladder for both the witch and the man. Not only is it her means of contact with the world beyond the tower; it is also the effectiveness of her power in relation to it, her phallic capacity to manipulate it:

I felt it switch the ground, the earth tugged at it,
once it returned to me knotted with dead warm birds,
once wrapped itself three times around the tower —
the tower quaked.

It is a "great net of hair" in which she would catch "a hawk, / a bird, and once a bear", and when she let it down for the man, it "hissed out / and spun like hail". However it also inflicted pain upon her: "My roots ached, / the blood dribbled on the stone sill" when "the glowing prince . . . the frame-faced bully boy" climbed it. The subject's only other definite action — strictly speaking her only definite action, since her hair seems to act of its own volition within this strange involition of hers; she herself seems incapable of either controlling or reaping the benefits of her hair's power — is in cutting her hair off and thus killing the Prince in his ensuing fall. Why does she do this?

The reason is that she is betrayed by what she has herself — by means of her hair — brought into her isolation. The first to arrive is the witch: "she was as much a part of me / as my own self; sometimes I thought, 'She *is* myself!" There is no reason given for the witch's access to Rapunzel's privacy, neither in the poem nor in the folktale. But within the poem the witch is indeed as much a part of Rapunzel as her own self, because she is sexually the other in relation to whom Rapunzel is constituted. Although "there was no mirror in the tower" Rapunzel has passed the Lacanian mirror-stage, the end of which "inaugurates, by the identification with the *imago* of the counterpart and the drama of primordial jealosy . . . the dialectic that will henceforth link the *I* to socially elaborated situations".[7] Rapunzel's drama is in not knowing this, in considering her subjectivity self-constituted and self-defining — a mistake made a century and a half earlier, and with similarly frigid results, by Thel in Blake's *The Book of Thel*. Thus she is not able to see the witch's appropriation of the prince's sexual activity as anything other than an expropriation from herself. Perceived by Rapunzel as totally alien to her own rigidly guarded subjectivity, sexuality thereby becomes bestial, inhuman, of conscious human significance only by its being repulsive:

I watched all night the beasts unsatisfied
roll in their sweat, their guttural cries
made the night thick with sound.
Their shadows gambolled, hunch-backed, hairy-arsed,
and as she ran four-pawed across the light,
the female dropped coined blood spots on the floor.

("Grave Fairytale" p. 91)

Rapunzel's response is to go frigid (the shears are "a stab of black ice") and to divest herself of her phallic hair, castrating herself. The result of this is to re-institute her isolation within a stink of (the prince's) death without now, it seems, any help of rescue, since she remains shorn of power, "bald as a collaborator". The reference is obviously to those who, during the 1939–45 war, were shorn if found collaborating with the Nazi regime imposed upon subject countries. In this instance Rapunzel is doubly guilty, she feels. First, by encouraging the visits of the Prince she has facilitated the entry of both the Prince and the witch into her tower, into her isolation, only to find them ignore and betray her, in their (bestial/sexual) involvement in each other. The second reason why she feels "bald as a collaborator" is that her attempt to rid herself of complicity with the "ingressors" has shorn her of her capacity to reconstitute herself as an identity or as a subject which is whole and faithful. To put it the other way round, it has confirmed her treacherous nature, her duplicity, her role as betrayer.

Rapunzel's repudiation of sexuality has reduced the black witch, her other, to "a little heap or rags . . . [which] grows smaller every year". The effect of her growth towards power has thus been to introduce her into the conditions which constitute power: there must be something to exercise power over or upon, there must be an other which thus constitutes the possibility of power. But she fails to see that her capacity for action — which is the same thing as her capacity for living and thus her capacity to be herself — is inescapably enabled by, and thus constituted by, the other. Interpreting the witch's sexuality as the loss of her own, Rapunzel destroys not only the Prince but also her other, the witch, and thus destroys the only and enabling condition of her power. Impotent, self-castrated, she remains in her tower, powerless, only half an identity.

A poem which is similar in style to "Grave Fairytale" is "Psyche's Husband" (*Greenhouse* p. 30). It is prefaced by two lines from Robert Duncan's *The Truth & Life of Myth*: "He is the Monster-husband who comes / to Psyche in the darkness of her wish-palace", but the poem draws as much on the tale of Beauty and the Beast as on Duncan or the original Psyche story from Apuleius. The opening setting is also reminiscent of that of "Miss Hewett's Shenanigans": the "myth-palace" in which Psyche waits has "marble halls", tapers, musak and carpets, while "a feast is laid". As such it contrasts with "the woodcutter's cottage . . . in the peaceful kingdom" where Psyche/the subject later lives. However, unlike Rapunzel, Psyche has not repudiated her sexuality when the poem begins, having born a child by her nighttime visitor. She is now waiting to greet him as a lover waiting for her beloved. It turns out, however, that the Eros of the Apuleian story is truly a beast:

> . . . the beast is upon me
> the stink from its snout   its sad pig eyes
> its fur ripples along my skin
> *kiss me*   it sobs   melodious-voiced   *kiss me*

This frightful revelation is enough to send Psyche "shrieking through the palace" in flight, significantly, though, snatching her baby with her as she leaves. Looking back, she sees that

> there is a toad with a horned head
> sadly plopping down the stairs behind me
> *kiss me*   it croaks   *kiss me.*

Apparently in retaliation for this repudiation of hers, the crow pecks her, drinking her blood, marking her as outcast from the myth-palace whose doormat spells an ironic "WELCOME". However "in the peaceful kingdom" she subsequently inhabits with her monstrous son, the crow seems to be her friend — as, indeed, do the toad and the beast. The end of this poem shares something of the quiet tone of the end of "Grave Fairytale", but it lacks the earlier poem's sense of total and irreversible isolation.

But of course the Prince/beast, Psyche's husband, has never been antagonistic to her. "It sobs", "it croaks", it supplicates, it wants to be loved. Furthermore, revolted as she is by it, in escaping its loathsome presence she takes with her their child who, by synedoche, signifies all the poem's aspects of animal sexuality or sexual animality: he has "the beast's snout   the toad's horn / & the crow's claw", while repeating his father's "kiss me". As in "Grave Fairytale", we therefore seem to have here another parable of power, but with significantly different results. Rapunzel's repudiation of sexuality entailed an annulment of her own power. But Psyche's rejection of her "husband" and of the "myth-palace" where she received him entails an embrace of maternal power which can metonymically reinstate the father within the child. Rapunzel's fate was the ultimate solitude resulting from self-castration; Psyche's is the loneliness of the phallic mother in relation to whom everything else is less than complete, less than human, less than beautiful.[8]

The strategy discernible in some of Dorothy Hewett's poetry for concealing the necessary gap between author and subject in the poem led me first to some discussion of the concept of "confessional poetry". I have now looked at three poems which render the "confessional" mode's apparent identification of author and subject increasingly difficult for the reader. I want to end by looking at a poem — actually a group of four closely linked poems — in which elements of fantasy and myth which impede such an identification are mixed with what seem to be direct revelations of the poet's privacies. Such a mixture is characteristic of much of Hewett's poetry, and serves to give the initial impression of a lively and deeply literate mind engaged in an honest and adventurous self-assessment by means of a wide-ranging sense of analogy. However, as I hope should be clear by now, such an interpretation, while clearly appealing to our common sense, is really an assimilation of the poetry to notions of realism which can still be rendered problematic by highlighting the textual nature of the Dorothy Hewett our reading of the poetry produces.

"The Labyrinth" is the final group of four poems in *Greenhouse* (pp. 99–104). Within that collection it serves as an appropriate culminating restatement of a number of the book's major themes: what is the value of love? of loss? of memory? of poetry? The labyrinth is both the Cretan one housing the Minotaur, and the lengthening accumulation of memories ("The labyrinth lengthens what remains? love!") Both labyrinths house their dangers: at the heart of the latter there is all that needs to be made sense of, and "even when the mirror shatters it's no solution / the thread of the past can never be broken". At the heart of the former are the castrating Cybele and her monstrous consort, the Minotaur: "the lurching monster lies / with the Ancestress".[9]

That the nature of this ambivalent content of the labyrinth is to be found in the subject's own present, and her memories of the past, is soon established. Acknowledging that "the labyrinth is a puzzle a maze / where you might get lost", she wonders just what is to be found there. Rapidly the "blurred visions" resolve through "misty rain / unrealizable loves" into something clearer:

> you arrive soft-footed out of the Spring
> Nureyev cheekbones blue shirt . . .

From this point on the poem moves largely within a contemporary world where the subject stands "in front of the boatsheds in the rain", or imagines herself as "a female Al Capone seeking / a miracle seeking the love / that will try once more". Those seeking a realist reading of the poem will find this the most accessible part, since it presents the subject dramatically involved in the familiar world of contemporary life. But presumably such a reading would have to designate those parts of the poem not of such a world as either metaphor or fantasy, bearing on the contemporary world of the subject's experience only analogically — unless, of course, the fantasy can be naturalized to a realist reading by means of some psycho-allegorical decoding such as I described earlier. The point that should be obvious is that a poem such as "The Labyrinth" — and in fact the whole of both volumes, *Rapunzel in Suburbia* and *Greenhouse* — resist such interpretation.

The "mirror" which the subject carries with her "into the labyrinth / to face the Cybele / to fight the Minotaur" seems to have the same function as that carried by Perseus when he slew Medusa: it protects her from the harmful effects of direct vision by necessarily mediating, and hence deferring, the presence of that which she will confront. The mirror, as we know, signifies self-recognition, and hence that seeing of oneself as constituted by/in the other which initiates the power of signification: in this instance it can be read as signifying the phallic power to signify itself, and in particular the power of art (that which we are not) to mediate the manifest world we call reality (that which it is not). But the gap thus opened within our apprehension of the world is not only the source of Lacanian desire. It can also can be the locus of isolation and loneliness, as when the subject imagines her departing lover "staring at [his] own reflection in the aircraft window". Or as when she reflects "I look in the mirror my hair turns white overnight." But if a window can reflect the loneliness of the present, it can also mediate the past:

> the garden in closed in infinity
> if you look through a narrow window
> you can photograph a girl reading under a clothesline
> a phosphorescent child with an ideal self
>   who is always beside her
> through the eyes of that child I still look
> at the world.

This window is found in the garden, the "Garden of Art" with its "heroes & lions / angels and gargoyles", and what the subject sees in it (that is, *in* as much as *through* it) is herself as young. It is not surprising then that in the poem's last part the subject declares "I must break the glass that reflects / the single image", since this "single image" is associated with solitude, solipsism, while the double image, the "child with an ideal self . . . always beside her" is not only the subject herself in the doubleness which constitutes her "identity". It is also the doubleness at the heart of the act of signifying, of language, of communicating. That is why "even when the mirror shatters it's no solution". The mirror, as art, is not the cause of this inescapable, constituting doubleness which can, in one mood, be read as alienation. To destroy the mirror would not change the essential condition of doubleness that it signifies any more than it would destroy history: "the thread of the past can never be broken". On the contrary, the mirror capitalizes on the condition of its own possibility, and in so doing it realizes its own power. Thus the poem ends:

the beast is garlanded   the Cretan girls toss on the horn
          the cock
I face the Minotaur   the moon turns on
                    my forehead
I stand in a planetarium whirling with stars.

The last line is not some kind of realistic, even defeated, "return to the mundane" after a momentary final voyage into a mythological past whose aim was either to invest the subject's own reality with a heroic flavour or to underscore the pathos of her defeat. In other words, the poem does not resile to the mundane. But neither does the poem end in some rococo apotheosis, some extravagant assimilation of the mundane present to the mythic past. Avoiding sentimentality, one would read its whole final section as a restatement of a mythic contemporaneity, of the persistence of strong archetypal patterns within modern suburban life as in ancient Crete. The fact that the past seems more dramatic and the present more mundane is due simply to the editorial hand of time: even a planetarium, for those alert to mythic continuities, is an image of the universe.

Concurrent with this reading, however, is its necessary and enabling other. If myth seems to be the essential structure of life such that conscious access to myth is a guide to meaning and assurance, it is none the less the product of an overlayering of texts, a grammar recognized rather than the speech it generates. To live with a sense of mythic assurance, to live in the present fullness of myth, is to live always with a sense that myth is prior — and hence other. Myth is recognized as such only by being prior — despite one's feeling that one's participation in it is present. As Duncan himself writes at the end of his book:[10]

  the soul   . recognizes wings
as flight long known   the color
  itself a universe   so near
only my hands counting   and eyes
  naming these things

holds at bay   what is   from me.

The last section of Hewett's "The Labyrinth" can afford the subject the assurance of mythic contemporaneity therefore only by a necessary recourse to the doubleness and discontinuity inseparable from, and in fact authorized by, myth's priority. It does this by entextualizing the subject as Artemis within a theatre (a planetarium) in which the mythic past, the universe, and she herself are accorded equal fictionality. Because of course the planetarium, read within this textuality — and, in fact, read also within the grammar of myth — "is" the universe, but the universe projected, the universe represented: that is, the universe as signified.

"The Labyrinth" is therefore truly a labyrinth. Constructed by an artist (Daedalus) to contain the monsters that are reality, it is reconstructed by an artist (Hewett) as that which her future subject — the "Dorothy Hewett in the poem" — must both penetrate (like Theseus) and escape (like its originary creator, Daedalus). It is thus the past recalled, as the prison from which she would free herself. She must go into it in order to get out; yet to get out, to be free of the Cybele and Minotaur, would mean to annul herself, to castrate herself, to blind herself, since it is "through the eyes of that child I still look / at the world" — and that child lives in the labyrinth, glimpsed through a window which is the subject's mirror rendered almost-transparent by her reflection on her past.

It is a labyrinth from which there is no successful escape — except in the exploration of it. Even the monsters of reality, Cybele and the Minotaur, can be found only within it, as can the departed lover: "Nureyev cheekbones   blue shirt / faded jeans / disguised as love". Love takes place there, though in this case in the past, and so does everything else. Because the labyrinth is the site of all things as they assume, or even approach, meaning. The labyrinth is the site of Rapunzel's imprisonment, and Psyche's "canopy of green leaves". It is the locus of revolutionary activity and its armchair nemesis. It is the ground of legal action against Dorothy Hewett's poetry and also of the strange activity which gets poems written. The labyrinth is discourse, discourse rendering itself always other than that which it is concerned with. Discourse is always, and can only be, predicated on division, duplicity, differentiation. Hewett's poetry demonstrates a firm conviction of the continuities of narrative pattern from mythic to present times. But it would not achieve anything of its present significance if she were not equally aware that no matter where the eternal pursuit of power is played out, it is only by inscribing herself within narrative, and hence within discourse, that she — and we — can have significant access to it. It is thus by her consequent involvement in discourse's labyrinthine duplicity that Dorothy Hewett's poetry reveals the way in which power can be comprehended, as distinct from merely suffered.

11

The Past Imperfect of Les A. Murray

And history,
So interior a science it almost seems
Like true religion . . .
– Peter Porter

To think about a writer's sense of the past is to do more than to think about how a writer views the past and to look at what kind of image of the past is created in the written work. It involves, in fact, thinking about the whole relationship, both conscious and unconscious, between a writer's art and the world it intervenes with. If this seems excessively general, it need only be pointed out that even if poetry is not always emotion recollected (whether in tranquillity or otherwise) it is only the poetry of the past, poetry already written, which we read. The act of writing a poem is that of inscribing the present outside itself, into a kind of past imperfect where its unfinished business will trouble readers in the future.

Virtually all poets, I would suggest, feel that the act of writing a poem somehow interferes with the normal process of time. A Horace or a Shakespeare claims that his art will defeat time's ravishing hand, being a monument more lasting than bronze or marble. Blake declares that "He who kisses the truth as it flies / Lives in eternity's sun rise", thus removing the whole debate from the realm of temporality altogether. On the other hand, Yeats's golden bird, "set upon a golden bough to sing . . . Of what is past, or passing, or to come", proclaims that art, engrossed in the past and the present, none the less has a prophetic function. But however we look at it, a poem bears upon time in much the same way as memory: something past which is not confined to the past, but which can emerge again in the present and take on new life there. Both poems and memories are aspects of the unfinishedness of the past, of — I wish to suggest — its imperfectness as distinct from its imperfection. The emergence of both of them into the present questions the intactness of the present, interrogating it with their imperfectness — which is apparently the imperfectness of what was once present and which, far from being finished, perfect, has come back from the past like the ghost of Hamlet's father in search of an appropriate, and illusory, finality. And just as memories can reveal by what they fail or refuse to recall, so too can poems signify by what they express silence about.

❧ ❧

Taken at its simplest, a concern with the past has been an explicit element in the work of a number of Australian poets. One immediately thinks of Kenneth Slessor, R.D. FitzGerald, James McAuley, or Francis Webb. These poets' interrogation of the stories or legends of navigators, explorers and precursors is frequently an attempt at locating moments of origin, moments whose apparently originary nature derives from their position at one end of a chain of temporal contiguity sustained by narrative. For example, Slessor's "Five Visions of Captain Cook" looks, among other things, towards the origin of Australia as a quasi-European culture in the South Seas. Webb's concern with explorer figures, particularly Edward John Eyre in "Eyre All Alone", on the other hand is an attempt at locating the originary moment of Grace within a redemptive ordeal of suffering in communion with the Australian continent.[1] For these poets, as for the novelists Patrick White and Thomas Keneally, the past and narrative go hand in hand, and from hand to hand. It is tempting to think that this narrativization of the past is not simply an attempt at locating and creating an Australian tradition, or identity, in any chauvinistic sense. It may also be seen as a manoeuvre to keep the past apparently accessible to the present. By asserting a metonymic contiguity of the past with the present, the moment of origin that the past is sensed to contain may be touched by narrative travel along the diachronicity of history. And perhaps this is, after all, of the nature of tradition. If the past is where we, both as a culture and as individuals, come from, then to lose all access to it would be such a drastic truncation of identity as to threaten identity entirely.

In the work of the poet Les Murray, however, the past figures in a somewhat different way. Murray has few poems in which the past is narrated: his free-ranging meditative, even ruminative, style can certainly narrate, but with the exception of his verse-novel, *The Boys Who Stole the Funeral*, narrative is not prominent. Even in *The Boys Who Stole the Funeral* the articulation of the story into sonnet-length segments arrests the forward movement of narrative, enabling lyric and meditative elements to subdue its linearity. Yet Murray is a poet who displays a striking sense of the past in his poetry, and he has written eloquently about it in a number of prose essays. That his sense of the past does not emerge as narrative is not unique to him, but it is worth noting that other contemporary poets with a comparable sense, such as David Malouf, Thomas Shapcott, Rodney Hall, and Roger McDonald, have all written about the past in conventional prose novel form. But the past, for Murray, seems more resistant to narrative than it does for these others, which is another way of saying that its mode of entering the present is different. It may simply mean that for Murray the past is more present.

Murray has written a number of prose pieces in which he discusses the past and what it means to him as someone living, and writing, in contemporary Australia. Of these pieces, one would want to pay particular attention to one entitled "On Sitting Back and Thinking about Porter's Boeotia" in his first prose collection, *The Peasant Mandarin*, and three from his second collection of essays, *Persistence in Folly*: "The Human-Hair Thread", "The Bonnie Disproportion" and "Starting from Central Railway — A Bush View of Sydney".[2] One would also want to pay some attention to his views on religion and the Roman Catholic church expressed in "Some Religious Stuff I Know About Australia", since his sense of the past has a distinctly religious dimension. However this latter essay's more explicit concern with the church, and its deployment of a more conventional Christian vocabulary largely absent from the poetry mark it as only marginal to the present discussion.

On the evidence of these prose pieces, one can see that Murray's sense of the past is an idiosyncratic amalgam of ancient non-Athenian Greek, Christian, Celtic and Australian Aboriginal elements strongly aligned with a deep belief in the abiding and traditional virtues of rural life. If this sounds like something of a jumble, I would want immediately to suggest that it is not. In fact, there is a deep consistency running through Murray's sense of the past, and all these elements are drawn into his thinking by the way they contribute to and shape a coherent view or pattern of belief.

Murray's childhood in the country had as its background the Free Presbyterian church. What to most people today would seem a sad aberration of the human spirit is described with almost amazing generosity in "The Bonnie Disproportion":

> The Murrays belonged to the strict non-conforming Free Presbyterian sect of Calvinism, which survives to this day in small pockets right along the east coast of Australia, from Geelong and St Kilda to Sydney and the northern rivers and thence up into Queensland. It is the true heir of the Convenants, this small church, still heavily predestinarian and given to an effortful plainness of observance intended as a rebuke to all papistical idolatry and opulence. Churches are utterly unadorned, and the only music allowed in them is unaccompanied singing of the Psalms; hymns

> are mere human songs, and an organ would be the devil's kist o' whistles. And yet the services have no silence in them either, no mystery, no awe; they are dry theological lectures interspersed with extempore prayers and the Psalms of David in Metre.
>
> (*Folly* p. 71)

It is little wonder that Murray's religious sense and his almost rococo enjoyment of linguistic richness should later lead him from such unadorned cheerlessness and into the Roman Catholic church. But the other pole of rural social life for members of the Free Presbyterians, as Murray points out in the same essay, was the house party, which served as a focus for the close-knit sense of community, of clan or tribe, which figures so prominently in his poetry:

> On the Sunday night, recitations and stories, and sometimes singing, were allowed. Many Australians have, away in the back of their memory, a feel for what is called in Gaelic *corracagailte*, which means a hearth fire when it has burned down to glowing coals late at night, and the deepest stories and the oldest, most profound traditions are brought out amid spellbound silence. It was our lens, that hearth, for looking back down the experience of our people right to the fields and attitudes of the Heroic age.
>
> (*Folly* p. 72)

This sense of a Celtic tradition which by-passes that of Anglo-Saxon or European Classical-Renaissance culture, and which has existed alongside it but which reaches further back and persists still in the quiet pockets of rural Australia, is central to Murray's work. His version of it is untinged by the nostalgic Irish nationalism so common in Australia, and it has come to him untouched by that puritanical version of Roman Catholicism which seems such a strange compatriot of the mythical Irish heroes. Its twin cardinal virtues are independence and community. That is why Murray sees urban life as inimical to it: cities smother a meaningful sense of community by being too large and too pressing, just as surely as they urge towards an anonymous conformity and stifle independence. It should be clear therefore that the high value Murray places on rural life does not stem from something uniquely Australian in it: he is not, for example, simply a belated follower of the earlier bush tradition with its associations of mateship, etc. On the contrary, he values rural life because it is the site and the perpetuator of a tradition and a group of values which predate not only Australia but the Roman-Christianization of Europe itself.

This tradition is not confined to Celtic culture, though its European version was brought to Australia by Irish and Scottish immigrants, Murray's ancestors among them. Murray calls it, in fact, a Boeotian culture, and claims that the culture of the Australian Aboriginals "is a Boeotian resource of immeasurable value for us all".[3] His essay, "On Sitting Back and Thinking about Porter's

Boeotia" discusses the notion at some length. By way of an extended preamble to a generous and searching appraisal of a poem by Peter Porter,[4] Murray contrasts the values of ancient Athens and its rival, the "rural, traditional-minded, predominantly small-holding Boeotia" (*P.M.* p. 174), birthplace of the poets Hesiod, Pindar, Corinna and (who knows? Murray implies) possibly Homer. "By contrast, the only great Athenian poets were dramatists. Athens' glory lay in her drama, her philosophers and her political theorists. All of these are urban . . ." (p. 175). Murray claims that Athenians "count" and their besetting vice is probably abstraction. But Boeotians "list" and "name".

> Boeotia, in her perennial incarnations, replaces theatre with dance or pageant — or sport; philosophy she subordinates to religion and precept, and in politics she habitually prefers *daimon* to *demos*. Mistrustful of Athens' vaunted democracy . . . she clings to older ideas of the importance of family and the display of individual human quality under stress. (P. 175)

In Murray's scheme of things, Athenian metropolitan values were the newcomers, spread later throughout Europe by Rome and subsequently to the rest of the world. But away from the metropolitan centres, Boeotia, "in her perennial incarnations" persists as a sub-culture, ignored, scorned or tolerated by the metropolis. Yet this "sub-culture" is in reality a deeply religious culture as old as civilization itself, whose centre is neither the Parthenon nor the Agora but "every place held sacred by any Boeotian" (p. 183).

This latter point should make it clear why Murray sees Australian Aboriginal culture as essential Boeotian. As the average Euro-Australian has only belatedly recognized, Aboriginal culture has, at its centre, a deeply religious attitude towards locality. This attitude has nothing to do with the possession of territory in the European (or, to use Murray's term, Athenian) sense. It springs, rather, from an individual or tribal spiritual identification with a specific place "*altjiranga*, that is, from all eternity". As Murray writes in "The Human-Hair Thread":

> In the Aranda view, the earth and the sky have existed *altjiranga*, that is, from all eternity. So have the supernatural beings who created the features of the earth and its human and animal inhabitants, and who continually reincarnate themselves in them. Some of the immense dignity of traditional Aborigines, when seen outside of degrading circumstances, obviously comes from their sense of being the present forms of eternally existing beings. A man who "owns" a certain ceremony or set of verses belonging to a sacred site does so because he *is* the supernatural being who indwells in that site.
>
> (*Folly* p. 10)

In such a culture, all myths are both eternal and eternally present. Our familiar distinction between past and present fails to hold, to be replaced by a kind of "sacred present" or "eternal" tense. Aboriginal myth narratives, properly speaking, do not describe events which took place in some remote "Dreamtime" which, consciously or not, most white Australians still think of as an indigenous Celtic twilight. (Murray's essay places specific emphasis on T. G. H. Strehlow's exposition of this common misunderstanding.) Nor do they act out again, verbally, events from the past, in the way I have suggested the narratives of other Australian poets do, asserting a diachronic contiguity through the chain of narrative. Instead, they are momentary realizations of narratives which have always been, and which always are — synchronically — in just the same way that their "owners" are the supernatural beings *altjiranga*, from all eternity.

Murray does not claim to be in full possession of this Aboriginal sense of spiritual presence (in both the metaphysical and the temporal sense), but his poetry and his essay "The Human-Hair Thread" both show a distinct familiarity with Aboriginal culture and an admirable sympathy with it and a willingness to learn from it. From the foregoing account, it should be clear how traditional Aboriginal culture tallies with his Celtic Boeotianism, being, in fact, yet another of its "perennial incarnations", thus providing a striking — and Australian — example of how the past is not past, and origin is always present. As he says, "Aboriginal art has given me a resort of reference and native strength, a truly Australian base to draw on . . ." (*Folly* p. 28). And if his poetry does not inhabit the mythic atemporality of Aboriginal poetry, it is none the less sustained by a sense of a past which is felt to be less past, and more contemporaneous, than in the work of most of his contemporaries. This is why Murray's sense of the past only rarely emerges in narrative: the past need not be gone through again because he feels it, albeit imperfectly, being gone through all the time.

Turning now to Murray's poetry, we can see how his Boeotianism has a double significance for his critique of Australian society. It entails a sense of the past as not past but co-present with, and within, the present. This, and its embodiment of "non-Athenian" values explains, as I have pointed out, his preference for proletarian rural community and clan, his suspicion of intellectual faddishness and urban internationalism, and his dislike of intellectual and social movements such as Feminism which challenge his radically conservative picture of the way human life should be lived. (I want to term Murray a radical conservative because I can think of no other way adequately to describe a man whose view of things is so independent, so coherent and yet also so explicitly pre-Athenian!) It stands behind his picture of two workmen at their tea-break in "The Mitchells", giving them something of an immemorial quality:

The first man, if asked, would say *I'm one of the Mitchells.*
The other would gaze for a while, dried leaves in his palm,
and looking up, with pain and subtle amusement,

say *I'm one of the Mitchells.* Of the pair, one has been rich
but never stopped wearing his oil-stained felt hat. Nearly everything
they say is ritual. Sometimes the scene is an avenue.[5]

(Murray has said of this poem that "I have a suspicion that one of the two Mitchells is an Aborigine" [*Folly* p. 15]). It informs the quality of sprawl in the poem of that name:

Sprawl is the quality
of the man who cut down his Rolls-Royce
into a farm utility truck, and sprawl
is what the company lacked when it made repeated efforts
to buy the vehicle back and repair its image.[6]

Although Murray claims that "Sprawl is really classless" and is "roughly Christian", despite the cut-down Rolls it seems predominantly working-class male:

Sprawl leans on things. It is loose-limbed in its mind.
Reprimanded and dismissed
its listens with a grin and one boot up on the rail
of possibility.

The self-possession that characterizes sprawl is supported, not by a sense of being heir to a long tradition, but by this sense of an immemorial centrality of human experience indwelling and, by and large, inalienable, ever-present. This is the quality that Murray considers Boeotian. His moving "Elegy for Angus Macdonald of Cnoclinn" sheds further light on its historical aspect in the final two stanzas:

The good does not go out of the past.
Angles of the moving moon and sun
elicit fresh lights from it continually;
. . . and the Otherworld
becomes ancestral, a code of history,
a style of fingering, an echo of vowels,
honey that comes to us from the lost world.[7]

What this is pointing to is a historical, psychological and even a spiritual equilibrium, and it is further defined in the poem "Equanimity":

> Whatever its variants of meat-cuisine, worship, divorce,
> human order has at heart
> an equanimity. Quite different from inertia, it's a place
> where the churchman's not defensive, the indignant aren't on the
>   qui vive,
> the loser has lost interest, the accountant is truant to remorse,
> where the farmer has done enough struggling-to-survive
> for one day, and the artist rests from theory —
> where all are, in short, off the high comparative horse
> of their identity.
> Almost beneath notice, as attainable as gravity, it is
> a continuous recovering moment . . .
> Christ spoke to people most often on this level
> especially when they chatted about kingship and the Romans;
> all holiness speaks from it.

(*P.O.* p. 24)

A sense of equanimity in fact characterizes almost the whole of Murray's most recent book, *The People's Otherworld*, from which "The Quality of Sprawl" and "Equanimity" are taken. There are, however, other notes in it as well, more disturbed and less at ease, and I will shortly turn to these by way of a conclusion. But before doing that, I want to look briefly at two sequences in which Murray's sense of the past figures prominently.

"Walking to the Cattle Place" (*S.P.*) is a sequence of sixteen poems which explores the centrality of cattle to a post-hunter/gatherer human civilization. As Christopher Pollnitz rightly points out, "The sequence is . . . deeply invested in the myths and the prestige of origins. It mines the childhood of the race and the poet's own childhood . . .".[8] But the strategy of the poem is not to delve back into the past so much as to reveal the past and the present as avatars of something immemorial:

> Far back as I can glimpse with descendant sight
> beyond roads or the stave-plough, there is a boy on cold upland,
> gentle tapper of veins, a blood-porridge eater,
> his ringlets new-dressed with dung, a spear in his fist,
>
> it is thousands of moons to the cattle-raid of Cooley
>
> but we could still find common knowledge, verb-roots
> and noun-bark enough for an evening fire of sharing
> cattle-wisdom.

(*S.P.* p. 63)

Today's children share "this deeply involved unpickable knot of feeling" with that early herdsboy:

At the hour I slept
kitchen lamps were sending out barefoot children
muzzy with stars and milk thistles
stoning up cows.
They will never forget their quick-fade cow-piss slippers
nor chasing such warmth over white frost, saffron to steam.
It will make them sad bankers.

(*S.P.* p. 61)

The modern world of banking and clerking ("It may subtly ruin them for clerks") lacks the nourishing, life-replenishing roots in that age-old and ageless concurrence of human and bovine interest that seems so essential to rural culture. The modern world is mechanical and reified, antagonistic to a rural Boeotian wholeness which will, none the less, persist despite it:

When Cloven Hoof and Wheel made war on a chair
and Hoof was burned to hide the holes in his back
that was indeed war
good people resigned from dancing and lived in the air
much wearing of black
then madness was easy. That day crumbles here. More future
in a little girl feeding the clean beasts rainbow cake.

It is a sight
to drain bad blood from whole capitals,
small calves butting her hands.

(*S.P.* p. 84)

"The cattle-place" that is being approached in this sequence is thus no particular farm, but rather that mythic state of mind and spirit which furnishes equanimity and which goes by the name of Boeotia: "Athens is lasting, but Boeotia is ever-new, continually recreated, always writing afresh about the sacred places and the generations of men and the gods" (*P.M.* p. 178).

Towards the end of "Walking to the Cattle Place" we read: "I am looking for the place where the names well out of / field stone". This is what happens in "The Buladelah-Taree Holiday Song Cycle" [*E.R.* p. 28] which is another sequence celebrating the rural life. In his essay "The Human-Hair Thread" Murray writes of this poem:

Around Christmas 1975, I conceived the idea of writing a cycle of poems in the style and manner of Berndt's translation of the Moon Bone Cycle. As I thought about it, I realised it would be necessary to incorporate in it elements of all three main Australian cultures, Aboriginal, rural and urban. But I would arrange them in order of distinctiveness, with the senior culture setting the tone and controlling the movement of the poem. What I was after was an enactment of a longed-for fusion of all three cultures, a fusion which, as yet perhaps, can only exist in art, or in blessed moments when power and ideology are absent.

(*Folly* p. 24)

It would indeed be a blessed moment if ideology were absent, rather than unconscious, and my underlying premise is that it never is.[9] Murray's attempted fusion of cultures is itself an ideological act, as is his arranging them in order of distinctiveness. In this arrangement, urban culture is clearly third best, while rural culture is shown as converging with the Aboriginal. Perhaps, more accurately, Aboriginal culture which was destroyed by white settlement is shown as re-emerging within rural culture, "ever new, continually recreated" in true Boeotian fashion. This is understandable if one agrees with Murray in his agreement with Peter Porter: ". . . our culture is still in its Boeotian phase, and any distinctiveness we possess is still firmly anchored in the bush" (*P.M.* p. 179).

One way this convergence occurs in Murray's poem (the only way that need concern us here) is in his Anglicization of Aboriginal place-naming practice, in which "names well out of / field stone" as a result of immemorial association. Thus the poem can talk of "the place of Bingham's ghost, of the Old Timber Wharf, of the Big Flood That Time" (*E.R.* p. 28), of "the place of the Plough Handles, of the Apple Trees Bending Over, and of the Cattlecamp" (p. 29), and of "the place of the Rail Fence, of the Furrows Under Grass, . . . of the Slab Chimney" (p. 31) and others.[10] In this kind of naming, a place and its significance are united and made accessible to continuing generations. The past is thus alive in the significance, the meaning, of place which children take in as readily as fruit:

> The trees are split and rotten-elbowed; they bear the
>   old-fashioned summer fruits,
> the annual bygones: china pear, quince, persimmon;
> the fruit has the taste of former lives, of sawdust and parlour
>   song, the tang of Manners;
> children bit it, recklessly
> at what will become for them the place of the Slab Wall, and
>   of the Coal Oil Lamp,
> the place of moss-grit and swallows' nests, the place of the
>   Crockery.
>
> ("Walking to the Cattle Place", *E.R.* p. 35)

Of this passage Murray writes:

> Section 11 continues the celebration of places, and describes the almost accidental acquisition of memory and significance by children; the children are learning ancestral things (and communing with them through the act of eating fruit) which will inform their sense of the world and of their country, and make it just a bit harder for them to become thoroughly alienated or effectively colonial. You might say they are absorbing the accidents of nationality.
>
> (*Folly* p. 26)

The point is that in this way of seeing locality, the past is as present as the features of the landscape itself, which means that it is not past at all, but indwelling, a quality of the present and not something other than it. Name and object named, signifier and signified, are apparently united as the gap between them is elided by a cancellation of the passage of time, which accumulates, rather than passes. Metaphoric rather than metonymic, paradigmatic rather than syntagmatic, Boeotia's perennial immanence is *altjiranga*.

Murray says in the same essay, "Aboriginal 'history' is poetic, a matter of significant moments rather than of development. To make it historical in our sense requires an imposition of western thinking" (*Folly* p. 27). Or as the poem says, "abandoned things are thronged with spirits" (*E.R.* p. 35). In Murray's poem the city dwellers on walkabout for the long weekend venture into this world and are momentarily replenished by it, even if they are only dimly aware why. At the end of their holiday they will re-enter "the heavy gut" of "that big stunning snake", the highway, and return to the city and their Athenian "Western thinking". But Boeotia will remain out there, watched over by a relaxed (equanimous) presence which, according to Murray's essay (*Folly* p. 26), places the region and its significance "in the universe":

> the Cross is rising on his elbow, above the glow of the horizon;
> carrying a small star in his pocket, he reclines there brilliantly,
> above the Alum Mountain, and the lakes threaded on the Myall
> River, and above the Holiday.
>
> (*E.R.* p. 38)

The (male) Cross places the region "in the universe" which, by implication is *his* universe, both by his brilliance and by the equanimity with which he carries "a small star in his pocket": one of the Pointers, perhaps, but a pointer also to our little world. Appearing in his own right only in the penepenultimate line of a long poem, the Cross signifies the transcendental signified as a ground of "perennial reincarnation" which can remove human destiny from the historical linearity, "that big stunning snake", that Murray identified with Sydney's holiday weekend, with its carloads of families leaving the city for their true origin, northern New South Wales: "Parasites weave quickly through the long gut that paddocks shine into" (*E.R.* p. 29).

❧ ❧

I mentioned earlier my premise that ideology is never absent from a text. It is most present when it is unconscious and therefore unnoticed. As Althusser pointed out, its presence is visible in what it omits from the text.[11] In Murray's case what is omitted from the text not only illuminates the ideology that forms the limits of its consciousness, it also bears directly on what we have been calling his sense of the past. It relates, in a strikingly immediate way, to his own origin.

The Cross, reclining brilliantly above the Holiday and carrying a small star in his pocket, points towards that pole which, in the southern hemisphere, is not marked by any star. The Cross shares his relaxed equanimity with Sprawl who "listens with a grin and one boot up on the rail / of possibility", and is "roughly Christian". An early avatar is the "fellow crying" in "An Absolutely Ordinary Rainbow" (*S.P.* p. 24) from whom a woman "receives the gift of weeping". Quite simply, in Murray's poetry the spiritual is remarkably male. This could, of course, be simply the result of subscription to western tradition, although the Roman Catholic church — of which Murray is an adherent — attempts a counterbalance in the prominence it gives to Mary, the Virgin "mother of God". But in Murray's poems, women and the female generally figure very little, and men and the male figure a great deal. Of the eight-two poems in the 1976 edition of his *Selected Poems*, only eighteen refer to women or use the feminine gender (six others refer to cows). His next collection, *Ethnic Radio*, added thirty-four more poems, of which seven make reference to the female. His later collection, *The People's Otherworld*, refers to it more frequently: in its forty-four poems, three of which are explicitly in memory of his mother, there are references to the female, or the feminine gender is used, in eighteen. Excluding *The Boys Who Stole the Funeral*, out of one hundred and sixty poems there is the barest reference to that "otherworld" which comprises the majority of Australia's population in only forty-three poems. Even this figure is arrived at by including the most cursory and conventional mention of the female, as in such phrases as "Ladies and gentlemen" (*C.P.* p. 127). Also worth noting is the fact that the city, which Murray disapproves of, is generally female, so that:

> When Sydney rules without the Bush
> she is a warders' shop
> with heavy dancing overhead
> the music will not stop
>
> and when the drummers want a laugh
> Australians are sent up.
> When Sydney and the Bush meet now
> there is no common ground.
>
> (*C.P.* p. 132)

In Murray's poetry, the people's Boeotian otherworld is predominantly male, inhabited by:

the warriors who have killed, and the warriors who eschewed
killing,
the solemn, the drily spoken, the life peerage of endurance;
drinking water from a tap,
they watch boys who think hard work a test, and boys who think
it is not a test.

(*E.R.* p. 34)

Murray's sense of the past sustains and informs a vision of the present which is significantly male-oriented, even male dominated. The Shorter Oxford Dictionary defines "equanimity" as "1. Fairness of mind or judgment, impartiality –1752. 2. Evenness of mind or temper; the quality of being undisturbed by good or ill fortune –1663". Murray's equanimity in the second sense depends on a rigorous separation of these two definitions such as to deny the first, the primary. It is not grounded on equalness, it seems, but on a persistent unequalness. This is highlighted by looking at the female figures in his verse novel, *The Boys Who Stole The Funeral*.[12]

This verse-novel is as male-dominated as the rest of Murray's poetry (one of the two male protagonists, we are told early on, is "famous for an epic fight with women" [p. 1]), but two women enter into the action. Gladys Dunn, "the remote and / country mother" who "sits up on her folded knees in her floral / skirt among the paisley of vegetable leaves and tendrils / and pretend trees of staked tomatoes" (p. 69) embodies all the rural virtues:

It is a pity we always had to be sensible
thinks Gladys Dunn, turning things back into her garden,
darkening the sweet-pea beds from a plastic bucket.
I've reached the age (again!) of taking stock.

She goes to the rust-still, algae-curdled dam
that is level with the garden, allows the bucket sinkage,
watches her daughter and Reeby approach past the feed-shed
and hauls up the bucket, brimming with loose shine and life-chains.

This is how I will meet everything in my life,
working at my jobs. (P. 51)

Gladys, like the other rural women we glimpse in the book, is practical, down to earth, creative — everyone's idea of a country aunty. She can sew a shroud as readily as she waters flowers:

I have to be competent again.
thinks Gladys Dunn, looking for rock salt
and bagging-needles and sheets,
well, it's a habit by this. (P. 12)

In contrast to such rural virtue is the feminist from the city, Noeline Kampff, who is the lover of one of the boys' fathers. She talks like this: "Who was that smartarse? Fucking ocker pig. You know him? . . . Fucking patriarchal Bjelke incest cretins? . . . They shit me? Is he staying?" (p. 47) and:

> I've found you you fucker I came
> all this way to find you you smashed my sisters down
> with a gaspipe you FASCIST it's time you were CONFRONTED.
>
> (P. 55)

She empties a bucket of beef blood over one of the boys (Reeby) and in turn has her face scalded with a kettle of boiling water by Gladys Dunn's daughter. The fact that Noeline Kampff is totally unbelievable as a character in the novel's narrative is not so relevant here as the fact that while the book shows a considerable diversity of male characterization, the women are presented only as polar opposites: rural earth-mother-aunt and urban fury. As long as the one verges on sentimentality and the other on absurdity, the female in *The Boys Who Stole The Funeral* can have no convincing central role in the narrative. Kevin Forbutt's final initiation thus takes place at the hands of two male spirits whose names conflate the Aboriginal and the Celtic cultures, Birroogun/Berrigan and Njimbin/Nimbin. *The Boys Who Stole The Funeral* remains a boys' story, with the female marginalized.

It is not my intention here to attempt a psychological explanation for this marginalization of the female in Murray's poetry, merely to draw attention to it and its consequences. But four poems point to a crucial absence at the centre of his poetry, the absence created by the death of his mother in 1951 when he was only thirteen. The earliest of these poems, "Cowyard Gates", tells of how the old family house has been demolished by a cousin who "didn't want an untidy widower ageing / on his new farm", and who is using the material scavenged from the old house for cowyard gates. The subject realizes that he has helped demolish the house too, for his own imaginative ends: "I had even ransacked it, / carried off slants of sunlight and of wind":

> . . . half demolished, it was almost an eddy
> standing there on the ridge,
> memory and loss in a grove of upright boards.
>
> Now Time's free to dissipate all the days trapped there:
> books in the sleepout, green walling of branches around
> our Christmas table, my mother placing and placing
> a tin ring on scone-dough, telling me about French.
> The first weeks of her absence.
>
> (*E.R.* p. 51)

Time has not dissipated, however, the mother's absence.

This central absence motivates the "Three Poems in Memory of

My Mother, Miriam Murray née Arnall" called, respectively, "Weights", "Midsummer Ice" and "The Steel". If one accepts for a moment, and cautiously, the claim to autobiographical candor made so clearly in the general title, one would say that "The Steel" is a poem of immense personal feeling, and one which took considerable courage to write. However it lacks the quality of Murray's best poetry, sounding aggrieved and argumentative in contrast to the equanimity of other poems in the same volume. Significantly, in this attempt to come to terms with the mother's death the poem resorts to narrative. The miscarriages suffered subsequent to the subject's own hurried birth and her eventual death through lack of prompt hospitalization are events from the past which do have to be gone through again in both anger and sorrow. The violent rupture of the family and the cruel intrusion of the mother's absence into the lives of the father and son stand where the mother's presence would otherwise be expected. This absence, this total unavailability of the mother, is the actual contrary of that immanence, that presence of the past within the present, which informs the metaphoricity of Murray's poetry. Or to put it another way, in this poem it is not the mother's presence but her absence which is present, an absence which cannot be eradicated, and which threatens the equanimity that Murray's sense of immanence sustains.

For the father, the result was a progressive turning away from the female:

> My father never quite
> remarried. He went back
> by stages of kindness to me
> to the age of lonely men,
> of only men, and men's company
>
> that is called the Pioneer age.
>
> (*P.O.* p. 35)

Whether the comparative absence of the female in Murray's poetry is in some comparable way the result of the pain of his mother's cruelly enforced absence can only be speculation. It is tempting to suggest however that this absence is what is left intact, almost as an object of reverence, between the opposing extremes of the country Aunt and the urban Virago in *The Boys Who Stole The Funeral*. Be that as it may, there is no doubt that her absence remained a powerful element, avoiding articulation within any poems by Murray until thirty years after the event of her death.

Turning to the two other poems in memory of his mother, "Weights" is a moving remembrance of a mother who could not bear weights, or children, after the subject's birth. In this poem the past lives on in the present, but so does absence:

She gave me her factual tone,
her facial bones, her will,
not her beautiful voice
but her straightness and her clarity.
(*P.O.* p. 30)

The other poem, "Midsummer Ice", is very fine indeed. Addressed to the mother, the poem recalls how as a child the son would carry ice in from the road to the ice chest, "the only utter cold / in all those summer paddocks". But, the son comes to realize, the mother is dead and, unlike him, can recall nothing:

I loved to eat the ice,
chip it out with the butcher knife's grey steel.
It stopped good things rotting
and it had a strange comb at its heart,
a splintered horizon rife with zero pearls.

But you don't remember.
A doorstep of numbed creek water the colour of tears
but you don't remember.
I will have to die before you remember.
(*P.O.* p. 31)

The last four lines are particularly significant. The son is divided from the mother by that "doorstep of numbed creek water the colour of tears" which is both death and the mark of her inescapable absence. Only by crossing that threshold himself can he reanimate the mother, enabling her to "remember" his childhood, and annul her absence. Her death, in other words, is the fatal rupture in the narrative line of his own life, and it can be annulled only by another, and equal, rupture on his part: "I will have to die before you remember".

It should now be possible to draw together the threads of this discussion of the sense of the past in Murray's poetry. On the one hand, we have seen how in his poetry the past is not, properly speaking, past at all, but indwelling, co-present with and within the present. The peculiar power of such a sense of the past is its ability to make origin seem accessible. This accounts for the poetry's confidence, and informs the moral values articulated in it. On the other hand, this sense has been sustained by the reticence of one major and painful element, by its refusal to be spoken. And where that painful past is now confronted and re-lived, it is as a cruel and premature intrusion of absence, of irreversible rupture and loss. Thus in Murray's poetry the sense of the past and the sense of its presence cannot be disentangled from the absence at its heart, the opulent immemoriality from painful personal loss, the sense of origin from irreversible and irreparable family rupture. Like the strangler fig of the northern New South Wales rain forests, the poetry weaves its baroque arabesques around an empty space which it both conceals and preserves. The poem "The Steel" ends by claiming that "Justice is the people's otherworld". One could also conclude that absence is the otherworld of presence, and Murray's poetry demonstrates how inseparable they are.

12

John Tranter: Absence in Flight

Since the start of the modernist era, the notion of a unified subject — identical within itself and free of external reference — has become untenable to many poets and other thinkers. And yet some such version of the Wordsworthian "egotistical sublime" has continued to leave its trace in much post-modernist poetry, almost as a reaction against the doubts, disillusions and evasiveness of classical modernism. In Australian poetry it can be seen most clearly today in the poetry of Les A. Murray, while its contrary can be perceived as a vital impetus in the poetry of Judith Wright or Dorothy Hewett. Yet extreme scepticism of a unified subject, a scepticism so extreme as to constitute in itself a disunification of it, also runs like a rift or fault-line through post-modernism, though rarely seen as clearly in Australian poetry, until recently, as in the poetry of the American poets Theodore Roethke, John Berryman and Robert Lowell. In the work of all three, this concern takes a psychological form rather than the social and historical form that gives to Pound's *Cantos* or Eliot's *The Waste Land* their plethora of cultural voices. Lowell's "I hear / my ill spirit sob in each blood cell, / as if my hand were at its throat"[1] for example, is a particularly tortured and psychologized version of Rimbaud's famous "It is a mistake to say: I think. One ought to say: I am thought . . . I is someone else. (*JE est un autre.*)"[2] The schizophrenic subject is a post-modernist equivalent of the modernist schizophrenic, or multiple, text.

More recently, the notion of the subject as construct has come back into prominence, particularly in relation to questions of gender. This inscribes the discussion again in social and ideological discourse, and in particular within the perennial nature/nurture debate, in terms roughly like the following. If we continue to regard the subject as something natural, something which can accept or resist — apparently at will — social, historical and ideological factors, then we remain at the mercy of what are, in reality, external determinants and constituents. Or, to put it even more simply: if we fail to see the subject as something which is constructed, then we will have no hand whatever in its construction, and will be mere passive objects of forces beyond our comprehension and control. On the other hand, if we recognize the true nature of the subject, an opportunity for intervention is opened. A fully autonomous, self-constructed subject is as impossible as a psyche without an unconscious; but some degree of control over the inevitable externality of subject construction is at least possible. I have earlier argued that when it comes to poetry every subject is a construct, having a textual rather than a virtual existence. However with the advent of modernism Pound and Eliot were early proponents of a poetry which foregrounded the subject in general as a multiple construct, internally different from itself, never actually present as itself. Any attempt at locating the "true" voice of Eliot or Pound present within the multiplicity of voices which is their poetry was misguided. On the other hand, earlier poets laboured to construct a subject which appeared to grow as naturally as a tree, and to sing as naturally as a bird. What was more, it was there for all to see.

In poetry, the apparently unified subject traditionally carried with it certain responsibilities. It was seen as the origin or source of the poem's utterance, which was not autonomous but the product of the poet's mind, or sensibility, or imagination, or psyche, call it what you will. Produced by the subject, the poem expressed, conveyed, enacted or otherwise made known to us — albeit often imperfectly — what the poet "had in mind". And the poet, being human, had in mind certain ideas or apprehensions about things which existed outside poetry or language. But we have already seen that the ostensible source of a poem's utterance is already a construct. And while it is theoretically possible that a reader may reconstitute exactly what some flesh and blood poet "had in mind" while writing the poem — just as it is theoretically possible that given enough time, typewriters and monkeys we may achieve a perfect rewriting of the works of Shakespeare — it is of no importance whatever, because it can never be ascertained or verified. Furthermore, the attempt to achieve such a reading reveals a mistaken notion of language as some pure medium of communication, like the totally unambiguous digital code used for musical recording, rather than an arbitrary system of signifiers deeply embroiled in the socio-historic circumstances of both authors and readers. The only poem of which the reader has knowledge is that which is constituted in his or her mind by the act of reading; and any claim that this is an Authorized Version — one which bears the sign and seal of the author's own authority — belongs rightly to the history of our insecurities rather than to literary criticism. Strictly speaking, Roland Barthes's claim for "the death of the author" does not mean that authors no longer exist.[3] It means that the role of "authorizing presence" which has been, from time to time, thrust upon authors by readers and critics is no longer sustainable — because it has always been an illusion, an illusion aided by the construction of an apparently unified subject who "stands in" for the author and obscures the fact of his or her absence.

In recent years a number of younger Australian poets have expressed distrust of the notion of poetry as a discourse bearing a moral or social message from an identifiable and unified subject, "the poet". The unofficial spokesman for these writers has been John Tranter, who collected the work of twenty-four of them in the anthology *The New Australian Poetry*.[4] In his introduction he discusses modernism in western art and literature, and aligns the work of the poets included in his anthology with this movement. In their poetry "words — the fragments of language the poet places in the special framework of a poem — have a reality more solid and intense than the world of objects and sense-perception", thus producing poetry which "demonstrates a value unencumbered by moralism, ego or social utilitarianism".[5] Tranter argues that this sets these poets apart from what he considered the prevailing moralizing atmosphere of Australian poetry at that time, an atmosphere typified by Vincent Buckley's poem "Golden Builders". A number of things about John Tranter's introduction to *The New Australian Poetry* are less than fully satisfactory, in particular the largely unexamined similarities and distinctions between modernism and post-modernism. There seems little point in discussing his arguments in detail, particularly in the light of the comment in an interview published in 1981 that his arguments are pragmatic rather than dogmatic.[6] However his running together of moralism, ego and social utilitarianism is of interest. Ego — what I have been calling the subject — is the central term here, the nucleus which keeps the other two in place. It is the source of moral opinion and the agent of social activity. If the subject's traditional constitution as identity is questioned, its function as author of moral and social concerns in poetry is also problematicized. Tranter puts it slightly differently in writing of a poem by John Forbes:

> Whatever else John Forbes may have intended his poem to do, it is at least certain that he is not concerned with persuading the reader to accept his view of human destiny; ethics, morality, religion and mythology are distinctly absent from the writer's concerns. (P. xxi)

One may well ask just what the writer's concerns are when they so studiously avoid such large areas of human experience, areas which were central to much of the poetry of Eliot and Pound, to mention only two of the classical modernists. If the answer is simply that such poetry shows that "words . . . have a reality more solid and intense than the world of objects and sense-perceptions" then we have more than a simple recipe for triteness and poetic narcissism.

We have a lack of understanding of the ineluctably linguistic, textual nature of all poetry.

It would be doing Tranter a disservice to argue that he falls into this simple trap. Instead, we would do better to accept the pragmatic nature of his argument, interpreting it thus as an attack on a certain role which poetry had assigned to it by a Christian/liberal humanist tradition dating back in English at least to Sir Philip Sidney's *The Defence of Poesy*. This is the role which insists that poetry both delight and teach,[7] and which led F.R. Leavis, an important influence in Australian university English departments and, according to Tranter, on Australian poetry of the 1950s and 60s, to praise Keats for his "moral and spiritual discipline".[8] Tranter is by no means alone in rejecting this role for poetry.[9] The humanist tradition which has sustained it has been under attack for much of this century, not the least by the contemporary American poets in whom Tranter has shown most interest, John Ashbery and Frank O'Hara in particular.[10]

It is not difficult to find an example from John Tranter's poetry to illustrate Archibald MacLeish's modernist and highly paradoxical statement of distrust of poetry as idea or opinion: "a poem should not mean, but be".[11] Although most of the poems in *Parallax*, his first book, are conventional enough in their procedures, later volumes take seriously Wallace Stevens's comment that "poetry should resist the intelligence / almost successfully".[12] The poetry's highly confident, dynamic rhythmic progression inducts the reader into a forward movement which we have come to associate with a clarity of purpose leading, in other poetry, to the disclosure of meaning. But in numerous poems an obscure reference, a plethora of proper names which may, or may not, refer to people or places, a frequently ambiguous or elliptic syntax, a predisposition for similes which reveal anything but similarity, and often a bewildering juggling of the discourse between possible speaking subjects or fragments of subjects — all this serves to defer meaning indefinitely. The result is often an obscurity which in the work of other poets might attract the charge of ellipsis or solipsism. However in Tranter's poetry this is accomplished with a purposive consistency which is not only stylistic but also stylish. Two examples will be enough for our purposes.

Crying in Early Infancy is a collection of one hundred sonnets published in 1977, and arranged in the order in which they originally appeared by the publisher, Martin Duwell of Makar Press, and not by Tranter himself.[13] While many of these sonnets are by no means unintelligible in terms of a conventional expectation of meaning in poetry, a number of them, including No. 92, are.

> Every frightened smile prepares
> blood for the borrowed floor and then
> morning on the street disrobe
> smiling as she glowered when
> you and Dick, do the repairs,
> fix the blue, the broken globe
> in that storm we know how
> to treat, now she licks her smile
>
> it's thunder, Dad, a heavy rain
> froth beside the drifting dhow
> the limpid waters of the Nile
> below, beside, a lark, a drain.
> Every newt with flickering fin
> guesses right, and turns it in. (P. 123)

Traditional strategies for deciphering this poem will not get us very far. The first three lines (to the word "street") present little problem, and thus offer the reader a (delusory) hope of successful understanding. Still, one would want to ask why the floor is "borrowed": are we being told of a situation in which someone has "borrowed" a room, a bed, for the night? A one night stand? This might explain the fact that the smile is "frightened" which in turn presages danger or damage ("blood"). But "disrobe" introduces the poem's first major dislocation. Is it second person present tense, or an imperative? The poem reveals no subject for "disrobe" yet provides no syntactical justification for it in relation to what has come before. And in fact syntactical uncertainty, indeterminacy, is one of the most obvious characteristics of this particular poem. However, other problems immediately arise at this point. Who is "she"? Who is/are "you": the speaking subject or someone addressed by the subject? We have no way of discovering who Dick is unless it refers to someone's penis ("you and [your] dick"?), nor who is being referred to as "Dad". As if this were not enough, the scene is suddenly located beside "the limpid waters of the Nile" even though it is generally well known that Nile water can hardly be described as "limpid". Perhaps the whole exercise is "a lark"? It would not be surprising then if the baffled reader, taking his cue from the newts, "turns it in", having guessed right: this line of approach is getting nowhere.

A poem such as this cannot be naturalized to the meaningful coherence that a reading of much other poetry establishes. More accurately, a poem such as this gains its whole point by infinitely deferring this coherence. For it should be recognized that without the reader's conventional expectation of constructing such a coherence the poem would lack all point whatever. I have argued elsewhere that reading is not an innocent activity, but an ideological act which, in Jonathan Culler's words is "charged with artifice".[14] One expectation central to both liberal and Christian humanist thought is that a text should be meaningful, that a reader should be able to "make sense" of it; thus it might not be fanciful to regard much twentieth century literary interpretation as based, ultimately, on the model of biblical hermeneutics. This would account for the frequent wish for a "final" reading, a total revelation of the "true" meaning. A poem such as the one we have been looking at thus gains its point by means of a kind of hermeneutic strip tease: offering to reveal all, promising glimpses of naked truth, it reveals only the surface of its own highly accomplished technique. Roland Barthes's comments on real, stage striptease in France seem apt here: ". . . we see the professionals of striptease wrap themselves in the miraculous ease which constantly clothes them, makes them remote, giving them the icy indifference of skilled practitioners, haughtily taking refuge in the sureness of their technique: their science clothes them like a garment".[15] It may be this quality of remoteness which has led Les A. Murray, for example, to criticize Tranter's poetry for being "disciplined out of any simplicity or largesse," since it eschews "the memory and aspiration of community" which, according to Murray, "have kept the best Australian poetry human".[16] Be that as it may, Tranter's poem seems the discourse of someone who refuses to "take part", who remains visibly absent.

Tranter has expressed his own awareness of this conspicuous impersonality, this absence, in his 1981 interview in *Meanjin*:

> On a personal level, I've always felt the need to maintain some kind of control over the way I think and act and speak. I don't know where that comes from but my personality is a reasonably self-aware, repressed one in a lot of ways. That comes through in the poetry. (P. 438)

This control takes on a formal aspect as well, apparent in many poems, which Tranter has described as follows:

> . . . I try one line of development and if that's no good I try another and see how far I can expand the original idea, and then I try to find a way of concluding that expansion and bringing it back to the start. Often my poems return in the last line or two to what has been posited in the opening, and I feel that's the way I have to get the poem completed. I have to tie one end up against the other so that it forms a circle, a box, or a complete unit.[17]

This formalist impulse, the desire to get the poems into a satisfying shape, is not surprising in a poetry which questions the shaping and concluding efficacy of statement or argument. It can be seen in the regular rhyme scheme of the sonnet I have been discussing. Even more significantly, it is found in the thoroughly traditional employment of a concluding couplet which appears to draw the preceding fragmented and unlocated discourse back into the frame of impersonal comment which the poem began with but which it somehow lost along its way. "Every frightened smile prepares . . ." approaches us with the apparent authority of generality: it is of the same order of statement as "Every person of good will . . ." or "Every guilty conscience must . . ." The poem's further development, however, undercuts this bland authority by revealing the disorder and fragmentation to which it can so readily give way. The concluding couplet marks a stop in that fragmentation: it is preceded by the poem's first full stop. "Every" repeats the poem's first word, marking that "return in the last line or two to what has been posited in the opening"; but with a difference. It is actually a return which denies return. Whereas the poem opened with what appeared to be the assurance of a general truth, the concluding couplet is not, in fact, confident generalization so much as descriptive of particulars ("Every newt with flickering fin / guesses right . . ."). And yet a further reversal occurs here too. Up to this point, the concluding couplet appears to be a statement of epistemological success, ("guesses right") of the kind which would underly such confident generality as that which begins the poem. But then the poem's final four words reverse this, acknowledging defeat ("and turns it in"). Starting with the kind of generalization that can be based only on epistemological confidence, the poem ends by echoing that confidence but only as a denial of it.

John Tranter's sixth collection, *Dazed in the Ladies Lounge*, was published in 1979. It contains a number of poems, each of thirty lines, which continue to resist the intelligence and which represent his most stylish and accomplished achievements in this mode. Five of these poems have alliterative titles linking prominent intellectual figures with various places in Australia which they have never visited: "Leavis at The London", "Sartre at Surfers Paradise", "Foucault at Forest Lodge", "Roland Barthes at the Poets Ball", and "Enzensberger at 'Exiles' ". With its reference to the German language and the Third Reich, only the last poem seems to be saying anything about the person mentioned in the title. "Leavis at The London" is typical of the others in that even the title is puzzling. If we are expecting to learn something about the English literary critic, editor of *Scrutiny* and baleful moralizing influence in Australian English departments and Australian poetry, the poem's opening lines are of little help:

> You need the money — your way of thinking's
> going out of fashion, and you're growing old.
> You need the make-up, and you need

the wake-up pills before the bombing run;
the flak is active tonight, you need
a glass of something sparkling and a deep
breath before you're ready for the fray.

(*S.P.* p. 149)

The question that immediately poses itself is just who is "you"? Is it F.R. Leavis, addressed by the poem's subject? Is it the reader, similarly addressed? Is it the poem's subject, being addressed by it/him/herself, the modern colloquial equivalent of "one"? It is true that Leavis's "thinking's / going out of fashion" but it is not true that he is going on a bombing mission. What has that to do, anyway, with the need for money, make-up and "a glass of something sparkling"? Does "you" refer to a number of different addressees, each with his/her separate needs? It might, but the poem does not enable us to distinguish them from each other. If the addressee is indeterminate — at least this far into the poem — can we determine just who is doing the addressing? Is it, as the title might suggest, Leavis? If it is, then all that the poem tells us about him by means of this strategy is that he sounds remarkably like Sartre, Foucault, Barthes and Enzensberger, and they all sound remarkably like the voice of the other John Tranter poems in this group. If the speaker is not Leavis, it is hard to determine who it is because of its refusal to position itself in relation to any addressee. Perhaps the next few lines will help to clear things up, as it seems that we catch a glimpse of someone:

On your way to the affair in the back seat
of a taxi you catch a face in the mirror —
bandages and a black eye, is that really
you? It's not Humphrey Bogart — you
should have gone to Acapulco like
mother said, but no, you had to take
the youth cure, then the bandage
loops across the screen spelling out
"Mad Dog" and you guess it's true.

Well, one can understand the need for "a glass of something sparkling" now; but who "is that really", whose face is seen in the mirror? Being a reflection, an image, it cannot be "really you", any more than the voice in the poem can be "really" John Tranter's or anything more than the poem's subject's. As if to underscore this deferral of presence, the bandaged face in the mirror unrolls on a screen (the media have intervened) to reveal no face, no identity, but to spell out a title, a signifier which "you" can only "guess" is true. This indeterminancy is further suggested by the comically ambiguous syntax of the first line and a half (is it "the affair", or "you", which is "in the back seat / of a taxi"?) and the mention of a film actor and a mother who could be the mother of both the addressor and the addressee or of either one of them (assuming, of course, that they are not one and the same). However it seems that indeterminancy can be dangerous, and that there is a "test of strength" which cannot be evaded or argued away:

> The shark pool looks inviting
> when they turn out the lights,
> but that's for after breakfast —
> breakfast on the terrace with the Krazy Kats,
> after the test of strength. Say goodbye
> to the Kodachrome mirage and the heavy
> petting, from now on your career
> shrinks to a point and your many enemies
> gather like a gerontology convention and
> whisper.

With the demise of the Kodachrome mirage we seem to be approaching closer to determinate meaning: perhaps age is the "test of strength" which cannot be denied, the moment of truth which comes to us all? This is certainly not stated in the poem, which even seems to deny it, as "breakfast on the terrace with the Krazy Kats" — which hardly seems an old person's way of starting the day — comes "after the test". Yet there is certainly — it seems — a stripping away of inessentials which is associated with getting older:

> After the Monkey Business, after
> a famous middle age there's nothing left
> but the engines turning over, the crew waiting
> in the moonlight — and when you take off
> the shadow on the speeding tarmac drops away.

Here is the return, towards the end of the poem, to what had been posited earlier: the reference to aircraft recalling the earlier "bombing run" and the "flak" (which is also a common metaphor for criticism of any kind). But if inessentials have been stripped away, what are we left with? Nothing, it seems, except a shadow which "drops away". The moment of truth, if and when it comes, reveals that truth will not be revealed.

The characteristic procedure of these poems, easily observed in "Leavis at The London", is to hurry the reader on, always on, preventing lingering or re-reading. This is achieved by the use of the second person which implies some kind of dramatic relationship between addressor and addressee which the reader is impelled to attempt to unravel, however unsuccessfully: "You need the money . . .", "Your good taste is so packed with reading . . .", "You are painfully conscious . . .", "You know it's dumb hippie magic, but . . ." are how some of these poems start. The language is colloquial, often slangy, and the sentences frequently run on over the line breaks, giving the impression of a voice in a hurry. This is accentuated by imagery which often refers to the world of fast cars, aircraft (often military), pop entertainment, movies, warfare. A thread of implied or impending violence runs through it, which also drives the reader forward in a search of comprehension. The result is a frenetic "surface" to the poetry which refuses to succumb to the reader's conventional or habitual desire for epistemological resolution, for hermeneutic satisfaction. This frenetic surface stands therefore as both contrast and counterpart to the impersonality on which I have already remarked, since it is the discourse of a subject which refuses to reveal itself except as a style of being concealed by a multiplicity of cultural codes without a centre.

Something like this is remarked by David Carter, in an excellent review of Tranter's *Selected Poems* in the journal *Scripsi.*[18] He observes that the "problem" with such poetry is not that it is non-referential, "but rather that it is *over*-referential . . . Rather than absence there is an abundance, an excess, or, in different terms, what looks like an overdetermination of its symbols". This excess of reference fails to resolve itself into a coherent subject, or what Carter calls a "self": "As signifieds seem to slide beneath signifiers so the self, *any* self which the poetry appears to uphold, is divided and dispersed, found everywhere and nowhere, like 'style' itself. Nevertheless, a hypothetical unconscious persists, felt in the process of reading as that which is resisted, displaced and over-laid." I am not so happy with the notion of a "hypothetical unconscious", which would seem to bear on the reader's desire to feel that *someone* or *something* is producing the poetry, rather than focussing on the poetry itself. Instead, I would prefer to say that in so far as the reader experiences this desire, Tranter's poetry problematicizes it — and the whole question of the subject in poetry — by offering the subject as nothing but a style of being not visible.

There is a danger of becoming predictably repetitive in poetry of the kind we have been looking at. If every poem were infinitely to defer meaning, or even the illusion of meaning, then at least in this respect every poem would be the same. And although the same can be argued for poems which do satisfy our hermeneutic imperative (that is, they all "get somewhere", so we already know in advance how they will end) nonetheless in many cases each poem "gets" somewhere different. Besides, poetry of epistemological striptease, fascinating and enticing as it is, depends on its opposite for its ability to function, every bit as much as does real striptease. If we had no desire for sexual fulfilment, its arousal-only-to-be-frustrated could not take place; if the desire to "make sense" of a poem were not a major factor in the reading of any poem, then a poem's resistance to this desire, its refusal to comply, would achieve nothing for either reader or poem. I am not implying here that such poetry is parasitic on conventionally "meaningful" poetry, nor that it is some kind of sport or game which poets can play in their less serious moments. On the contrary, it represents the other side of the discourse of that poetry, the side which it is one of the tasks of the more conventionally "meaningful" poetry to obscure, even to appear to conquer. Yet as T.S. Eliot's "Burnt Norton" puts it:

> Words strain,
> Crack and sometimes break, under the burden,
> Under the tension, slip, slide, perish,
> Decay with imprecision, will not stay in place,
> Will not stay still.[19]

Within the coherences of more conventional poetry one can read the threat of incoherence; and within the incoherence of some of John Tranter's poetry, as in John Ashbery's, one is tantalized by the possibilities of coherence — but coherence deferred. In the world of visual art, the paintings of the late Armenian-American Arshile Gorky are as close an equivalent as I can suggest. There are also distinct similarities with the current vogue in sculpture for building machine-like objects which function mechanically, but to no conceivable mechanical end.

However not all of Tranter's poetry is as enigmatic as my account might suggest. Many of the sonnets in *Crying in Early Infancy* can be construed into meaning in a thoroughly traditional manner, which perhaps accounts for the popularity of that book among critics who are sympathetic to Tranter's work.[20] These sonnets certainly contain obscurities of reference, and almost all of them are characterized by that impersonality which unsympathetic critics such as Les A. Murray would consider an evasion of human communality. But a number of recognizable themes recur in these sonnets: art (including pop art and entertainment), alienation, a general sense of malaise (it would be interesting to count the number of headaches that are suffered in Tranter's poetry), and war:

> In a crude circle of dust and stubbled grass
> children are playing soccer. All else
> is olive brown and blue reduced to powder.
> Outside the boundary the referee
> draws a line, cutting off an easy talent
> from originality. A small dog like a movie star
> drags a grown man across the field,
> and his friends follow, asking what to do
>
> with the stricken afternoon, and why is the man
> crying. The circle of burnt grass grows
> smaller, and somehow the game is accommodated
> in the grip of politics. In a dark brick

building on the other side of the world
a man is carefully inspecting a clip of bullets. (P. 111)

John Tranter has rather disingenuously denied that *Crying in Early Infancy* is "a book written in the surrealist mode with dreamlike poems", claiming that "That's not true at all. It's not a catalogue of dreams, it's a collection of poems!"[21] Of course it is a book of poems, but a number of them, like No. 60, work to create a dreamlike fluidity which in this case generates a claustrophobic tightening such as one experiences in nightmares. The "crude circle" of the soccer field shrinks to "the grip of politics" in the third last line. The dust and burnt grass slip easily into a suggestion of warfare, as does the game of soccer, which is itself a contest ritualized by the presence of a referee. It may be the case that the man is crying because he realizes that warfare is a contest without a referee who "draws the line". The claustrophobic effect is further generated by the shrinking of the outdoor, summer-struck playground or playingfield to "a dark brick / building" in which the minute inspection of "a clip of bullets" is being menacingly performed by an anonymous man. This poem thus works by means of the same referential "slippage" as the two other poems we have looked at. But whereas in those the result was a deferral of meaning, this sonnet generates a tightening sense of menace all the more intense for its apparent inexplicability and anonymity, as things refuse to stay peacefully in place.

There are a number of poems of this kind which would serve to conclude this discussion. The cheerfully satirical and parodic "Ode to Col Joye" (*S.P.* p. 138) displays one aspect of Tranter's poetry which a concentration on the less referentially located poetry might serve to neglect: the witty, deft, satirical mode, often choosing as its targets contemporary Australian poets. In fact a satirical streak runs through a great deal of the poetry, producing an intriguing blend of acerbic astringency and irreverent fun. Or there are the two ambitious sequences, "The Alphabet Murders" (*S.P.* p. 69) and "Rimbaud and the Modernist Heresy" (*S.P.* p. 126). The first is a complex, elusive poem which seems to characterize itself at the start of its eighteenth section:

Reaching the excuse for verbal intemperance we find
the best argument persuades us to strain out from poverty
to excess, though the profit of this striving
is not in the final chapter but in the zooming
between two worlds of action, neither being of interest
without the gasping towards the other, which is the circus
where we get whatever valuables we come across
and it is not "reality" nor "art" that keeps us hot
but the idea of "hurtling", down the road between
the promise and the freaky now. (P. 83)

And although, as the poem goes on to acknowledge, Yeats did not work this way, it is not very far from Wallace Stevens's claim that "Natives of poverty, children of malheur, / The gaiety of language is our seigneur".[22] The latter poem, "Rimbaud and the Modernist Heresy", is an extended consideration of the French writer as poet, rebel, renegade, and radical. It is one of Tranter's more pressing poems, acting out a radical assessment of its own possibilities. The sequence starts and ends with what seems a firmly locatable subject:

Sitting by the river under damp trees
I listen to the wind in the leaves
whispering hatred and loneliness . . . (P. 126)

and

Learning, where the deeply human
is the object of a fierce knowledge,
can reach an imitation of the style of love,
but in that future under whose arrogant
banner we have laboured for our own rewards
we shall both be gone into that
unforgiving darkness. (P. 137)

Such a subject constitutes or situates itself as the romantic rebel; but like the historical Rimbaud, and like the poem itself, it refuses to stay fixed. The result is a poem which seems both deeply concentrated and remarkably elusive, the subject again revealing itself as that which has no visible nature of its own with which to authorize such roles as that of romantic rebel. These roles come to it from outside, from culture or from history, and are not an expression of the subject but an impression on it. The subject itself appears only, as I said before, in a style of remaining invisible within their multitudinous flux.

Rather than examine these rather long poems in any detail, however, my ends will be as well served by looking at a later poem which was awarded first prize in a national competition run by the *Australian* newspaper in 1985. Written since the publication of *Selected Poems*, "Lufthansa" is too long to quote in full, but brief enough to encompass in this discussion.[23]

Since one must oversimplify, we can start by saying that the poem is "set" within an aeroplane flying over the Alps, as the subject drinks a glass of lemonade, observes the skill of the aircrew which keeps them safe, and thinks of a woman called Katharina who is "sleeping elsewhere / under a night sky growing bright with stars". From such a resume, it should be clear that the subject of this poem is firmly located as an "I" who appears in the third line and whose observations and musing form the substance of the poem. Although the "I" becomes, in the ninth line, "you", and then later "we", "us" and "me", this fluctuation between pronouns articulates a casual colloquialism rather than the subject's multiplication or fragmentation. (Still, the fact that it can address itself as "you" indicates — as surely as the colloquialism does — the subject's lack of identity with itself. However, this is not foregrounded in this poem.)

At the poem's centre lies the question, "And what is this truth that holds the grey / shaking metal whole while we believe in it?" The lines immediately following this question fail to locate any salvational truth:

> The radar keeps its sweeping intermittent promises
> speaking metaphysics on the phosphor screen;
> our faith is sad and practical, and leads back
> to our bodies . . .

And in fact the search for truth is abandoned as "the Captain / lifts us up and over the final wall" of the threatening Alps and the subject recalls Katharina, perhaps tenderly, perhaps gratefully. Is this all the "truth" that is needed to keep us safe — our bodies, and the memory of human friendship? Such an answer seems inadequate. Memory, after all, is not truth, any more than it is the *ding an sich*. Memory is what stands in for truth: the memory of Katharina occupies the space made available to it by her physical absence. Furthermore, in this poem, memory is entrusted to the "grey / shaking metal" along with the subject who holds or experiences it: they are simultaneously vulnerable.

In effect, "Lufthansa" is constructed back to front. What keeps the concern going — the poem on its journey across silence, just as much as the plane on its flight over the "ice reefs" of the Alps — is the skilful exercise of technique. The first half of the poem is a celebration of it:

> I'm struck by an acute feeling of precision —
> the way the wing-tips flex, just a little
> as the German crew adjust the tilt of the sky.

A similar skill characterizes the cabin crew:

> you notice how the hostess, perfecting a smile
> as she offers you a dozen drinks, enacts what is
> almost a craft: Technical Drawing, for example,
> a subject where desire and function, in the hands
> of a Dürer, can force a thousand fine ink lines
> to bite into the doubts of an epoch, spelling
> Humanism.

This is the same skill which maintains "the smile behind the drink / trolley and her white knuckles as the plane drops / a hundred feet". Precision, skill, craft: fusing desire and function, they bite into doubt just as Dürer's etchings bit into the doubts of the late Middle Ages and helped to spell out Humanism. This is what keeps "the grey / shaking metal whole while we believe in it". The poem has answered the question before it has been asked. But the question is asked where it is, because the subject desires something more metaphysically satisfying than the provisional, than the practice of skill or technique. This is why the poem continues by searching for an absolute which will replace the "sweeping intermittent promises" which both hold out the possibility of a wholeness of truth, and testify to its absence.

It may well be that Humanism was a lie, dear gorgeous nonsense etched with a mixture of skill, determination and delusion over the face of the abyss. Whatever it was, it certainly was not truth — any more than poetry, which proceeds with its own mixture of precision and unjustified confidence to navigate the pitfalls of life and the hazards of language. Yet both Humanism and poetry were, and continue to be, effective praxis. It is too early to tell whether "Lufthansa" marks a rapprochment with Humanism on John Tranter's part. David Carter comments in his review of *Selected Poems* that some of the latest poems return "to the representation of a 'slice-of-life' or a brief dip inside character . . . Perhaps this represents an attempt at sentiment, a search for a kind of 'breakthrough' that the premises of the earlier poems seem to deny or resist."[24] Certainly "Lufthansa" conforms to this pattern, while holding no illusions about any successful outcome to a search for truth. And apt though it may at first seem to be, Frank O'Hara's famous statement that "You just go on your nerve"[25] does not sum it up. As the moment of danger passes and the plane approaches "a dictionary of shelter", the subject's demand for truth is supplanted by memories of friendly contact. Memory speaks out of absence, it exists only by virtue of the absence, the non-presence of what is remembered, including truth. But here it is not the absence of the subject, as in many earlier poems, that accomplishes the poem's direction. It is someone else's absence that facilitates memory in the subject, so that memory supplements skill, or nerve, or technique — such as that of the efficient aircrew — and humanizes them. This is how "desire and function" combine at this point in the poem, bringing it to a poise, a repose, "under a night sky growing bright with stars". No destination has been reached, least of all truth. Everything is all, still, up in the air. But for the moment, even if the poem is still " 'hurtling', down the road between / the promise and the freaky now", we feel that it is being guided by more than meticulous skill.[26]

13

"*Innocence Had Lost Its Voice*": *Poetry of the Great War*

In his introduction to *Shadows from Wire* Geoff Page remarks that "rarely since the 1914–18 war ended has Australian interest in it been higher", and he continues by citing a number of recent films and books which have both expressed and stimulated that interest. *Shadows from Wire* and *Benton's Conviction*, his recently published novel, and a further anthology of Australian war poems, *Clubbing of the Gunfire* edited by Chris Wallace-Crabbe and Peter Pierce, are all further evidence of this interest.[1] One intriguing characteristic of this interest is the difficulty those who evince it have in accounting for it. As Page puts it, "For reasons not easily explained the 1914–18 war and the states of mind of those engaged in it have increased greatly in significance for Australians in recent years."

Wallace-Crabbe and Pierce, in their introduction, are more speculative but no more conclusive when they claim that around 1973 "Great War themes became suddenly important, as it were spontaneously". And they continue:

> It may be that the sheer process of time had made these materials imaginatively vivid at last. It may be that the cessation of Australia's military involvement in South-East Asia both released and provoked the writers' imagination. Or it may be that these writers silently influenced one another. (P. 12)

Whatever the case, these writers continue, "the impact of that first major war was both concentrated and powerful; the mythology presents it as our first true blooding". They point out, however, that so far the Second World War has had no comparable effect within Australian writing.

It is hard to see why "the sheer process of time" should single out the Great War for such elevation into mythic significance. Myths are not made by time but by history, by readings of history. It is perhaps more likely that by the mid-1970s Australian writers and historians became aware that Australian participants in the Great War were rapidly becoming scarce, and that the memories of those who were still alive were rapidly becoming unreliable. Interest in the Great War may have spearheaded what has now become something of a national obsession with the lives and memories of those ancestors and precursors who are about to pass over the horizon into silence, and whose thoughts, memories and even delusions must be captured before it is too late. The invasion of Sunset Homes with tape recorders has become something of a sunrise industry. It also has something to do with a search for origin.

If we ask the question "The origin of what?" in the context of the Great War, then it may be wise to avoid sociological or historical speculation and turn to the poetry itself. If the poetry of the Great War did indeed produce a mythology, as Wallace-Crabbe and Pierce suggest, then present-day poems such as those in *Shadows from Wire*, written long after the event and by nobody remotely involved in it physically, may be construed as constituting a re-reading of that event and a de-formation or re-formation of the myth. Something like this can certainly be concluded from Geoff Page's decision to exclude all poetry written during the Great War itself from his anthology because he found "the quality of these latter poems to be depressingly low" (p. 9). And judging from the evidence collected in *Clubbing of the Gunfire*, he is right in this. Australian poets were even less equipped than their British counterparts with the means to articulate the enormity of that conflict.[2] There was certainly nobody of the artistic stature of a Wilfred Owen or an Isaac Rosenberg, or even of a Siegried Sassoon or Edmund Blunden. But their poetry is not without interest, even if that interest lies at least partly in what the poetry fails to speak. Page's effective silencing of poetry written during the Great War can understandably be justified in terms of its aesthetic ineptitude; but it can also be seen as an expression of the notion that those poets did not say their experience correctly, the right way — the way, that is, that present-day poets can say it. An earlier (phase of the) myth is thus silenced by a later one which displaces or effaces it. I will look briefly at these two moments of Great War poetry in an attempt to find out what is happening here.

Any discussion of myth today would necessarily call to mind such names as Northrop Frye, Claude Levi-Strauss and Roland Barthes. Any thorough discussion of their definitions of myth is beyond my means here. I hope that for the moment it might be sufficient to say that my own understanding of myth approximates to Barthes's definition of it as a second-order semiological system whose function is to naturalize what is in fact ideology,[3] although I would wish to add Derrida's dictum that each signified becomes in its turn yet another signifier in an endless chain of signifiers. Such an addition may seem at first sight to destroy the distinctive semiological character of Barthes's notion of myth, since it destroys the notion of metalanguage or, more accurately perhaps, makes all language a metalanguage. But the effect may be, instead, to restore to myth the diachronicity which Barthes's synchronic account deprived it of,[4] and which seems implicit in most other theories of myth.

Roughly, one could say that for traditional notions of myth (and I would include Frye here) the myth of myth itself is that of the Eternal Return, in which the narrative embodiment of some timeless, primordial, or archetypal ur-text finds its way into the world of discourse only to founder, as inevitably it must, in such a lapsed world, and fall, like Persephone into the underworld, into silence. This, however, is only the dark phase of the myth, which continues with the rebirth of a new narrative avatar of the ur-text which meets the same fate, and so on *ad infinitum*. Implicit in this picture of things is that the ur-text itself remains unchanged, being a timeless truth, an archetypal pattern, which willy-nilly dramatizes itself in discourse, over and over again. This truth may be a scientifically verifiable fact such as "Life has a tropism to perpetuate itself in a process which incorporates death" or some indisputable truism; but although it is common to call the ur-text itself myth, I would contend that this is a confusion. Myth occurs only when that truism takes on the flesh of language, when it becomes narrative and discourse, as indeed it must if we are to talk about it at all. The tale of Persephone, the story of the Corn God, the crucifixion and resurrection of Christ: these are the myths, not the ur- or archetypal pretext itself, which can perhaps be understood as an abstraction from the particular myths rather than as the *langue* which generates the variant mythic *paroles*.

Roland Barthes's account of myth, on the other hand, seems to be stubbornly secular. The difference comes about because of his introduction of the term "ideology" between the ur-text and the myth narrative. In his account, myth renders the ideology invisible, which is another way of saying that myth gives to contingent and even patently false texts the air of an eternal truthfulness. Whether this is as true of the great primordial dramas examined by Frye as it is of the "urban" and "cultural" myths Barthes examined is not particularly relevant here, though it would be an interesting exercise to attend to their ideological and cultural (as distinct from their "archetypal") dimensions. If one bore rigorously in mind that myth is the "writing out" (or "speaking out") in discourse rather than the ur-text which can be abstracted from these instances, then it is possible that the cultural specificities and ideological nature of these instances might emerge as less accidental or contingent than Frye, for example, would consider them to be. However more to my point here is that in all cases myth is a second statement, what Barthes calls a metalanguage, existing wholly within the world of discourse which is neither eternal nor necessarily truthful, and certainly never eternally truthful. Myth narratives may thus, as we saw earlier, fall into the underworld only to be born again in a new incarnation of the ur-text. But they must also, as other texts do, pass that invisible line dividing signifier from signified and be themselves subject to re-readings, misreadings and transformations. Considered in this light, myth, which naturalizes ideology by rendering its ideological nature invisible, may be seen as a series of displacements each capable of further displacement. In the case of Australian poetry concerning the Great War, the later poetry (that written about it today) demystifies the earlier and takes its place, transforming the myth rather than dispelling it.

It is hard to know quite how to read C.J. Dennis's poem "The Push" seriously today.[5] Yet its jingoism and its exaltation of Australianness are precisely those qualities which would guarantee its popularity when it was written:

> We've slung the swank fer good an' all; it don't fit in our plan;
> To skite uv birth an' boodle is a crime.
> A man wiv us, why, 'e's a man becos 'e is a man,
> An' a reel red-'ot Australian ev'ry time.
> Fer dawg an' side an' snobbery is down an' out fer keeps.
> It's grit an' reel good fellership that gits yeh friends in 'eaps.

Poetry that wears its heart so resolutely on its sleeve is in little need of demystifying: the message is loud and clear and, of course, not new. Temper democratic, bias offensively Australian:

> 'e lobbed wiv 'em on Egyp's sandy shore.
> Then Pride o' Race lay 'olt on 'im, an' Mick shoves out 'is chest
> To find 'imself Australian an' blood brothers wiv the rest.

It is warfare which has revealed the true gold in the heart of Ginger Mick: "Becos the bugles wailed a song uv war, / We found reel gold down in the 'earts uv orl our Ginger Micks". And mateship has been elevated to a religious dimension:

> Shy strangers, till a bugle blast preached 'oly brother'ood;
> But mateship they 'ave found at last; an' they 'ave found it good.

The recurring image throughout the poem is that of goldmining: "Ev'ry feller is a gold mine if yeh take an' work 'im right." War does that work, cutting through the overburden of birth, wealth, social position and so forth to reveal the true values of maleness and Australianness. A positive value is thus assigned to warfare, which is seen not as a site of bloodshed and suffering, but as that which removes the dross and worthless elements in order to reveal the heart of gold at the core of the Australian male. The War, in other words, performs the same function as the bush or the outback in much nineteenth century popular fiction and, like the bush, it is no place for a woman. The poem's elevation of maleness and male mateship is achieved at the expense of the female and of any notion of male-female relationships, and is in marked contrast to the Second World War poems of Kenneth Mackenzie in the same anthology. A man's "a man becos 'e is a man" and because he is not a woman, or a child. The good is defined as Australian, male, proletarian and egalitarian, in contradistiction to non-Australian, female, middle class and educated (note the poem's spelling) and hierarchic. The poem's democratic egalitarianism is thus enabled by a series of hierarchic assumptions which it attempts to conceal by failing to talk about them. Needless to say, it takes little perspicacity today to discover these assumptions.

A poem by Rae Desmond Jones in *Shadow from Wire*[6] provides us with another look at the Great War soldier. "The Photograph" takes as its object a young man much like Ginger Mick, and Jones reveals the negative aspect of the qualities Dennis's poem praised: the soldier's naivety, his vanity, his lack of education and his innocence:

> tom smiles proud
> of his uniform
>
> aware of
> his prominence in
> a rural scene
>
> hat set askew
> rakish & cliche,
> i almost hear
>
> the beer is
> rotten but the
> girls is fine. (P. 74)

The photographer, "who was doubtless / shrewd" (being French), and "some later / sophisticate" who has defaced the photograph by drawing a moustache and spectacles on it have already passed judgment on Tom's vanity, "and sentenced / him to eternity / or the scrapheap". But contrary to their cynicism, the poem then goes on to speculate on the subsequent fate of this soldier, who "looks as / though he would / love horses, / dogs & a glass / of beer". Did he die in bed, an old man? Was he injured and did he then live on, a cripple? Was he revisited by nightmares of the fighting? The poem answers none of these questions, all of which mark possible fates of the Great

War soldier, but which are of little real interest today because, as the poem concludes:

> i think i
> like him & feel a
> bit sorry because
>
> whether good or
> bad his likeness is
> sentimental junk
>
> which should be
> burnt.

Even as a mature or old man, Tom is naive, vain, ignorant and possibly incapable of learning much from his experience; but, for all that, not a bad sort of a bloke, the poem seems to be suggesting. Still, to cling to the photograph as though it has worth in itself is to be sentimental. That aspect of our (Australia's) past which Tom signifies belongs to the past, and "should be / burnt", expunged from the present. The fact that the poem does quite the opposite is not really a contradiction here; what Jones has done is to re-draw Tom's portrait in a likeness that Tom would never recognize.

We have come a long way from Dennis's paeon of praise to the golden-hearted Australian male. What has been gained, or lost, in between the two poems? Certainly, a degree of jingoism has been lost, and the naive faith that war ennobles and is in itself noble. And a certain realism has been gained, by which I mean a disillusioned, rather than a sentimental, comprehension of the facts of modern war. But Hal Porter's poem, "After September 21, 1914 AD", spells it out in its final stanza:

> Sunbonnet girls in pinafores
> still skipped; those funny men still chattered
> on gramophones — but innocence
> had lost its voice, no longer mattered:
> no innocence at all since then,
> never such innocence again. (P. 16)

A similar message can be read from the end of Alan Gould's "From Pozières":

> For seven weeks much iron fell.
> Nowhere was safe; some survived.
> Fewer returned to homes they knew.
> Some say the old world dies. For us
> nothing is the same. (P. 44)

And even today's schoolboys, in David Malouf's "Report from Champagne Country" (p. 46), are "pissed off with honour / boards and manhood's rare, impulsive gift" and the "gold-leaf heroes" commemorated in school assembly halls. One is reminded here of Wallace Stevens's "metal heroes that time granulates", such as the General Du Puy in *Notes towards a Supreme Fiction* of whom it can eventually be said that "Nothing has happened because nothing has changed, / Yet the General was rubbish in the end."[7]

Time and again, the poems in *Shadows from Wire* stress the loss of innocence when faced with the realities of war, a message which is also part of the burden of Roger McDonald's novel *1915* and David Malouf's *Fly Away Peter*. Chris Wallace-Crabbe writes in "The Shapes of Gallipoli":

> Horror grows more
> familiar than our blurred
> mothers and wives.
> Bivouacking in the Dandenongs
> I never thought of this for conclusion,
> the name of which is Death
> but it was a fellow from school that wrote,
> The bugles of England were blowing o'er the sea
> And how could I stay?
> To stay on Gallipoli was easy,
> as worm-fodder, as flybait,
> as honour. (P. 34)

In Roger McDonald's "1915", the poem, not the novel:

> No mother comes to help, although
> a metal voice is whining
> "boys, relax", as one
> by one they totter to their knees. (P. 21)

And in Les Murray's "Lament for the Country Soldiers":

> They didn't see the badge upon their hat
> Was the ancient sword that points in all directions.
> The symbol hacked the homesteads even so. (P. 14)

The soldiers' innocence is here constituted in their blindness to the double-edged sign of their calling, to its inevitable capacity to cut both ways. This "other side" of war emerges in another photograph, finally, as Thomas A. Shapcott writes of his father in "War":

> Proudly he sat for his photo in the glib slogan
> of his army uniform, before he sailed.
> The other side of war re-shaped that soldier,
> and the later pictures stare bleakly, exiled. (P.82)

It is, of course, entirely possible, even probable, that the generation of 1915 was more innocent than later generations. After all, few

Australians had first-hand knowledge of war and even less comprehension of modern war. It would have been as impossible for them as for their European counterparts to forsee the immense carnage, and the apparently interminable misery of mud and cold in Europe, or the stupid futility of Gallipoli. It is also true that many men joined up in what might well have been as much a rush to escape the boredom of everyday life in the Antipodes as it was a response of filial valour to the bugles of England calling o'er the sea. But that is not my point. Today's poets and novelists are not writing history, they are not researching and revealing the Great War with any particular pretensions to a scientific objectivity and impersonality.[8] Present-day poetry (as well as novels such as *1915* and *Fly Away Peter*) is engaged in constructing a new myth of the Great War — not in order to get closer to the "truth" of that particular historical moment, but in order to serve the needs of the present. This new myth re-reads the old in order to distort it, constituting the War as the moment of destruction of a primal innocence. This means, of course, that essential to the myth is the innocence destroyed, an innocence which Australia as a nation, and its young men in particular, had — so the myth runs — in the early days of this century (in the early days of our nationhood, one could say) and which later generations, it seems, have no longer, and cannot recover. As Shapcott's poem says, "wars do not finish: it is not over", and the scars, although "wilted over", remain scars. This is, in fact, the burden of Vance Palmer's fine poem "The Farmer Remembers the Somme":

> I have returned to these:
> The farm, and the kindly Bush, and the young calves lowing;
> But all that my mind sees
> Is a quaking bog in a mist — stark, snapped trees,
> And the dark Somme flowing.[9]

"After such knowledge" as another poet wrote shortly after the Great War, "what forgiveness?"

The phrase, that Australia "came of age" in the Great War, points to this same myth, which is homologous with the expulsion from Eden. Childhood is the age of innocence, and it ends, as it did for our first parents, with the taste of the knowledge of good and evil, and an awareness of death. Ginger Mick's heart of gold, "The physical perfection / Of those young soldiers, / The flower of the armies", belong to "the bonzer *stoushing* days / the *spirited* and *clean-cut* days"[10] which we can never re-enter, and which are as remote from us as its slang is outdated. Present-day poetry, therefore, creates a myth of the fall and the expulsion from Eden. By corollary it also creates a myth of a golden age of "innocence present" some time in the now unreachable past, separated from today's absence of innocence by the great divide of the Great War.

The creation of such a myth of the past is, of course, essentially a way of defining the present. Far from being disinterested history (if there can be such a thing) the poems in *Shadows from Wire* are highly motivated. Generally they declare themselves as the product of a harder, more cynical, less idealistic and less foolish world which can none the less be moved to compassion, indignation and pity. It is tempting to agree with Wallace-Crabbe and Pierce that this may be indeed the legacy of the Vietnam War and its accompanying protest movement, this affirmation of an ability not to be fooled by the promoters of war, xenophobia and patriotism. And when we turn to the section "Asian Wars 1950–1972" in their anthology *Clubbing of the Gunfire* we find, not surprisingly, a number of similarities with the recent poetry which deals with the Great War, despite the fact that Roger McDonald and David Campbell are the only poets in this section who are also represented in *Shadows from Wire*. The enemy, in this part of the Wallace-Crabbe and Pierce anthology, is not the Viet Cong but the politicians, a mindless bureaucracy and the military machine itself. As A.D. Hope puts it most succinctly and most memorably:

> Linger not, stranger, shed no tear;
> Go back to those who sent us here.
> We are the young they drafted out
> To wars their folly brought about.
> Go tell those old men, safe in bed,
> We took their orders and are dead. (P. 197)

Charles Higham writes:

> Five politicians count
> Their gains. They pierce a map
> With pins. Each wound is faint
> But deep. (P. 190)

R.D. FitzGerald denounces the "arrogance and greed" which is at the core of "the military creed / which tests all worth in terms of war" (p. 178) while Bruce Beaver declares:

> I would say No to patriotism's
> inflated toad anywhere —
> No to the nationalistic lie in the rotten teeth
> of all democracies, communes,
> imperialist church and police states. (P. 186)

And later in the same poem Beaver claims:

> There is no just war among ourselves,
> only the cannibalistic incursions
> of the inveterately immature

which raises the interesting question: If Australia "came of age" in the Great War and shed its innocence, how is it that there is an inveterate immaturity which embroils us in further wars? The answer would seem to be that coming of age was not a reality but indeed a myth (in the common meaning of the word as a cherished delusion), a myth which is sustained by relocating the enemy within, rather than outside, the nation — an ideological act *par excellence*.

Christopher Brennan, in "The Chant of Doom", had no doubt as to where to find the enemy:

> we read
> How the hosts of darkness burst,
> Ravishing, thro' Belgium first,
> Then with gather'd wrath amain
> Sweeping on the storied Seine,
> Sworn to wreck and ravin. (P. 41)

The rabble-rousing fury of Brennan's Great War poetry is legendary, and I imagine that it has less to do with patriotism than with the nationality of his wife. But there was nothing unusual at that time in Brennan's firm location of the enemy outside Australia and, in this instance, outside the Empire. In this he was joined by that well known nationalist Henry Lawson. But Harley Matthews's poem "True Patriot" (p. 49), which deals with the Great War, already finds the fanaticism of the idiotically patriotic Corporal and the "blood-mad generals" more of a danger than the official enemy. However it is only Kenneth Slessor's "An Inscription for Dog River" among the poems from the Second World War which sounds this note of bitter disaffection. Speaking of their commander, the dead proclaim:

> We, too, are part of his memorial,
> Having been put in for the cost,
>
> Having bestowed on him all we had to give
> In battles few can recollect,
> Our strength, obedience and endurance,
> Our wits, our bodies, our existence,
> Even our descendants' right to live —
> Having given him everything, in fact,
> Except respect. (P. 148)

Significantly, when John Millett's "Tail Arse Charlie" (p. 140) lays blame on the Allied airmen ("They are the ones / who fire-bombed Essen and Leipzig / ripped Hamburg from the memory of the world — / boiled park lakes / tore babies from mothers' hands with fire-winds") it is in a poem written thirty-five years after the event, and after the Vietnam War as well.

Generally, in the poems from the Second World War collected by Wallace-Crabbe and Pierce, the stress is on the pathos of war, epitomized by Slessor's "Beach Burial" or in Clive Turnbull's "Do This for Me, Then" which ends:

I remember a girl alone in the dusk,
I remember fine rain falling in green places.
I have put away the noise and the glare and the smell,
the swirl and the rise and fall, the faces.
Now I am tired.
I would be left to sleep in the quiet dark
down the soft years to heal me here alone.
Do this for me, then:
do not move the stone. (P. 154)

This pathos is mixed too with a sense of enormous vulnerability, as in David Campbell's classic, "Men in Green", or in Francis Webb's memorial to dead airmen in "Dawn Wind on the Islands":

Here, where they died, oblivion will burn
The moth-winged bomber's glass and gristle; weirs
Of time will burst, burying them; the sun
Casually mock a cross of stars.
And I have watched them die, wedged fast, below
The tumbling barracks and the yellowing page,
Each day more helpless and more desperate.
At dawn these agonies break loose and grow
Out of the rotted boards, the voices rage:
Cry, cry, but feel — but never forget. (P. 151)

In another fine poem, pathos is mixed with a resonant admiration of true heroism, as in John Manifold's equally classic "The Tomb of Lt John Learmonth, A.I.F." which repudiates armies or patriotism in a fine purification of courage:

I could as hardly make a moral fit
Around it as around a lightning flash.
There is no moral, that's the point of it.

No moral. But I'm glad of this panache
That sparkles, as from flint, from us and steel,
True to no crown nor presidential sash

Nor flag nor fame. (P. 120)

There is place for neither flag-waving patriotism nor for xenophobic hatred of the opposing armed forces in this poetry, which is surprising when one considers the moral enormity of the Third Reich and the long-lasting bitterness felt by some towards the Japanese. This suggests that the Second World War is not, in Australian poetry, a conflict in which morality and politics align but one, rather, into which politics hardly enters at all. The battle is not against the Axis powers, but for survival in the face of a capriciously malign universe acting virtually without human agency — as the last line of David Campbell's "Men in Green" makes clear:

And I think still of men in green
  On the Soputa track,
With fifteen spitting tommy-guns
  To keep the jungle back.   (P. 129)

Some of the most unusual Australian poems dealing with the Second World War are by Kenneth Mackenzie: "The Tree at Post 4", "Searchlights" and "Dawn, Post 3". All three are love poems, in which the woman that the poet loves takes over the particulars of war, transfiguring them into articles of love, before retreating again into the absence forced on her by the poet's military duties. Thus, in "Searchlights", when the poet sees

    the searchlights splitting the moonlight,
coldly caressing each other deep in the zenith
of almost-midnight, loving one another

like chill blue hoses of fireless flame gone amorous

he thinks of his beloved, whose

warm brown legs were the splayed beams,
the sultry heat of the room was night, fluid
and smooth against the searching limbs like milk.

And just as the searchlights "sought for a winged enemy", "inside / you sought and fought that way, too, and you won / now and again". In "The Tree at Post 4" the tree marking "this blazing desert of a post" transforms into the woman, then back again. Love, and imagination, it seems, can transcend war, but only temporarily. None the less, such transformation can sustain one even when it is over. Significantly, this transformation is a capacity of the female, whose identity is characterized by a radical instability, a tropism to participate in metaphor. The woman becomes the searchlights or the tree at the sentry post, transforms them into herself and empties them of their warlike significance in a sustaining, creative protean fluidity which contrasts markedly with her figuration elsewhere.

If we turn back now to poetry about the Great War written recently — to the poems in *Shadows from Wire*, in fact — we find the female projected in a somewhat different light. More precisely, the female takes on two figurations: Mum back at home, most probably on a farm,[11] and the woman in Geoff Page's "Home Front", which is brief enough to quote in full:

After the morning in Martin Place
with sidestepping faces and a clutch of white feathers
her tram sways home past harbour street-ends
uneasy with so much conviction.

The afternoon is given to verses:
tomorrow socks. Nouns are flags
heroically abstract and verbs
are tight with rightful anger

and she will speak of the Somme
as *a river of pure love*
a river from which perhaps
right now a telegram with name attached

will shatter her resolve forever
or make it iron with grief. (P. 54)

This, in effect, is the female as enemy, aider and abetter of the "blood-mad generals", handing out white feathers, penning patriotic verses for the newspapers, urging on the war and the appalling bloodshed by a kind of shrill ignorance. In her hands language and patriotism are confounded ("Nouns are flags") in a constriction of "rightful anger" which misreads "blood" as "love". She appears also in "The Clarrie Dunn Fragments" reprinted from Les Murray's *The Boy Who Stole the Funeral*, where her enemy signification is unmistakable:

Ah well. Did I tell you about the civvy
suit I borrowed, one London leave?

It got me a white feather, that,
outside a Bond Street shop
from a hoity-toity dame. She screamed
when I grabbed her, neck and crop,

and pitched her through the window glass.
I would not be Offered Up. (P. 100)

Such a woman "Offers Up" the young men for slaughter; she is aligned with the England ("hoity-toity" and in London) of Empire, of whom Lawson wrote approvingly, "She's England yet, with little to regret — / Ay, more than ever, she'll be England yet".

One would possibly expect this figure of the domineering and demanding female to be identified in some cogently systematic way with England, the colonial power, the Mother which the maturing ex-colony could now reject and whose power it could now come to evade. Such an identification would serve to expel this version of the enemy from within our midst, would make it (her) external. But, as we have already seen with "Home Front", this is not the case. And in "Poppy Day" by Graeme Kinross Smith she appears in a rejuvenated form as the young child — female — who like her precursors cannot believe that war and death are real:

> She has an answer:
> just think if we could
> tickle their tummies
> and make them stretch
> and fix them —
> that's a way.
> Ah no, my sweet, I say,
> dead, you're dead;
> you cannot come alive again. (P. 90)

The poem concludes, "The danger now I see / is that I half believe / this bloodless, sad perspective." The child's naivety in this poem both tantalizes the poet and saddens him by its lack of realism, its lack of maturity. It is bloodless, in that it denies the reality of bloodshed; but also because it lacks the substance of real life. To use the words of Bruce Beaver, this is the inveterate immaturity which we, as a nation, carry within us, and from which wars can still spring. It may be true, as Hal Porter's poem proclaimed, that "Innocence / had lost its voice". But the past perfect tense is significant. We may agree that, for the nation as a whole, "never such innocence again" will be ours. And yet . . . and yet . . . Innocence springs always anew, almost as though human nature has an inbuilt resistance to learning the bitter facts of life or, confronted with them, will learn them only reluctantly, as at the end of Shapcott's poem "War":

> And we, in the comfortable bedrooms,
> taken for granted always, innocent,
> were forced among the spaces of his acts and words
> to where his gains burned through like punishment. (P. 82)

The new myth of the Great War is primarily, as I said, a myth of the present. In this myth, the Great War is the cataclysmic moment in our collective past inaugurating the loss of an unsullied or simple, unambiguous innocence. The death of innocent young men narrativizes the death of innocence as "golden innocence" (the old myth), and its internalization as both a childlike unworldliness and as naivety, immaturity, gullibility, vanity: the enemy within. The mark of our new maturity is that we recognize the enemy now, not as external, but as internal. It is, in fact, precisely in the transition of the enemy from a foreign foe to an element internal to our own constitution that we have the tasting of the fruit of the knowledge of good and evil and the expulsion from Eden. Judith Wright's poem "The Killer", not included in either of these anthologies, expresses it succinctly:

> But nimble my enemy
> as water is, or wind.
> He has slipped from his death aside
> and vanished into my mind.
>
> (*Five Senses* p. 42)

However it seems that the poetry which constitutes this new myth of the Great War is mostly written by men. Of the thirty-two poems in *Shadows from Wire*, only two are written by women; and Christine Churches and Dorothy Hewett are the only women among sixteen male contributors. This could be the result of editorial bias, though my own reading among contemporary Australian poetry suggests otherwise. It could be argued, perhaps, that war involves men more than women, although I would not like to be the one to argue it. In fact, Geoff Page's "Inscription at Villers-Bretonneux" comments on this:

> Headstones
> speak a dry consensus. Just one
> breaks free: "Lives Lost, Hearts Broken —
> And For What?" I think of the woman
>
> and those she saddened by insisting —
> the Melbourne clerk
> who must have let it through. (P. 94)

Whatever the reasons (and I am sure they are important, and deserve more careful attention than I can give them here) women seem freer of the constraint to write about the Great War than many of our male poets and novelists. Consequently, the Great War myths seem to be almost entirely a male creation, and it may be worth pondering the fact that within the new version of this myth the enemy is seen as embodied either in males unlike ourselves — the generals and the politicians — or, very frequently, in females unlike our mothers.[12] The recognition that the enemy is somehow internal constitutes our maturity. But the enemy is not ourselves, for all that — because we, the makers of this discourse, happen to be male. In this particular myth, maturity and loss of simple innocence seem for many writers still to involve a nostalgia for the dumbly maternal and a distrust of or a hostility towards the essentially ambivalent figuration of the feminine. In her role as antagonist who can also suffer, the Great War woman bears a not entirely accidental resemblance to the figure of Nature which I discussed in my third chapter.

Chris Wallace-Crabbe wrote in "The Shapes of Gallipoli" that "At the core of the myth this truth is coiled like a snake, / that the men who enact it cannot see what pattern they are tracing" (p. 36). This is indeed a truth, and Wallace-Crabbe declares it with dignity and persuasiveness. The ambiguity of his concluding lines is also worth pondering:

> The men who spoke Australia did not know what they wrought
> for it was only defined by the completion of their lives.
> Icarus gave little thought to where it was he fell.
> We remember the spasmodic fire of ghostly riflemen
> and the funeral rites of Hector, tamer of horses,
> and the shallow sea, lapping still.
> Then let our crooked smokes climb to their nostrils,
> whose nostrils, time alone will prove,
> interminable seasons
> passing over

Time will not, in fact, prove anything, as the poem's tentative tone suggests. And "the men who spoke Australia" are not the "ghostly riflemen" of Anzac or the Somme any more than they are Hector. They are, and can only be, the poets themselves, perhaps too involved in "what pattern they are tracing" to see immediately the exact nature of the myth they are creating. Poetry's ambition to speak the myth of Australians at war is not, and probably never could have been, simply a speaking out of something already determined, an articulation of what is there, of an archetypal deep structure in the nation's consciousness generating a subsequent series of "interpretations" each of which, Persephone-like, would return to their deep source to be refreshed for a new birth into discourse. On the contrary, the making of this myth is rather like the making of war, the assimilation of an earlier myth for the purpose of reducing and reforming it for a new purpose, twisting it askew to serve the needs of the present. It thus has to do with need and power — and is inescapably an ideological act. The same must be said for any discourse which attempts to discuss it, which attempts to reveal its nature as a discourse in an endless chain or texture of discourses — including this one.

Notes

Notes to Chapter 1

1. Fredric Jameson, *The Political Unconscious* (Ithaca, N.Y.: Cornell University Press, 1981), passim, and in particular on pp. 48-49.
2. Barbara Johnson, *The Critical Difference* (Baltimore: Johns Hopkins University Press, 1980), p. 5.
3. Paul De Man, "Semiology and Rhetoric" in Josué Harari, ed., *Textual Strategies* (Ithaca, N.Y.: Cornell University Press, 1979), p. 139.
4. T.S. Eliot, *Selected Essays* (London: Faber, 1951), p. 15.

Notes to Chapter 2

1. Geoffrey Dutton, ed., *The Literature of Australia* (Ringwood: Penguin, 1964; revised edition 1976). The revised edition repeats the practice of the first.
2. John Docker, *In a Critical Condition* (Ringwood: Penguin, 1984).
3. Fredric Jameson, *The Political Unconscious* (Ithaca, N.Y.: Cornell University Press, 1981), p. 35. Whenever the word history — and, in fact, culture — is used in the present essay, it is to be understood in the light of Jameson's formulation.
4. Elaine Showalter, *A Literature of Their Own* (Princeton, N.J.: Princeton University Press, 1977), p. 13.
5. Harold Bloom, "Coleridge: The Anxiety of Influence" in W.K. Wimsatt, ed., *Literary Criticism: Idea and Act* (Berkeley: University of California Press, 1974), p. 513.
6. Ibid., p. 518. See also, Harold Bloom, *The Anxiety of Influence* (New York: Oxford University Press, 1973) and *A Map of Misreading* (New York: Oxford University Press, 1975).
7. Les A. Murray, *The Peasant Mandarin* (St Lucia: University of Queensland Press, 1978), p. 189.
8. Les A. Murray, ed., *The New Oxford Book of Australian Verse* (Melbourne: Oxford University Press, 1986).
9. John Tranter, ed., *The New Australian Poetry* (St Lucia: Makar Press, 1979), p. xxv.
10. Leonie Kramer, ed., *The Oxford History of Australian Literature* (Melbourne: Oxford University Press, 1981), p. 23.
11. Ibid., p. 272.
12. Jameson, *Political Unconscious*, p. 225.
13. Kramer, *Oxford History*, p. 391.
14. Ibid., p. 409.

15. Ibid., p. 410.
16. Among critical studies, Vivian Smith's chapter on poetry in the Leonie Kramer, ed., *Oxford History* is only one of the most recent examples. Introductions to recent anthologies also bear out my point. For example, see the introduction to Chris Wallace-Crabbe, ed., *The Golden Apples of The Sun* (Melbourne: Melbourne University Press, 1980): ". . . it has given me considerable delight to embark on a choice of the best, the most challenging and the most spirited Australian poems of this century" (p. 1); to Rodney Hall, ed., *The Collins Book of Australian Poetry* (Sydney: Collins, 1981): "The true poets are those who, far from ambitious to be 'great', dedicate themselves to the service of the language and as a result touch its richness" (p. 7); and Robert Gray and Geoffrey Lehmann, eds., *The Younger Australian Poets* (Sydney: Hale and Iremonger, 1983): ". . . we have chosen only those poets who we feel can manage a precise, communicative use of language and who have something moving or interesting to say. We have looked for, along with literary values, whatever impressed us as human ones" (pp. 14 and 15). As a close examination of this latter introduction will show, to be explicit about locating "literary" values in the proximity of "human" values is not the same as being explicit about their actual relation, nor about the origin or nature of either.
17. James McAuley, *A Map of Australian Verse* (Melbourne: Melbourne University Press, 1975).
18. Jonathan Culler, *The Pursuit of Signs* (Ithaca, N.Y.: Cornell University Press, 1981), p. 127.
19. Π. O., ed., *Off the Record* (Ringwood: Penguin, 1985) and Susan Hampton and Kate Llewellyn, eds., *The Penguin Book of Australian Women Poets* (Ringwood: Penguin, 1986).
20. *Off the Record*, p. 3.
21. M.H. Abrams, *A Glossary of Literary Terms*, 4th ed. (New York: Holt, Rinehart, Winston, 1981). On the other hand, the book includes explicit definitions of fiction, drama and novel.
22. See, for example, his essay "Free Verse: A Post-Mortem" in A.D. Hope, *The Cave and The Spring* (Adelaide: Rigby, 1965), pp. 38-50.
23. See note 3 above.
24. Roland Barthes, *S/Z*, trans., Richard Miller (New York: Hill & Wang, 1974), p. 10.
25. That this problem is neither simply theoretic nor new is shown by Douglas Sladen in his introduction to *A Century of Australian Song* (London: Walter Scott, 1888): "What is the raison d'être of this book? A Scotch paper, well known for the soundness of its criticisms, in referring to it, laid down that to be of any value it must be confined to the productions of Australian natives. This, then, would be an anthology of Australian verse into which admission was denied to Adam Lindsay Gordon" (p. 2).

Notes to Chapter 3

1. Charles Altieri, *Enlarging the Temple* (Lewisburg: Bucknell University Press, 1979). See, particularly, the introduction and chapter 1.
2. S.T. Coleridge, *Biographia Literaria* (London: J.M. Dent, 1906, 1949), p. 164.
3. Wordsworth's most succinct statement of this position is his famous "Tintern Abbey".
4. Altieri's terms, "immanentist" and "symbolist", can be seen to correspond loosely to Lacan's imaginary and symbolic, though one would not want to push the similarities too closely. Although akin to Coleridge's notion of symbolism, Christopher Brennan's symbolism led in a different direction, as we shall see in the next chapter.

5. Quoted by Altieri, *Enlarging the Temple*, p. 47. Eliot's essay appears in Frank Kermode, ed., *Selected Prose of T. S. Eliot* (London: Faber & Faber, 1975), pp. 175-78.
6. Ibid., p. 17.
7. Henry David Thoreau, *Walden and Civil Disobedience* (New York: Norton, 1966), p. 61.
8. Henry Lawson, *Prose Works* (Sydney: Angus & Robertson, 1948), p. 89.
9. Thoreau, *Walden*, p. 27. Thoreau's relish of the natural particulars of Walden Pond accounts for a large part of his book.
10. Both stories are in Barbara Baynton, *Bush Studies* (Sydney: Angus & Robertson, 1965).
11. Joseph Furphy, *Such Is Life* (Sydney: Angus & Robertson, 1944).
12. Nathaniel Hawthorne, *The Scarlet Letter* (New York: Norton, 1978), p. 147.
13. Ibid., p. 151.
14. Ralph Waldo Emerson, *The Selected Writings* (New York: Modern Library/Random House, 1950), p. 14.
15. Ibid., p. 15.
16. Ibid., p. 20.
17. William Wordsworth, *Poetical Works* (Oxford: Oxford University Press, 1956), p. 165.
18. See, for example, Galway Kinnell's remarkable poem "The Bear" in his *Body Rags* (Boston: Houghton, Mifflin, 1968), p. 61 or the poetry of Robert Bly.
19. G.A. Wilkes, *The Colonial Poets* (Sydney: Angus & Robertson, 1974).
20. Included in Wilkes, *Colonial Poets*, p. 15.
21. Judith Wright, *Preoccupations in Australian Poetry* (Melbourne: Oxford University Press, 1965), p. 9.
22. Ibid., p. 5.
23. Robert Hughes, *The Art of Australia* (Harmondsworth: Penguin, 1970), p. 54.
24. David Campbell, *Selected Poems* (Sydney: Angus & Robertson, 1978), p. 77.
25. Les A. Murray, *Selected Poems* (Sydney: Angus & Robertson, 1976), p. 138.
26. A.D. Hope, *Selected Poems* (Sydney: Angus & Robertson, 1973), p. 122.

Notes to Chapter 4

1. Axel Clark, *Christopher Brennan: A Critical Biography* (Melbourne: Melbourne University Press, 1980).
2. Sturm, Terry, ed., *Christopher Brennan* (St Lucia: University of Queensland Press, 1984. Portable Authors Series).
3. Ibid., p. 381.
4. A.R. Chisholm and J.J. Quinn, eds., *The Prose of Christopher Brennan* (Sydney: Angus & Robertson, 1962).
5. Wallace Stevens, *The Necessary Angel* (New York: Random House/Vantage, 1951), p. 31. It is interesting how closely Freud's comments on art in *Civilization and its Discontents*, trans. Joan Riviere, rev. ed. (London: Hogarth Press, 1963) tally with Stevens:

   > . . . satisfaction is obtained from illusions, which are recognized as such without the discrepancy between them and reality being allowed to interfere with enjoyment. The region from which these illusions arise is the life of the imagination . . . At the head of these satisfactions through phantasy stands the enjoyment of works of art. (P. 17)

6. For a fuller discussion of Stevens, see my essay "The Late Poems of Wallace Stevens" in R.J. Bell and I.J. Bickerton, eds., *American Studies: New Essays from Australia and New Zealand* (Sydney: Australian New Zealand American Studies Association, 1981). The later, more post-modern aspects of Stevens's poetry are distinctly reminiscent of that sense of an obscure but immanent order

which is epitomized by Wordsworth's famous description of the Simplon Pass in Book 6 of *The Prelude*. However, one would want to stress that Stevens never fully abandoned his earlier, more Coleridgean, notion of the imagination as that power which creates a symbolic coherence in the absence of an order manifest in the tangible world. He differed from his fellow modernist Americans, Pound and Eliot, however, in stressing the existential and provisional nature of this fictive order.

7. Chisholm and Quinn, *Prose*, p. 19. The essay is dated 1901.
8. Brennan chastises Wordsworth for the "obscure way" a symbolist notion of correspondences lies behind his attitude to nature, adding that "his state of mind on this subject remains, like his poetic expression for the most part, lumbering, blundering, and unformed" (*Prose* p. 54). The implication is that Wordsworth's thought and poetry were too encumbered with the things of this world.
9. See, for example, Clark, *Christopher Brennan*, pp. 193-97.
10. A.R. Chisholm and J.J. Quinn, eds., *The Verse of Christopher Brennan* (Sydney: Angus & Robertson, 1960). The poems in the section "Poems, 1913" are numbered, and I cite them here by poem number rather than by page number.
11. Jacques Lacan, *Ecrits, A Selection*, trans. Alan Sheridan (New York: Norton, 1977), p. 5. For fuller details see Lacan's essays in *Ecrits*, "The Mirror Stage as Formative of the Function of the I", pp. 1-7; and "The Function and Field of Speech and Language in Psychoanalysis", pp. 30-113.
12. The French philosopher Jacques Derrida has mounted a sustained attack on the "metaphysics of presence" underlying this notion of a transcendental signified, which he sees as characterizing Western metaphysical thought since the time of Plato. In Derrida's words Plato, in the *Phaedrus*, has Socrates privilege the spoken over the written word because of its supposed capacity to "erase itself or become transparent, in order to allow the concept to present itself as what it is, referring to nothing other than its presence". (Jacques Derrida, *Positions*, trans. Alan Bass (Chicago: University of Chicago Press, 1981), p. 22.) But, he argues, building on the earlier work of Ferdinand de Saussure, "The sign is only the supplement of the thing itself" and "Immediacy is derived . . . all begins through the intermediary" (Jacques Derrida, *Of Grammatology*, trans. Gayatri Chakravorty Spivak (Baltimore: Johns Hopkins University Press, 1976), pp. 145-57). Derrida's argument is too complex and, perhaps, by now too well-known for me to give more than these brief comments on it. My main intention at this point is to highlight this moment of its similarity with Lacan's. For both, immediacy is a delusion — for Lacan, because of the nature of the subject and its relation to its other; for Derrida, because of the nature of language itself.

    For a particularly clear explication of Lacan's thought on language, see Fredric Jameson, "Imaginary and Symbolic in Lacan: Marxism, Psychoanalytic Criticism and the Problem of the Subject" in Shoshana Felman, ed., *Literature and Psychoanalysis* (Baltimore: Johns Hopkins University Press, 1982), pp. 338-95. For Derrida, and for Ferdinand de Saussure, see Jonathan Culler, *On Deconstruction* (Ithaca, N.Y.: Cornell University Press, 1982); and Christopher Norris, *Deconstruction: Theory and Practice* (London: Methuen, 1982).

Notes to Chapter 5

1. John Tranter, ed., *The New Australian Poetry* (St Lucia: Makar Press, 1979). Tranter's claim that "we are still involved in the modernist revolution" (p. xx) has some truth to it, but is an oversimplification.
2. Fredric Jameson, *The Political Unconscious* (Ithaca, N.Y.: Cornell University Press, 1981), p. 225.
3. Kenneth Slessor, *Poems* (Sydney: Angus & Robertson, 1944; 2nd ed. 1957), p. 57. All quotations from Slessor are taken from this edition without further citation.

4. The allusion to the dotty house in Thomas Love Peacock's novel *Headlong Hall* is obvious. My present interpretation of this section of the poem presupposes this, but also takes seriously the poem's own attempt at characterizing what its title signifies. In any one comprehensive reading of the poem, we presumably shuttle between a "Peacockian" (or outsider's) interpretation — one which will necessarily be ironic — and the one I give here, which regards Slessor's "Headlong Hall" as signifying something genuinely worth having. The result of this shuttling is nostalgia.
5. A. K. Thomson, ed., *Critical Essays on Kenneth Slessor* (Brisbane: Jacaranda, 1968), p. 71.
6. Ibid., pp. 128-29.
7. Northrop Frye, *The Anatomy of Criticism* (Princeton: Princeton University Press, 1957, 1973), p. 186.
8. Ibid., p. 193.
9. Ibid., p. 187.
10. Whether speech can *ever* be originary/original and the manifesting of presence is, of course another matter. (See chapter 4, note 12.) This does not in any way reflect on the subject's *longing* for such presence, which would be for him a triumphant victory over death, loss and meaninglessness.
11. N.B. Coleridge's dictum in chapter 23 of the *Biographia Literaria* (London: J.M. Dent, 1906, 1949) that the imagination "dissolves, diffuses, dissipates, in order to re-create; or where this process is rendered impossible, yet still at all events it struggles to idealize and to unify. It is essentially *vital*, even as all objects (*as* objects) are essentially fixed and dead". Slessor's "Five Bells" is virtually a dramatization of this passage, with Joe Lynch remaining dead despite the struggle of the poet's vital imagination to be united with him again.
12. Wallace Stevens, *The Necessary Angel* (New York: Random House/Vantage, 1951), p. 36.

Notes to Chapter 6

1. A.D. Hope, *The Cave and the Spring* (Adelaide: Rigby, 1965), p. 44. Other works by Hope quoted here are: *Selected Poems* (Sydney: Angus & Robertson, 1973), *New Poems 1965–1969* (Sydney: Angus & Robertson, 1969), *A Late Picking* (Sydney: Angus & Robertson, 1975), *The New Cratylus* (Melbourne: Oxford University Press, 1979); and *The Pack of Autolycus* (Canberra: ANU Press, 1978).
2. R. F. Brissenden, "Art and the Academy — The Achievement of A. D. Hope" in Geoffrey Dutton, ed., *The Literature of Australia* (rev. ed. Ringwood: Penguin, 1976), pp. 406-26.
3. "Vivaldi, Bird and Angel" is found in *New Poems 1965–1969*, pp. 59-74. This passage is on pp. 62-63.
4. Dutton, *Literature of Australia*, p. 416.
5. See, for example, Ferdinand de Saussure, *Course in General Linguistics*, trans. P. Owen (London: Fontana, 1974), p. 120: ". . . in the linguistic system there are only differences, with no positive terms" and (p. 117): ". . . we discover not ideas given in advance but values emanating from the system. When we say that these values correspond to concepts, it is understood that these concepts are purely differential, not positively defined by their content but negatively defined by their relations with other terms of the system." For a lucid and brief guide to these theories, see Jonathan Culler, *Ferdinand de Saussure* (London: Fontana, 1976, 1980).
6. Plato, *Phaedrus* (Harmondsworth: Penguin, 1973), pp. 274-79.
7. Jacques Derrida, "Plato's Pharmacy" in *Dissemination*, trans. Barbara Johnson (Chicago: University of Chicago Press, 1981), pp. 61-171.

8. Jacques Derrida, *Of Grammatology*, trans. Gayatri Chakravorty Spivak (Baltimore: John Hopkins University Press, 1976), p. 157.
9. Dutton, *Literature of Australia*, p. 425.
10. Hope, *A Late Picking*, p. 22.
11. Hope, *The New Cratylus*, p. 131.
12. Hope, *Selected Poems*, pp. 91-99.
13. Hope, *A Late Picking*, pp. 41-43.
14. For a fascinating supplement to the argument that follows, one should read Hope's acute essay on male-female relations as they appear in Milton and Tennyson, ' "She for God in him" ' in *The Pack of Autolycus*, pp. 169-86. Hope's approach to Milton in this essay is not entirely dissimilar from my approach to Hope.
15. Julia Kristeva, *Desire in Language*, trans. Gora, Jardine and Roudiez (New York: Columbia University Press, 1980), p. 238.
16. Hope, *Selected Poems*, pp. 122-26.
17. Barbara Johnson, *The Critical Difference* (Baltimore: Johns Hopkins University Press, 1980), p. 5.

Notes to Chapter 7

1. For Derrida's discussion of Plato's *Phaedrus*, see "Plato's Pharmacy" in Jacques Derrida, *Dissemination*, trans. Barbara Johnson (Chicago: University of Chicago Press, 1981), pp. 61-171.
2. Poems discussed or mentioned here come from the following books by Judith Wright: *Collected Poems, 1942–1970* (Sydney: Angus & Robertson, 1971) [referred to as *CP* in text]; *Fourth Quarter and Other Poems* (Sydney: Angus & Robertson, 1976); and *Phantom Dwelling* (Sydney: Angus & Robertson, 1985).
3. Although it is tempting to see in "Naked Girl and Mirror" a poetic equivalent of the process described in Lacan's essay "The mirror stage as formative of the I" (*Ecrits*, pp. 1-7) I feel that drawing too close a parallel would be a distortion, if for no other reason than the obvious one that Wright's poem deals with a moment of puberty. However I have employed some of Lacan's terms in order to invoke the suggestive similarities between the two texts.
4. To employ Julia Kristeva's terms, this would be a move from the semiotic to the symbolic. See especially "From One Identity to Another" in Julia Kristeva, *Desire in Language*, trans. Gora, Jardine and Roudiez (New York: Columbia University Press, 1980), pp. 124-47. But see my note 3 above for a word of caution. It may be that by signalling puberty as this move from pre-Oedipal narcissism to the Oedipal symbolic, Wright's poem is revealing a curious example of Freud's compulsion to repeat.
5. Derrida, *Dissemination*, p. 133.
6. Lacan, *Ecrits*, p. 104.
7. A very different poem of Judith Wright's, "Dotterel" (*Collected Poems* p. 182), serves also to emblematicize this quality, particularly in the penultimate stanza:

    Water's edge, land's edge
    and edge of the air —
    the dotterel chooses
    to live nowhere.

8. See Jacques Derrida, *Positions* (Chicago: University of Chicago Press, 1981), p. 33.
9. For example, consider Lacan's: "The unconscious is that part of the concrete discourse, in so far as it is trans-individual, that is not at the disposal of the subject in re-establishing the continuity of his conscious discourse" (*Ecrits* p. 49). Jonathan Culler's formulation, "The unconscious is the excess of what one says over what one knows, or of what one says over what one wants to say", is

possibly more immediately intelligible. (*On Deconstruction* [Ithaca, N.Y.: Cornell University Press, 1982], p. 127). However, threat, censorship and antagonism are implied in Lacan's further comment (*Ecrits* p. 50): "The unconscious is that chapter of my history that is marked by a blank or occupied by a falsehood: it is the censored chapter."

10. Derrida, *Dissemination*, p. 76.
11. That such a dream is impossible is acknowledged in "Summer", a poem in *Phantom Dwelling* (p. 144) in which she contrasts herself with non-human creatures: "In a burned out summer, I try to see without words / as they do. But I live through a web of languages."

Notes to Chapter 8

1. *Poetry Australia* 56 (September 1975).
2. David Campbell, "Francis Webb" in Geoffrey Dutton, ed., *The Literature of Australia* (Ringwood: Penguin, 1976), pp. 500-508.
3. Leonie Kramer, ed., *The Oxford History of Australian Literature* (Melbourne: Oxford University Press, 1981), p. 411.
4. William H. Wilde, Joy Hooton and Barry Andrews, eds., *The Oxford Companion to Australian Literature* (Melbourne: Oxford University Press, 1985), p. 734.
5. Francis Webb, *Collected Poems* (Sydney: Angus & Robertson, 1969), p. vii. *C.P.* indicates this volume throughout this chapter.
6. Ibid., p. viii.
7. Ibid., p. ix.
8. S. Kierkegaard, *The Sickness unto Death*, trans. Walter Lowrie (Oxford: Oxford University Press, 1941), pp. 111-12.
9. John Tranter, ed., *The New Australian Poetry* (St Lucia: Makar, 1979). A fuller discussion of John Tranter is to be found in chapter 12 of the present work.
10. Wallace Stevens, "The Idea of Order at Key West" in *The Collected Poems of Wallace Stevens* (London: Faber, 1955), p. 128.
11. Although in some respects similar, the Cook figure in "Five Visions of Captain Cook" is not a modernist hero. Albeit posthumously, his daemonic force is claimed to have changed the world: "So Cook made choice, so Cook sailed westabout, / So men write poems in Australia".
12. Frank Kermode, ed., *Selected Prose of T.S. Eliot* (London: Faber, 1975), p. 177.
13. T. S. Eliot, "The Waste Land" in *The Complete Poems and Plays of T. S. Eliot* (London: Faber, 1969), p. 59.
14. The Book of Exod. 3.
15. W.E. Henley's poem "Invictus" was extremely popular and widely anthologized, for example in Sir Arthur Quiller-Couch, ed., *The Oxford Book of English Verse 1250–1918* (Oxford: Oxford University Press, 1900, 1939), p. 1027. It is perhaps not too much to see in this poem's popularity a last defiant cry of the illusory unified subject.
16. The *Weekend Australian*, 12-13 Apr. 1986, "The Weekend Magazine", p. 15.
17. Michel Foucault, "What Is an Author?" in Josué V. Harari, ed., *Textual Strategies* (Ithaca, N.Y.: Cornell University Press, 1979), p. 150.
18. Dutton, *Literature of Australia*, p. 503.
19. Jacques Lacan, *Ecrits: A Selection*, trans. Alan Sheridan (New York: Norton, 1977), p. 30.
20. See Note 11 to chapter 4 above.
21. The Gospel according to St. Luke. 4.
22. Jacques Derrida, *Dissemination*, trans. Barbara Johnson (Chicago: University of Chicago Press, 1981), p. 76.
23. See Jacques Derrida, ". . . That Dangerous Supplement" in *Of Grammatology*,

trans. Gayatri Chakravorty Spivak (Baltimore: Johns Hopkins University Press, 1976), pp. 141-64.

24. This reading of Webb's text need not blind us to its contradictory nature. The fact that Harry is attempting to write a letter at all suggests, strictly speaking, that he is already experiencing that condition of desire which must be mediated by language, by "the word" which Lacan epigrammatically describes as "already a presence made of absence." (*Ecrits* p. 65). Only by desire, it seems, can the absence of desire be signified.

Notes to Chapter 9

1. This must have been particularly so after the appearance in the *Bulletin* of her famous acrostic castigating all editors.
2. For a particularly clear introduction to this question, I would refer the reader to Antony Easthope, *Poetry as Discourse* (London: Methuen, 1983). Also see Jacques Lacan, *Ecrits*(New York: Norton, 1977), in particular the essays "The Mirror Stage as Formative of the Function of the I" (pp. 1-7) and "The Function and Field of Speech and Language in Psychoanalysis" (pp. 30-113). Also of relevance is Michel Foucault, "What Is an Author?" in Joshué Harari, ed., *Textual Strategies* (Ithaca, N.Y.: Cornell University Press, 1979), p. 141; and, of course, Roland Barthes' famous essay "The Death of the Author" in *Image Music Text* (London: Fontana, 1977), p. 142.
3. Vivian Smith, for example, lays considerable stress on the "autobiographical or personal" aspect of her "poems of poignant psychological experience" in his comments in Kramer (ed.) *The Oxford History of Australian Literature*.
4. In this essay I have taken poems from Gwen Harwood's *Selected Poems* (Sydney: Angus & Robertson, 1975), and *The Lion's Bride* (Sydney: Angus & Robertson, 1981). (Indicated in the text as *S.P.* and *Lion's Bride*, respectively.)
5. Perhaps at my peril I have been trying to avoid the awkward neologisms "the subject of the enounced" and "the subject of enunciation" which might make this discussion clearer, but at the expense of the English language. By the identity of the poet's voice I mean, of course, the subject of enunciation. For a clear discussion of these subjects, see Antony Easthope, *Poetry as Discourse*, pp. 30-47.
6. Clearly, what we are prepared to accept as "normal talk" in poetry is relative to the poem's formality. For example, in a highly formal poem (one in heroic couplets, or in tightly rhymed quatrains, perhaps) only a small loosening of the formal requirements may be needed to give the effect of non-poetic discourse. In free, unrhymed verse, more drastic measures, such as the deployment of colloquialisms, or even of slang, may be required.
7. In addition to everything else, at the most basic level the "I" of the poem is a written "I" simulating speech, not speech itself. And as Derrida has pointed out so clearly, even speech occupies the space created by the inevitable deferral of presence, being itself no more than another mode of signifying. See Jacques Derrida, *Of Grammatology* (Baltimore: Johns Hopkins University Press, 1976), esp. pp. 144-52, and the essay "Plato's Pharmacy" in *Dissemination* (Chicago: University of Chicago Press, 1981), pp. 61-171.

Notes to Chapter 10

1. The volumes of Dorothy Hewett's poetry discussed here are *Windmill Country* (Melbourne: Overland, 1968); *Rapunzel in Suburbia* (Sydney: Prism, 1975); and

Greenhouse (Sydney: Big Smoke Books, 1979). (Indicated in this chapter as *Windmill Country*, *Rapunzel* and *Greenhouse*, respectively.)

2. The American influences most relevant here would be Robert Lowell and Allen Ginsberg, though one must also include Frank O'Hara. The latter's example was particularly important for Bruce Beaver, whose *Letters to Live Poets* (Sydney: South Head Press, 1969), was an important early contribution to the confessional style in Australian poetry.
3. For the early use of that term, see M.L. Rosenthal, *The New Poets* (New York: Oxford University Press, 1967). Rosenthal characterizes Robert Lowell's poetry as confessional in that it deals with "explicit themes . . . usually developed in the first person and intended without question to point to the author himself" (p. 26). It is thus "one culmination of the Romantic and modern tendency to place the literal Self more and more at the centre of the poem" (p. 27). Both statements seem problematic today. I have put the term "confessional poetry" always within quotation marks because, as I hope the present discussion makes clear, it is not only misleading but something very like a contradiction in terms.
4. Brian Kiernan, in "Seeing her own Mischance", *Overland* 64 (1976) pp. 16-22, is reluctant to apply the term "confessional" to Hewett's poetry. Nonetheless his comment that "there is the sense that there are many Dorothy Hewetts" produced by her work points in that general direction. In another article in the same issue of *Overland*, (pp. 24-29) Bruce Williams approaches the problem of "confessional" poetry more explicitly and more circumspectly: " 'Confessional': a misleading tag for a poet, suggesting undisciplined outpourings. It suggests that the medium between self and reader is rubbed out to convey the real experience. But this notion of real experience is always chimerical." Williams goes on to discuss the notion from the angle of the poet's, rather than the reader's, production of texts. "The confessional poet pushes at the boundaries that divide poetry from direct communication (that necessary fiction) for a purpose: to win new territory for poetry . . . There is a widespread wish to destroy the category of art itself. Raging against the repressiveness of our society, and against the decadence of academic formalism (which turns lively, shapely poems to ice) poets long for the direct touch, a form of communion through words."
5. Bruce Beaver's *Letters to Live Poets* is another example. This book's explicit reference to moods of acute depression and revulsion acted as a powerful corrective to the notion that poetry should embody only morally acceptable attitudes, that it should be a record of all the best that was thought and felt.
6. In the Grimms' version, Rapunzel is given at birth to the witch in payment for her father's theft of vegetables from the witch's garden to satisfy the appetite of his pregnant wife. At puberty she is shut in a tower where the witch visits her by climbing up her hair. Hearing her sing, the King's son falls in love with her. Discovering how the witch visits her, he does the same until the witch one day discovers Rapunzel's secret. She cuts off the girl's hair and banishes her to a desert. That evening when the king's son visits, the witch lets down the severed hair for him to climb. Discovering his loss, the man leaps from the tower and is blinded. Only after wandering for years does he come across Rapunzel, whose tears restore his sight. Meanwhile she has had twins, presumably by him; and they then live happily.
7. Jacques Lacan, *Ecrits, A Selection*, trans. Alan Sheridan (New York: Norton, 1977), p. 5.
8. For a discussion of the phallic mother, see "The signification of the phallus" in Lacan, *Ecrits*, pp. 281-91. Also "Motherhood according to Bellini" in Julia Kristeva, *Desire in Language*, esp. p. 238, where she claims that symbolic coherence is vested in the mother because "she warrants that everything is, and that it is representable".
9. It should be remembered at this point that although I have interpreted the labyrinth as the subject's lengthening accumulation of memories which houses

power in its ambivalently destructive/creative aspect, it is also the creation of that most famous of mythical artists, Daedalus. One should also remember that Cybele and the Minotaur are constituted textually, to be read only in the mirror of the intruding subject, as — indeed — is Daedalus. This apparent contradiction could serve to point out another path to the unravelling of the nature of the labyrinth from the one I follow in this article, a path which would lead to the same conclusions.

10. Robert Duncan, *The Truth and Life of Myth* (Michigan: Sumac Press, 1968), p. 78.

Notes to Chapter 11

1. Webb's immanentist view places him closer to Murray than his narrative conventions readily allow in "Eyre All Alone". This accounts for the poem's dislocation of linear narrative into a series of lyric moments. See my earlier discussion of Webb in chapter 8.
2. Les A. Murray, *The Peasant Mandarin* (St Lucia: University of Queensland Press, 1978), and *Persistence in Folly* (Sydney: Angus & Robertson, 1984). (Referred to, respectively, as *P.M.* and *Folly* throughout this chapter.)
3. Murray, *The Peasant Mandarin*, p. 183.
4. "On First Looking into Chapman's Hesiod" in Peter Porter, *Collected Poems* (Oxford: Oxford University Press, 1983), p. 211.
5. Les A. Murray, *Selected Poems* (Sydney: Angus & Robertson, 1976), p. 126. Indicated as *S.P.* in this chapter.
6. Les A. Murray, *The People's Otherworld* (Sydney: Angus & Robertson, 1983), p. 29. Indicated as *P.O.* in this chapter.
7. Les A. Murray, *Ethnic Radio* (Sydney: Angus & Robertson, 1977), p. 44. Indicated as *E.R.* in this chapter.
8. Christopher Pollnitz, *Southerly* 1 (1981): p. 55.
9. Fredric Jameson's *cri de coeur* applies as much to poetry as to critical texts: "It should not, in the present intellectual atmosphere, be necessary laboriously to argue the position that every form of practice . . . presupposes a form of theory . . . whose denial unmasks it as ideology." Fredric Jameson, *The Political Unconscious* (Ithaca, N.Y.: Cornell University Press, 1981), p. 58.
10. This is not so far from white rural practice as might be thought by those who grew up in the city. In my own childhood an otherwise undistinguished bend in the road was known by all of us as "the place where Charlie Carruthers killed his father" after a fatal car smash.
11. Louis Althusser, *Lenin and Philosophy and Other Essays* (London: New Left Books, 1971), p. 28.
12. Les A. Murray, *The Boys Who Stole the Funeral* (Sydney: Angus & Robertson, 1980).

Notes to Chapter 12

1. Robert Lowell, "Skunk Hour" in *Life Studies* (London: Faber, 1959), p. 103.
2. The quotation from Rimbaud comes from a letter to Georges Izambard dated 13 May 1871, and is printed in Oliver Bernard, ed., *Rimbaud* (Harmondsworth: Penguin, 1962), p. 6.
3. Roland Barthes, "The Death of the Author" in *Image Music Text*, trans. Stephen Heath (London: Fontana, 1977), p. 142.
4. John Tranter, ed., *The New Australian Poetry* (St Lucia: Makar Press, 1979).
5. *The New Australian Poetry*, p. xxiv.

6. Interview with Jim Davidson, *Meanjin* 4 (1981): ". . . most of the arguments I've had about literature are really pragmatic, conditional arguments that are there for the time being because they're needed." He also says in the same interview, "One thing that must be said about the polemical arguments about Modernism in the anthology is that they're not to be taken too seriously . . . So the discussion of it was very basic, and not really worth going into in any great detail." (P. 429)
7. See Sir Philip Sidney: "These be they that, as the first and most noble sort may justly be termed *Vates*, so these are waited on in the excellentest languages and best understandings, with the foredescribed names of poets; for these indeed do merely make to imitate, and imitate both to delight and teach, and delight to move men to take that goodness in hand, which without delight they would fly as from a stranger, and teach, to make them know that goodness whereunto they are moved . . .". "The Defence of Poesy" in *Selected Poetry and Prose*, Robert Kimbrough, ed. (San Francisco: Rinehart Press, 1969), p. 111.
8. F.R. Leavis, *Revaluation* (London: Chatto & Windus, 1956), p. 272.
9. ". . . this quasi-religious rhetoric is a natural outgrowth of Australian university English departments, and is probably inevitable, given their peculiar ancestry: by Matthew Arnold, out of Doctor Leavis, via Victorian England. Common-Room Humanism is as apt to sermonise as any other fervid minority belief." Tranter, *The New Australian Poetry*, p. xxii.
10. Compare "I hadn't read Ted Berrigan up until a couple of years ago, although I do admit to having been influenced by John Ashbery and Frank O'Hara over the last five years. I think those influences are fairly liberating ones." *Meanjin* 4 (1981), p. 23.
11. Archibald MacLeish, "Ars Poetica" in *New and Collected Poems* (Boston: Houghton Mifflin, 1976), p. 106.
12. Wallace Stevens, *Opus Posthumous* (London: Faber, 1959), p. 171.
13. All except one of the poems referred to in this essay are to be found in John Tranter, *Selected Poems* (Sydney: Hale and Iremonger, 1982). Page numbers throughout this chapter refer to this edition, cited as *S.P.*
14. Jonathan Culler, *Structuralist Poetics* (Ithaca, N.Y.: Cornell University Press, 1975), p. 129.
15. Roland Barthes, *Mythologies* (London: Jonathan Cape, 1972), p. 86.
16. Les A. Murray, *The Peasant Mandarin* (St Lucia: University of Queensland Press, 1978), p. 196.
17. Martin Duwell, ed., *A Possible Contemporary Poetry* (St Lucia: Makar Press, 1982), p. 33.
18. David Carter, "John Tranter: Popular Mysteries", *Scripsi* vol 2, no 4 (1984), pp. 117-22.
19. T.S. Eliot, *The Complete Poems and Plays of T.S. Eliot* (London: Faber, 1969), p. 175.
20. See for example Rae Desmond Jones: "*Crying in Early Infancy* is Tranter's finest piece of work so far, not least because it is engaged in tormented dialogue with anti-art . . . Tranter is less concerned with purely verbal effects than with the serious, puritanical need to test stringently the art that is so valuable to him." "The Ambiguous Modernist: Themes in the Development of the Poetry of John Tranter", *Australian Literary Studies* vol 9, no 4 (October 1980), pp. 500-501.
21. Duwell, *A Possible Contemporary Poetry*, p. 32.
22. Wallace Stevens, *The Collected Poems* (London: Faber, 1955), p. 322.
23. Judith Rodriguez and Andrew Taylor, eds., *Poems, Selected from The Australian's 20th Anniversary Competition* (Sydney: Angus & Robertson, 1985), p. 85; and Les A. Murray, ed., *The New Oxford Book of Australian Verse* (Melbourne: Oxford University Press, 1986), p. 324.
24. Carter, "John Tranter", p. 122.
25. Frank O'Hara, "Personism" in *The Selected Poems of Frank O'Hara*, ed. Donald Allen (New York: Random House, 1974), p. xiii.

26. John Tranter's own comments on "Lufthansa", in a letter to the author, are of considerable interest. They were written in response to the present chapter, and are reproduced in full:

"Lufthansa". I generally like what you do with this (sometimes rather difficult) poem. The main thrust is right on target: more on that later. A slight gap occurs, though, I feel, between two of the quotes you make, and I'd just like to look at that for a moment. Your quote on p.169 "The radar keeps . . . and leads back / to our bodies . . ." breaks off at (what is to me) an interesting point; your quoting of the remainder of the passage half-way down p.169 ("This is the same skill which maintains 'the smile behind the drink trolley . . .' Precision, skill, craft: fusing desire and function, they bite into doubt . . .") takes up another point. It seems to me that in between something has been missed; or perhaps I'd like the poem to make a particular point at that stage (intentionalist fallacy strikes again).

In this poem, I'd like it to seem that where our faith leads (for what it's worth) is exactly back "to our bodies, to the smiles behind the drink / trolley and her white knuckles as the plane drops / a hundred feet . . ." Without being too Baden-Powell about it, the radar can help and guide (as can the church, the state, or the Lufthansa Technical Training College, I suppose), but in the end it's how we manage to live inside our sad and terminally imperfect bodies, white-knuckled but still smiling because that's your job and it matters here and now to other frightened people, that counts. Hence the sudden intrusion of the sunlight, and the toast to an absent friend, at this point, I suppose. Though in fact the real-life thoughts and events were noticed in the order in which they appear in the poem — although that's irrelevant, too, dammit.

It's not that I want to be theological, for God's sake. Others have ploughed that field dry. But something John Scott said a few years ago keeps recurring to me; as far as I can remember, he said something like: now that we poets have got on top of Modernism and then post-modernism and can do all that stuff, what do we do with it? It has to be more important than designing wallpaper. I'd like to find some way to fuse those discoveries and techniques with a humanism that's not Common-Room Humanism, that can take in the best that contemporary thinking can come up with. And one that handles our local, and our trans-national, society today, not just Victorian England, or the Bush, or Woodstock.

It seems to me that Cavafy, for all his limitations, is as important a poet as Frank O'Hara, with all his; and that O'Hara would have accepted that without question (indeed, he probably did.) And of course we have to go beyond Cavafy — and Auden — and Ashbery, I suppose. (Is there poetry after Ashbery?) But without turning our backs on the value of what Cavafy *et al.* were doing.

That's why I feel the points you make towards the end of the paper are right on target; but for a poet it's a tricky row to hoe, and you need more than just the ability to go on your nerve, as you point out.

Notes to Chapter 13

1. Geoff Page, ed., *Shadows from Wire* (Canberra: Australian War Memorial, 1983); Geoff Page, *Benton's Conviction* (Sydney: Angus & Robertson, 1985); and Chris Wallace-Crabbe & Peter Pierce, eds., *Clubbing of the Gunfire* (Melbourne: Melbourne University Press, 1984).
2. The absence of any tradition of home-grown Australian poetry concerning itself with war is demonstrated by the invocation of Dante in Frederic Manning's

"Grotesque" (*Clubbing of the Gunfire*, p. 69 – by no means a bad poem), by the Catullan "Hail and farewell to those who fought and died" of J. Le Gay Brereton's "The Dead" (p. 61) and most unhappily by Leon Gellert's classical apostrophe to "The Wrecked Aeroplane" (p. 45):

> Unhappy craft of Daedalus reborn,
> That liest with white wings torn . . .

which sidetracks into a Poe-like "Forlorn! Forlorn!" White raven indeed!

3. Roland Barthes, *Mythologies*, trans., A. Lavers (London: Jonathan Cape, 1972). The relevant essay is "Myth Today" (pp. 109-59). For Northrop Frye's highly influential account of myth in relation to literature, see his *Anatomy of Criticism* (Princeton, N.J.: Princeton University Press, 1957), passim.
4. Barthes, *Mythologies*, p. 137.
5. Wallace-Crabbe and Pierce, *Clubbing of the Gunfire*, p. 74.
6. Page, *Shadows*. Until specified, further page references are to this anthology.
7. Wallace Stevens, *Collected Poems* (London: Faber & Faber, 1954), p. 392.
8. The question of whether history can attain the condition of a "science" is of course older than Nietzsche. One would hope that at present nobody would quibble with the assertion in chapter 2, following Fredric Jameson, that all history is available to us only as text, an assertion which brings it into the same arena of discourse as myth but which does not equate the two.
9. Wallace-Crabbe and Pierce, *Clubbing of the Gunfire*, p. 62.
10. Ibid., pp. 35 and 40. The quotations are from poems by Chris Wallace-Crabbe and Les Murray.
11. Geoff Page's "Small Town Memorials", "Harney", and Les Murray's "Lament for the Country Soldiers", and "Troop Train Returning" are only a few which emphasize the rurality of the soldiers and their family background. Not surprisingly, the negative urban feminine has a counterpart in a positive rural one.
12. Not all other women embody the enemy. For the whore as mother-replacement, the super-mother away from home, see the phantasies in Page's "Trench Dreams" and Wallace-Crabbe's "The Shapes of Gallipoli". And of course, as Mackenzie's and Shapcott's poems indicate, not every version of the new myth displays the bias I am pointing to here, which is a tendency rather than an invariant practice.

Bibliography

SOME CONTEMPORARY ANTHOLOGIES OF AUSTRALIAN POETRY

Dutton, Geoffrey, ed., *The Heritage of Australian Poetry*. South Yarra: Currey O'Neil, 1984.

Elliott, Brian, ed., *The Jindyworobaks*. St Lucia: University of Queensland Press, 1979.

Gray, Robert and Lehmann, Geoffrey, eds., *The Younger Australian Poets*. Sydney: Hale & Iremonger, 1983.

Hall, Rodney, ed., *The Collins Book of Australian Poetry*. Sydney: Collins, 1981.

Hall, Rodney and Shapcott, Thomas W., eds., *New Impulses in Australian Poetry*. St Lucia: University of Queensland Press, 1968.

Hampton, Susan and Llewellyn, Kate, eds., *The Penguin Book of Australian Women Poets*. Ringwood: Penguin, 1986.

Heseltine, Harry, ed., *The Penguin Book of Australian Verse*. Ringwood: Penguin, 1972.

———., *The Penguin Book of Modern Australian Verse*. Ringwood: Penguin, 1981.

Jennings, Kate, ed., *Mother I'm Rooted*. Fitzroy: Outback Press, 1975.

Kramer, Leonie and Mitchell, Adrian, eds., *The Oxford Anthology of Australian Literature*. Melbourne: Oxford University Press, 1985.

Murray, Les A., ed., *The New Oxford Book of Australian Verse*. Melbourne: Oxford University Press, 1986.

Page, Geoff, ed., *Shadows from Wire*. Canberra: Australian War Memorial, 1983.

Π. O., ed., *Off the Record*. Ringwood: Penguin, 1985.

Shapcott, Thomas W., ed., *Australian Poetry Now*. Melbourne: Sun Books, 1970.

———., *Contemporary American and Australian Poetry*. St Lucia: University of Queensland Press, 1976.

Tranter, John, ed., *The New Australian Poetry*. St Lucia: Makar, 1979.

Wallace-Crabbe, Chris, ed., *The Golden Apples of the Sun*. Melbourne: Melbourne University Press, 1980.

Wallace-Crabbe, Chris and Pierce, Peter, eds., *Clubbing of the Gunfire*. Melbourne: Melbourne University Press, 1984.

Wilkes, G.A., ed., *The Colonial Poets*. Sydney: Angus & Robertson, 1974.

POETS

Christopher Brennan

XVIII Poems. Sydney: Privately stylographed by the author, 1897.

XXI Poems (1893–1897): Towards the Source. Sydney: Angus & Robertson, 1897.

Poems. Sydney: G.B. Philip, 1914. Facs. ed. *Poems [1913]*. Introd. G.A. Wilkes. Sydney: Sydney University Press, 1972.

A Chant of Doom and Other Verses. Sydney: Angus & Robertson, 1918.

XXIII Poems (a selection from *Poems [1913]* with three previously uncollected poems). Ed. J.J. Quinn. Sydney: Australian Limited Editions Society, 1938. Facs. ed. Sydney: Sydney University Press, 1972.

The Burden of Tyre. Sydney: Privately printed, H.F. Chaplin, 1953.

The Verse of Christopher Brennan. Ed. A.R. Chisholm and J.J. Quinn. Sydney: Angus & Robertson, 1960.

The Prose of Christopher Brennan. Ed. A.R. Chisholm and J.J. Quinn. Sydney: Angus & Robertson, 1962.

Christopher Brennan: Selected Poems. Ed. A.R. Chisholm. Australian Poets Series. Sydney: Angus & Robertson, 1966.

Selected Poems. Sel. G.A. Wilkes. Sydney: Angus & Robertson, 1973. Reprint A & R Modern Poets, 1979. Reprint 1985.

Musicopoematographoscope and Pocket Musicopoematographoscope: Prose – Verse – Poster – Algebraic – Symbolico – Riddle. Introd. Axel Clark. Sydney: Hale & Iremonger, 1981.

Christopher Brennan. Ed. Terry Sturm. Portable Australian Authors. St Lucia: University of Queensland Press, 1984.

Charles Harpur

Thoughts. A Series of Sonnets. Sydney: W.A. Duncan, 1845.

Songs of Australia — First Series. (Broadsheet.) Sydney: Welch, c. 1850.

The Bushrangers, A Play in Five Acts, and Other Poems. Sydney: W.R. Piddington, 1853.

A Poet's Home. (Broadsheet.) Sydney: Hanson and Bennett, 1862.

A Rhyme. Braidwood, NSW, c. 1864.
The Tower of the Dream. Sydney: Clarson, Shallard, 1865.
Poems. Ed. H. M. Martin. Melbourne: G. Robertson, 1883.
Selected Poems of Charles Harpur. Ed. K.H. Gifford and D.F. Hall. Melbourne: Arura Writers, 1944.
Rosa: Love Sonnets to Mary Doyle. Ed. C.W. Salier. Melbourne: Hutchinson, 1948.
Charles Harpur. Sel. and Introd. Donovan Clarke. Australian Poets Series. Sydney: Angus & Robertson, 1963.
Charles Harpur. Ed. Adrian Mitchell. Three Colonial Poets. Book I. Melbourne: Sun Books, 1973.
The Poetical Works of Charles Harpur. Ed. Elizabeth Perkins. Sydney: Angus & Robertson, 1984.

Gwen Harwood

Poems. Sydney: Angus & Robertson, 1963.
The Fall of the House of Usher. Music by Larry Sitsky, libretto by Gwen Harwood. 1965.
Poems: Volume Two. Sydney: Angus & Robertson, 1968.
Lenz. Music by Larry Sitsky. Libretto by Gwen Harwood. 1974.
Selected Poems. Sydney: Angus & Robertson, 1975. Reprint 1981, 1983. Rev. ed. incorporating poems from *The Lion's Bride*. A & R Modern Poets, 1985.
The Lion's Bride. Sydney: Angus & Robertson, 1981.

Dorothy Hewett

What About the People! (with Merv Lilley). Northbridge, NSW: National Council of the Realist Writers Groups, 1961.
Windmill Country. Melbourne: Overland, 1968.
Rapunzel in Suburbia. Sydney: Prism, 1975.
Greenhouse. Sydney: Big Smoke Books, 1979.

A.D. Hope

The Wandering Island. Sydney: Edwards and Shaw, 1955. Reprint 1956.
Poems. London: Hamish Hamilton, 1960. New York: Viking Press, 1961.
A.D. Hope. Sel. Douglas Stewart. Introd. by the author. Australian Poets Series. Sydney: Angus & Robertson, 1963.
Australian Literature 1950–1962 (a brief survey). Melbourne: Melbourne University Press, 1963.
Dunciad Minimus. An Heroick Poem. Canberra: Privately produced. Australian National University Press, 1963.
The Cave and the Spring: Essays on Poetry. Adelaide: Rigby, 1965.

Reprint San Francisco: Tri-Ocean Books, 1965; Chicago: University of Chicago Press, 1970, 1971. 2nd ed. Sydney University Press, 1974.

Collected Poems 1930–1965. Sydney: Angus & Robertson, 1966. New York: Viking, 1966. Reprint. Sydney: Angus & Robertson, 1967, 1968. 2nd ed. 1972.

New Poems 1965–1969. Sydney: Angus & Robertson, 1969. New York: Viking, 1970.

Dunciad Minor: An Heroick Poem. Melbourne: Melbourne University Press, *1970*.

A Midsummer Eve's Dream: Variations on a Theme by William Dunbar. (Essays.) Canberra: Australian National University Press, 1970. New York: Viking, 1970; Edinburgh: Oliver and Boyd, 1971.

A.D. Hope Reads from His Own Work. Poets on Record Series, no. 8. (Record and booklet.) St Lucia: University of Queensland Press, 1972.

Collected Poems 1930–1970. (2nd ed. of *Collected Poems 1930–1965*.) Sydney: Angus & Robertson, 1972. 1st paperback ed. Sydney: Angus & Robertson, 1972. Reprint 1975. Reprint A & R Modern Poets, 1977.

The Damnation of Byron. Illustrated by Virgil Burnett. Stratford, Ont.: Pasdeloup Press, 1973. Ltd ed.

Selected Poems. Preface by the author. Sydney: Angus & Robertson, 1973. Reprint 1974, 1975.

Native Companions: Essays and Comments on Australian Literature, 1936–1966. Sydney: Angus & Robertson, 1974.

Judith Wright. Australian Writers and Their Work. Melbourne: Oxford University Press, 1975.

A Late Picking: Poems 1965–1974. Sydney: Angus & Robertson, 1975. Reprint Sydney: Wentworth Press, 1975. Ltd ed.

A Book of Answers. Sydney: Angus & Robertson, 1978.

The Pack of Autolycus. (Essays.) Canberra: Australian National University Press, 1978.

The Drifting Continent. Illustrated by Arthur Boyd. Canberra: Brindabella Press, 1979.

The New Cratylus: Notes on the Craft of Poetry. Melbourne: Oxford University Press, 1979.

Antechinus: Poems 1975–1980. Sydney: Angus & Robertson, 1981.

The Tragical History of Doctor Faustus by Christopher Marlowe; purged and amended by A.D. Hope. Canberra: Australian National University Press, 1982.

The Age of Reason. Melbourne: Melbourne University Press, 1985.

Les A. Murray

The Ilex Tree (with Geoffrey Lehmann). Canberra: Australian National University Press, 1965.

The Weatherboard Cathedral. Sydney: Angus & Robertson, 1969.

Poems Against Economics. Sydney: Angus & Robertson, 1972.

Lunch and Counter Lunch. Sydney: Angus & Robertson, 1974.

Selected Poems: The Vernacular Republic. Sydney: Angus & Robertson, 1976. New York: Persea Books, 1982.

Ethnic Radio. Sydney: Angus & Robertson, 1977.

The Peasant Mandarin. Prose Pieces. St Lucia: University of Queensland Press, 1978.

The Boys Who Stole the Funeral. A Novel Sequence. Sydney: Angus & Robertson, 1980. Reprint 1982.

Equanimities. Cophenhagen: Razorback Press, 1982.

The Vernacular Republic: Poems 1961–1981. Sydney: Angus & Robertson, 1982. Rev. ed. of *Selected Poems: The Vernacular Republic*. Reprint 1984.

The People's Otherworld: Poems. Sydney: Angus & Robertson, 1983.

Persistence in Folly. Sydney: Angus & Robertson, 1984.

Kenneth Slessor

Thief of the Moon. Sydney: the hand press of J.T. Kirtly, 1924. Reprinted with Lindsay's illustrations, as: *Earth-Visitors*. London: Fanfrolico, 1926.

"Five Visions of Captain Cook"; in *Trio: A Book of Poems* by K. Slessor, H. Matthews, and C. Simpson. Sydney: Sunnybrook Press, 1931.

Cuckooz Contrey. Sydney: Frank Johnson, 1932.

Darlinghurst Nights and Morning Glories: Being 47 Strange Sights . . . Set Forth in Sketch and Rhyme by "Virgil" [i.e., Virgil Gavan Reilly] *and Kenneth Slessor*. Sydney: Frank Johnson, 1932. Reprint. Sydney: Angus & Robertson, 1981.

Funny Farmyard: Nursery Rhymes and Painting Book. Sydney: Frank Johnson, 1933.

Five Bells: XX Poems. Decorations by Norman Lindsay. Sydney: Frank Johnson, 1939.

One Hundred Poems: 1919–1939. Sydney: Angus & Robertson, 1944. Reprint 1947, 1951. 2nd edition as:

Poems. Sydney: Angus & Robertson, 1957. Reprinted many times, most recently as: *Selected Poems*. A & R Modern Poets. Sydney: Angus & Robertson, 1986.

Bread and Wine: Selected Prose. Sydney: Angus & Robertson, 1970.

Backless Betty from Bondi. Ed. Julian Croft. Sydney: Angus & Robertson, 1983.

John Tranter

Parallax and Other Poems. Sydney: South Head Press, 1970. (*Poetry Australia*, no. 34).
Red Movie and Other Poems. Sydney: Angus & Robertson, 1972.
The Blast Area. Gargoyle Poets, no. 12. St Lucia: Makar Press, 1974.
The Alphabet Murders. Sydney: Angus & Robertson, 1975.
Crying in Early Infancy: 100 Sonnets. St Lucia: Makar Press, 1977.
Dazed in the Ladies Lounge. Sydney: Island Press, 1979.
The New Australian Poetry, ed. John Tranter. St Lucia: Makar Press, 1979.
Selected Poems. Hale & Iremonger, 1982.

Francis Webb

A Drum for Ben Boyd. Illustrated by Norman Lindsay. Sydney: Angus & Robertson, 1948.
Leichhardt in Theatre. Sydney: Angus & Robertson, 1952.
Birthday. Adelaide: *Advertiser* Printing Office, 1953.
Socrates and Other Poems. Sydney: Angus & Robertson, 1961.
The Ghost of the Cock. Sydney: Angus & Robertson, 1964.
Collected Poems. Preface by Herbert Read. Sydney: Angus & Robertson, 1969; enlarged by the inclusion of "Early Poems 1942–1948". Sydney: Angus & Robertson, 1977.
Francis Webb Reads from His Own Work. Poets on Record Series. (Record and booklet.) St Lucia: University of Queensland Press, 1975.

Judith Wright

The Moving Image. Melbourne: Meanjin Press, 1948. Reprint 1962, 1965.
Woman to Man. Sydney: Angus & Robertson, 1949. Reprint 1967.
The Gateway. Sydney: Angus & Robertson, 1953.
The Two Fires. Sydney: Angus & Robertson, 1955.
Birds. Sydney: Angus & Robertson, 1962. 2nd ed. Sydney: Angus & Robertson, 1967. 3rd ed. London: Angus & Robertson, 1978.
Charles Harpur. Australian Writers and Their Work. Melbourne: Oxford University Press, 1963. 2nd rev. ed. 1977.
Five Senses: Selected Poems. Sydney: Angus & Robertson, 1963. 2nd rev. ed. Sydney: Angus & Robertson, 1972. Reprint A & R Modern Poets, 1976. Reprinted most recently 1985.
Judith Wright. Sel. and introd. by the author. Sydney: Angus & Robertson, 1963. Reprint 1967.
City Sunrise. Brisbane: Shapcott Press, 1964. Ltd ed.
Preoccupations in Australian Poetry. (Essays.) Melbourne: Oxford University Press, 1965.

The Other Half. Sydney: Angus & Robertson, 1966.
Henry Lawson. Great Australians. Melbourne: Oxford University Press, 1967.
Collected Poems 1942–1970. Sydney: Angus & Robertson, 1971. Reprint 1974. Reprint A & R Modern Poets, 1975.
Alive: Poems 1971–1972. Sydney: Angus & Robertson, 1973. Reprinted most recently 1985.
Judith Wright Reads from Her Own Work. Poets on Record Series, no. 9. (Record and booklet.) St Lucia: University of Queensland Press, 1973.
Because I Was Invited. (Essays.) Melbourne: Melbourne University Press, 1975.
Fourth Quarter. Sydney: Angus & Robertson, 1976.
The Double Tree: Selected Poems 1942–1976. Boston: Houghton Mifflin, 1978.
Phantom Dwelling. Sydney: Angus & Robertson, 1985; London: Virago, 1986.

REFERENCES

Abrams, M.H. *A Glossary of Literary Terms*, 4th edition. New York: Holt, Rinehart and Winston, 1981.
Althusser, Louis. *Lenin and Philosophy and other Essays* trans. Ben Brewster. London: New Left Books, 1971.
Altieri, Charles. *Enlarging the Temple*. Lewisburg: Bucknell University Press, 1979.
Barthes, Roland. *Image Music Text* trans. Stephen Heath. London: Fontana, 1977.
______. *Mythologies* trans. Annette Lavers. London: Jonathan Cape, 1972.
______. *S/Z* trans. Richard Miller. New York: Hill and Wang, 1974.
Baynton, Barbara. *Bush Studies*. Sydney: Angus & Robertson, 1965.
Beaver, Bruce. *Letters to Live Poets*. Sydney: South Head Press, 1969.
Bell, R.J. and Bickerton, I.J. eds. *American Studies: New Essays from Australia and New Zealand*. Sydney: Australian and New Zealand American Studies Association, 1981.
Bloom, Harold. *The Anxiety of Influence*. New York: Oxford University Press, 1973.
______. "Coleridge: The Anxiety of Influence" in W.K. Wimsatt ed. *Literary Criticism: Idea and Act*. Berkeley: University of California Press, 1974.
______. *A Map of Misreading*. New York: Oxford University Press, 1975.
Brissenden, R.F. "Art and the Academy: The Achievement of A.D.

Hope" in Geoffrey Dutton ed. *The Literature of Australia*. Ringwood: Penguin, 1964; rev. ed. 1976.

Buckley, Vincent. *Essays in Poetry, mainly Australian*. Melbourne: Melbourne University Press, 1957.

_____. "The Poetry of Kenneth Slessor" in A.K. Thomson ed. *Critical Essays on Kenneth Slessor*. Brisbane: Jacaranda, 1968.

Campbell, David. *Selected Poems*. Sydney: Angus & Robertson, 1978.

_____ . "*Francis Webb*" in Geoffrey Dutton ed. *The Literature of Australia*. Ringwood: Penguin, 1976.

Carter, David. "John Tranter: Popular Mysteries" in *Scripsi* vol. 2, no. 4, 1984, p. 117.

Clark, Axel. *Christopher Brennan: A Critical Biography*. Melbourne: Melbourne University Press, 1980.

Coleridge, S.T. *Biographia Literaria*. London: J.M. Dent, 1906, 1949.

Culler, Jonathan. *Ferdinand de Saussure*. London: Fontana, 1976.

_____. *On Deconstruction*. Ithaca: Cornell University Press, 1982.

_____. *The Pursuit of Signs*. Ithaca: Cornell University Press, 1981.

_____. *Structuralist Poetics*. Ithaca: Cornell University Press, 1975.

de Man, Paul. "Semiology and Rhetoric" in Josué Harari ed. *Textual Strategies*. Ithaca: Cornell University Press, 1979.

Derrida, Jacques. *Dissemination* trans. Barbara Johnson. Chicago: University of Chicago Press, 1981.

_____. *Of Grammatology* trans. Gayatri Chakravorty Spivak. Baltimore: Johns Hopkins University Press, 1976.

_____. *Positions* trans. Alan Bass. Chicago: University of Chicago Press, 1981.

Docker, John. *In a Critical Condition*. Ringwood: Penguin, 1984.

Duncan, Robert. *The Truth and Life of Myth*. Michigan: Sumac Press, 1968.

Dutton, Geoffrey ed. *The Literature of Australia*. Ringwood: Penguin, 1964; rev. ed. 1976.

Duwell, Martin ed. *A Possible Contemporary Poetry*. St Lucia: Makar Press, 1982.

Easthope, Antony. *Poetry as Discourse*. London: Methuen, 1983.

Eliot, T.S. *The Complete Poems and Plays of T.S. Eliot*. London: Faber, 1969.

_____. *Selected Essays*. London: Faber, 1951.

_____. *Selected Prose of T. S. Eliot* ed. Frank Kermode. London: Faber, 1975.

Emerson, Ralph Waldo. *The Selected Writings*. New York: Modern Library/Random House, 1950.

Felman, Shoshana ed. *Literature and Psychoanalysis*. Baltimore: Johns Hopkins University Press, 1982.

Foucault, Michel. "What Is an Author?" in Josué Harari ed. *Textual Strategies*. Ithaca: Cornell University Press, 1979.

Freud, Sigmund. *Civilization and Its Discontents*, trans. Joan Riviere. London: Hogarth Press, 1963.

Frye, Northrop. *The Anatomy of Criticism*. Princeton: Princeton University Press, 1957.

Furphy, Joseph. *Such Is Life*. Sydney: Angus & Robertson, 1944.

Harari, Josué ed. *Textual Strategies*. Ithaca: Cornell University Press, 1979.

Hawthorne, Nathaniel. *The Scarlet Letter*. New York: Norton, 1978.

Hope, A.D. "Slessor Twenty Years After" in A.K. Thomson ed. *Critical Essays on Kenneth Slessor*. Brisbane: Jacaranda, 1968.

Hughes, Robert. *The Art of Australia*. Harmondsworth: Penguin, 1970.

Jameson, Fredric. *The Political Unconscious*. Ithaca: Cornell University Press, 1981.

______. "Imaginary and Symbolic in Lacan: Marxism, Psychoanalytic Criticism and the Problem of the Subject" in Shoshana Felman ed. *Literature and Psychoanalysis*. Baltimore: Johns Hopkins University Press, 1982.

Johnson, Barbara. *The Critical Difference*. Baltimore: Johns Hopkins University Press, 1980.

Jones, Rae Desmond. "The Ambiguous Modernist: Themes in the Development of the Poetry of John Tranter" in *Australian Literary Studies* vol. 9, no. 4, October 1980, p. 497.

Kiernan, Brian. "Seeing her own Mischance" in *Overland* no. 64, 1976, p. 16.

Kierkegaard, S. *The Sickness unto Death* trans. Walter Lowrie. Oxford: Oxford University Press, 1941.

Kinnell, Galway. *Body Rags*. Boston: Houghton Mifflin, 1968.

Kramer, Leonie ed. *The Oxford History of Australian Literature*. Melbourne: Oxford University Press, 1981.

Kristeva, Julia. *Desire in Language* trans. Thomas Gora, Alice Jardine and Leon S. Roudiez. New York: Columbia University Press, 1980.

Lacan, Jacques. *Ecrits: A Selection* trans. Alan Sheridan. New York: Norton, 1977.

Lawson, Henry. *Prose Works*. Sydney: Angus & Robertson, 1948.

Leavis, F.R. *Revaluation*. London: Chatto & Windus, 1956.

Lowell, Robert. *Life Studies*. London: Faber, 1959.

McAuley, James. *A Map of Australian Verse*. Melbourne: Melbourne University Press, 1975.

MacLeish, Archibald. *New and Collected Poems*. Boston: Houghton Mifflin, 1976.

Norris, Christopher. *Deconstruction: Theory and Practice*. London: Methuen, 1982.

O'Hara, Frank. *The Selected Poems of Frank O'Hara* ed. Donald Allen. New York: Random House, 1974.

Page, Geoff. *Benton's Conviction*. Sydney: Angus & Robertson, 1985.

Plato. *Phaedrus* trans. Walter Hamilton. Harmondsworth: Penguin, 1973.

Pollnitz, Christopher. "The Bardic Pose: A Survey of Les A. Murray's Poetry" in *Southerly* no. 4, 1980, p. 367; no. 1, 1981, p. 52; and no. 2, 1981, p. 188.

Porter, Peter. *Collected Poems*. Oxford: Oxford University Press, 1983.

Pound, Ezra. *The Cantos of Ezra Pound*. London: Faber, 1975.

Quiller-Couch, Sir Arthur ed. *The Oxford Book of English Verse 1250–1918*. Oxford: Oxford University Press, 1900, 1939.

Rimbaud, Arthur. *Rimbaud* ed. Oliver Bernard. Harmondsworth: Penguin, 1962.

Rodriguez, Judith and Taylor, Andrew eds. *Poems, Selected from The Australian's 20th Anniversary Competition*. Sydney: Angus & Robertson, 1985.

Rosenthal, M.L. *The New Poets*. New York: Oxford University Press, 1967.

Saussure, Ferdinand de. *Course in General Linguistics* trans. P. Owen. London: Fontana, 1974.

Showalter, Elaine. *A Literature of Their Own*. Princeton: Princeton University Press, 1977.

Sidney, Sir Philip. *Selected Prose and Poetry* ed. Robert Kimbrough. San Francisco: Rinehart Press, 1969.

Sladen, Douglas ed. *A Century of Australian Song*. London: Walter Scott, 1888.

Smith, Vivian. "Poetry" in Leonie Kramer ed. *The Oxford History of Australian Literature*. Melbourne: Oxford University Press, 1981.

Stevens, Wallace. *The Necessary Angel*. New York: Random House/ Vintage Books, 1951.

______. *The Collected Poems of Wallace Stevens*. London: Faber, 1955.

______. *Opus Posthumous*. London: Faber, 1959.

Taylor, Andrew. "The Late Poems of Wallace Stevens" in R.J. Bell and I.J. Bickerton eds. *American Studies: New Essays from Australia and New Zealand*. Sydney: Australian and New Zealand American Studies Association, 1981.

Thomson, A.K. ed. *Critical Essays on Kenneth Slessor*. Brisbane: Jacaranda, 1968.

Thoreau, Henry David. *Walden and Civil Disobedience*. New York: Norton, 1966.

Webb, Francis. *Poetry Australia* Commemorative Issue. Sydney: South Head Press, no. 56, September 1975.

Wilde, W. H., Hooton, J., and Andrews, B. eds. *The Oxford Companion to Australian Literature.* Melbourne: Oxford University Press, 1985.

Williams, Bruce. "Dorothy Hewett: Confession and Beyond" in *Overland* no. 64, 1976.

Wimsatt, W.K. ed. *Literary Criticism: Idea and Act.* Berkeley: University of California Press, 1974.

Wordsworth, William. *Poetical Works.* Oxford: Oxford University Press, 1956.

FURTHER READING

The journal *Australian Literary Studies* (University of Queensland) regularly publishes bibliographical data on Australian poetry, including the writers discussed in this volume.

For readers interested in pursuing the more theoretical issues, I recommend the excellent bibliographies in the following:

Culler, Jonathan. *On Deconstruction.* Ithaca: Cornell University Press, 1982.

______. *Structuralist Poetics.* Ithaca: Cornell University Press, 1975.

Easthope, Antony. *Poetry as Discourse.* London: Methuen, 1983.

Harari, Josué ed. *Textual Strategies.* Ithaca: Cornell University Press, 1979.

Hošek, Chaviva, and Parker, Patricia eds. *Lyric Poetry.* Ithaca: Cornell University Press, 1985.

Tompkins, Jane ed. *Reader-Response Criticism.* Baltimore: Johns Hopkins University Press, 1980.

Index